THE GUINNESS BOOK OF

GOLF

FACTS AND FEATS

THE GUINNESS BOOK OF
GOLF
FACTS AND FEATS
SECOND EDITION

DONALD STEEL

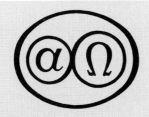

Guinness Superlatives Ltd,
2 Cecil Court, London Road,
Enfield, Middx.

Acknowledgements

The author and publishers wish to record their gratitude for particular help given by:

Asia Golf Circuit (Lily Kim Hall)
ETPD (Bill Hodge)
Golfers' Handbook (Percy Huggins)
LGU (Jennie Cobb)
LPGA of America (Ruffin Beckwith)
US Golf Association (Patrick Leahy)
USPGA
R and A Championship Records 1860–1980 (Peter Ryde)

Title page illustration: **A golf match on Blackheath, 1870**
(Illustrated London News)

Editor: Beatrice Frei
Design and Layout: David Roberts

Copyright © Donald Steel
and Guinness Superlatives Ltd 1980, 1982

First published in 1980

Second edition 1982

Published in Great Britain by Guinness Superlatives Ltd, 2 Cecil Court,
London Road, Enfield, Middlesex

Set in 9/10pt Plantin
Photoset, printed and bound by Redwood Burn Ltd, Trowbridge, Wiltshire
Colour separation by Newsele Litho, Milan

British Library Cataloguing in Publication Data

Steel, Donald
    The Guinness book of golf facts and feats.—
    2nd ed.
    1. Golf—Records
    I. Title
    796.352'09   GV1001

    ISBN 0–85112–242–6
    ISBN 0–85112–257–4 Pbk

Contents

Introduction

When it comes to researching just how, when and where golf had its origins, it is too easy to become swallowed up in fathomless waters. For our purposes, it is safe to say that the game is at least five centuries old and that the first dramatic tales of competition concern the old challenge matches for which there were frequently high stakes.

However, championship golf is distinctly modern. The British Open, launched by the Prestwick Club, was first played in 1860 and all the early records and achievements concern British golfers. Not until after World War I did the United States assume the playing dominance so familiar today and it was still later that many of the events highlighted in this book took place.

For example, the women's professional tour in the United States, the Asia circuit, the World Cup and the World Amateur team championships have all sprung to life since World War II, a period when the game has developed out of all recognition. Even as recently as the 1950s the only lucrative circuits were in Great Britain and the United States and you had to be very good to make anything approaching a living. Now, a young tournament professional can seek to prove himself on additional circuits in the Far East, Australia, New Zealand, Europe, South Africa and South America.

One result of this expansion has been a rapid increase in the number of records, facts and feats that have to be chronicled. No other game has quite such an assortment of records and everyone who plays is intrigued by this variety.

This is because only a tiny proportion of golfers play competitively and anyone enjoying a few holes with friends is quite liable to perform a feat which the greatest players have been unable to match. It is one of the few active pastimes in which four generations, however good or bad, can take part at the same time—thanks to the handicapping system.

While a number of names in these pages may, therefore, strike few immediate chords, the real interest and the main focus of attention is upon the great players and their great deeds; those men and women whose skill has set them apart.

Allowance must be made, as in any sport, for changing times and particularly for the enormous advance in equipment. What might Willie Park or Willie Anderson have done with the benefit of a ball that flew

further, or how many more putts might they have holed on greens as highly manicured as those of today? Yet it is fascinating to see how many old records survive.

Young Tom Morris remains the youngest winner of the British Open, having won in 1868 at the age of 17 years and 5 months; and there has not been anyone since to threaten his record although young golfers today can do remarkable things. Nevertheless, we are not yet accustomed to golfers being past their best at 16 like swimmers and gymnasts.

One day, Young Tom may be deposed, but it is hard to envisage another golfer succeeding his father as Open Champion as happened with the Morrises. It is rare even for father and son to take part in a modern British or American Open although Gary and Wayne Player were exceptions in 1979 at Lytham and 1982 at Pebble Beach.

Of the other records which may never be broken, Bobby Jones's Impregnable Quadrilateral must head the list. I never cease to wonder at his achievement of winning the Open and Amateur championships of Britain and America in the same summer (1930); or how Byron Nelson won eleven straight tournaments on the US professional tour in 1945.

Into this highly improbable bracket we can place the 19 major victories of Jack Nicklaus (17 as a professional) although after that at St Andrews in 1978, he felt himself to be more vulnerable. All the same he will not be overtaken in a hurry; nor will Harry Vardon's six victories in the British Open.

The American Open record of victories is shared by Nicklaus, Willie Anderson, Bobby Jones and Ben Hogan with four apiece and, if Nicklaus is unable to beat it before he is through, it will be some while before anyone else does.

I have mentioned the effect of modern equipment on the downward spiral of scoring but it should also be remembered that prize-money is an imperfect measurement of achievement and reference is made to it mainly because the earnings of others exert a strange fascination. To illustrate this, Nancy Lopez in three years exceeded the $359 323 which took Mickey Wright 23 seasons to accumulate (1955–78). In that time Wright won 82 tournaments, a record Lopez is unlikely to beat.

Inevitably, a large part of this book involves Britain

and America, the leading golfing nations in competitive and championship terms. However, every attempt has been made to cover as large a part of the globe as possible and due regard has been paid to records from other countries. The theme is also facts and feats and here the hardest part has been to decide what to leave out.

This is a work of reference, a book to settle arguments and one that can be picked up for five minutes to induce the reaction 'fancy that'. When delving into the past, it is astonishing what unusual feats have been performed. These pages are intended to provide something for everyone—the champions, the addicts, the club players who comprise the vast and honourable majority; and those who are always promising to play a little more but never quite manage it. Perhaps this book will act as the spur.

In order to avoid repetition and also aid readability the nationalities, and dates of birth and death, where known, are included in the names index.

Golfing Countries

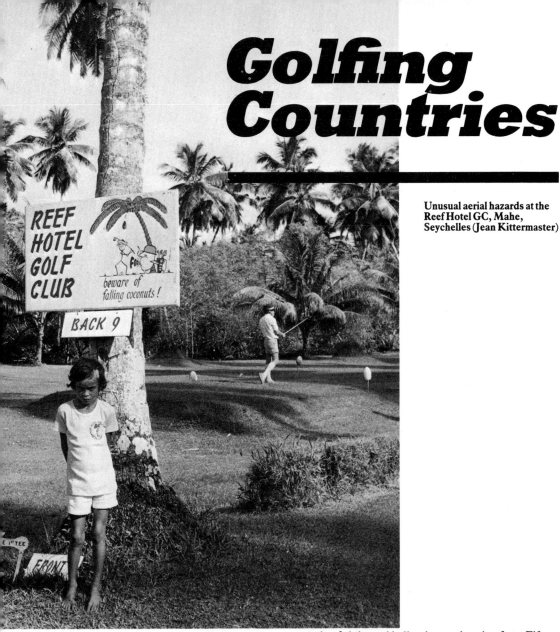

Unusual aerial hazards at the Reef Hotel GC, Mahe, Seychelles (Jean Kittermaster)

Afghanistan One course was known in Kabul before the Russian invasion in 1979.

Argentina Lomas was the first club in 1892, the introduction of the British who were said at the time to be 'devoted to a strange sort of amusement'. There are now 130 Clubs and 40 000 golfers, the best known of the Clubs being The Jockey Club, Olivos and Hindu—all around Buenos Aires—and Mar del Plata.

The best known professionals are Jose Jurado, Roberto de Vicenzo, Tony Cerda and Vicente Fernandez.

Australia One of the foremost golfing nations of the world since the Hon James Graham brought his own supply of clubs and balls when emigrating from Fife to Melbourne in 1847. There are unreliable reports of golf being played earlier than that.

Hopes of establishing the game were foiled by the gold rush but, after one or two now famous Clubs made 'false starts', Royal Melbourne GC, founded in 1891, is the oldest with complete continuity.

There are about 1390 courses and an estimated 340 000 golfers.

Austria Emperor Franz Josef I was the originator of golf in Austria, giving land for an annual rent of 1 krone for a course at Wien-Krieau in 1901. This became the home of the Golf Club Wien (Vienna).

Austria now boasts 20 courses and a golfing population of about 3000.

Bahamas First golfing pioneer was a Scottish officer, Alexander Campbell, commander of a British military force in Nassau who laid out a simple course around what is now Fort Charlotte. This was in the late 18th century, a hundred years before golf was played in North America. Campbell, a Glaswegian, was once a caddie boy. Nowadays, sophisticated developments have sprung up all over the Bahamas, including many of the smaller islands. For two years (1970 and 1971), the Bahama Islands Open formed part of the USPGA tour.

Barbados Has two courses founded after World War II by British influence. Has about 550 local resident golfers although the numbers are swelled considerably by the large number of tourists.

Belgium With only 15 courses and 5000 golfers, the game is for the lucky few although it has thrived largely because of the interest shown by the Royal Family. In 1903, King Leopold II said that British businessmen must have 'the opportunity of playing one of their favourite sports' and duly made land available at Ostend, Terveuren and in the Ardennes.

Royal Antwerp, founded in 1888, was Belgium's first course.

Bermuda As a British possession since 1684, it has a rich golfing heritage. There are more courses (eight) per square mile than anywhere else in the world. These include Mid Ocean, Belmont, Riddell's Bay, Castle Harbour and the most recent 18-hole creation, Port Royal, which is run by the government. The game is played by 3000 of the islanders.

Abiko Golf Club, Japan (Courtesy of Golf Digest, Japan)

Bolivia One of the most remote golfing nations, it nevertheless boasts nine courses including some of the highest in the world. The course in the mining town of Oruro is about 12 000 ft above sea level. The highest in the world, in Peru, is more than 14 000 ft above sea level.

Botswana The best course in a land whose chief industry is diamonds, is Gaborone; this is the scene of the Kalahari Diamond Classic, part of the African Safari circuit. It is situated on the edge of the Kalahari Desert. There are about five other Clubs, mostly small.

Brazil One of the strongest golfing nations of South America although, for such a big country, its 45 courses and 7000 golfers is nothing compared to Britain. São Paolo GC is the oldest, dating from about the turn of the century, when a group of British engineers working for the railway company sowed the early seeds.

Bulgaria Only one course, a few miles from Sofia but hopes for more in the form of tourist developments.

Burma As in many another country, golf in Burma owes its origins to the British community who saw the game as one of the lighter sides of their colonial rule. There are currently about 50 courses, mostly 9 holes, but there are 15 000 golfers.

Canada Golf came to Canada before America. No doubt the fur traders of the Hudson Bay Company played some form of golf before the official start of the Royal Montreal Club in 1873 (Royal since 1884), but that was 15 years before the official start in the United States.

As was only to be expected, the early pioneers were Scots and the Royal Montreal Club was chiefly responsible for the spread of the game to over 950 Clubs by 1951 and something like 140 000 golfers. The Royal Canadian Golf Association has been the governing body since 1896.

Chile Although not as popular as other games, golf has a significant following with 31 courses and over 7000

Tropical delight, Sandy Lane, Barbados

Scarcely recognisable today. The view from the 4th green on the Old course at Sunningdale, April 1906 (BBC Hulton Pic. Lib.) *Below:* The 7th hole at Vale do Lobo, Portugal which is in danger of suffering coastal erosion (Phil Sheldon)

players. The best course in the country is Los Leones in Santiago.

China The People's Republic of China virtually put an end to golf but, until 1949, golf had thrived ever since the British introduced the game towards the end of the last century. However, as interest waned here, it mul-

tiplied enormously in Taiwan or the Republic of China largely, at first, through the Americans who were stationed there and then afterwards when it was maintained locally.

Their professionals quickly showed themselves to be outstanding players and profited from the develop-

(Plakatsammlung, Kunstgewerbemuseum, Zürich)

(Plakatsammlung, Kunstgewerbemuseum, Zürich)

ment of the Far East or Asian tour. There are now 14 courses, double the number ten years ago, and 25 000 golfers. Arnold Palmer is at present planning a new course in the People's Republic.

Colombia Colombian golf began in 1917 in Bogota with the founding of the Country Club of Bogota. Altogether there are 29 courses and 7000 golfers.

Czechoslovakia Golf was a fashionable game in that country from the time the first Club was founded in Karlovy Vary (Carlsbad) in 1904 until the time of the Russian invasion in 1968. In pre-war years, their tournaments were popular with golfers from overseas including Henry Cotton who twice won their Open championship. Czechoslovakia was one of the founder members of the European Golf Association in 1937.

Less is known these days about golf in the country but there are eight courses and about 1000 golfers.

Denmark Official golf in Denmark originated at the Copenhagen GC at the end of the last century but progress was slow throughout the country. By the mid-1950s, there were only a dozen or so clubs but Denmark has kept in step with the remarkable expansion that has taken place in the world since then. There are now about 45 courses and 20 000 golfers.

Dominican Republic There are four courses in the Republic but local members still only number about 500. There is, however, good demand from tourists.

Egypt British influence led to golf being introduced to the country over 60 years ago. It prospered at Gezira, Alexandria and Khedivial but interest has waned in the last 25 years and there are still only four courses.

Finland A Dane, Charles Jensen, took golf to Finland in 1930 when 9 holes were built at what is now the Helsinki Club although it was not until 1952 that it was extended to 18 holes. Thirty years later there are 15 courses and about 2500 players but the season is short even if there is some compensation that golf in midsummer can be played by the light of the midnight sun. One course on an airfield site has only 6 holes.

Fiji Only two 18-hole courses although 15 courses in all.

France One of the first countries outside Britain and India to have an established Club. That was at Pau in 1854 but though the French Open dates from 1906 and has had many famous winners, golf in France still remains a fairly exclusive and expensive sport. There are 113 courses and almost 40 000 golfers.

Germany Until 1981, no German had ever won their Open championship which was first played in 1912 at Baden Baden where a nephew of Theodore Roosevelt was President. However, the influence of Bernhard Langer could spur a new wave of interest and cause an increase of the country's 42 000 golfers and 146 Clubs in 1980.

The first courses were built in 1895 but a few years earlier, members of London society frequenting the German spas were in the habit of taking their clubs with them; this caused an eyebrow or two to be raised among the locals, particularly when the golfers began taking divots in neighbouring parks.

Ghana The ten courses in Ghana today owe their popularity to the days before independence (1957), when overseas influence was strong.

Greece The tourist industry has produced a spread of interest in the game, there being courses at Glyfada in Athens, Corfu and Rhodes. The population of Greek golfers is around 400 but the Greeks were host to the 1979 World Cup.

Guatemala Four courses and 700 golfers.

Holland Nobody now will be able to prove the origins of golf but many believe it may have started in Holland. It depends on whether a game played centuries ago was a true fore-runner of golf or one with strong similarities. However, the modern part of Dutch golf began with the founding of the Haagsche GC in the Hague in 1893.

Several more followed in the next few years and the Dutch Open started in 1919 but though many courses were severely scarred during the German occupation in World War II, the game thrives once more on 25 courses. The membership of these Clubs is about 11 000.

Hong Kong Royal Hong Kong GC lies not far from the border of communist territory but from the day in 1889 when the first course was established on ground that was in constant use by the army for drill and polo, there has been significant expansion in this golf-crazy part of the world, despite land being in short supply.

Iceland A four-month season hardly suggests that golf is a national sport, but since 1934 ten Clubs have grown up and from the 1000 or so golfers, international teams are sent to several European events.

India As might be expected in the days of the Raj, Indian golf has historic roots. Royal Calcutta, founded in 1829, is the oldest Club in the world outside Britain and, by the turn of the century, India had a dozen Clubs.

Their Amateur championship is 90 years old and the India Golf Union now has over 100 Clubs and 10 000 members on its books. Currently, the Indian Open is part of the Asian circuit for professionals.

Indonesia In a part of the world where the game has grown faster than anywhere else in recent years,

Indonesia has 50 courses and 20 000 players.

Iran A new course, the Imperial CC in Teheran was opened in 1970 to replace an old sand course and there are two further developments planned in Persepolis and on the shores of the Caspian Sea but recent events in Iran may well have destroyed all this.

Iraq British interest in and around Baghdad set its golfing sights on a 13-hole sand course in 1925 which was subsequently abandoned, but the Iraq Petroleum Company and the Basrah Petroleum Company ran sand courses which were mainly for company staff.

Ireland For a relatively small island, Ireland has 240 courses and 120 000 golfers although the Golfing Union of Ireland, like the Irish Rugby Union, incorporates north and south. There have been many notable Irish golfers and the courses that abound around the Irish coast have few equals.

Israel The Caesarea Golf and Country Club, opened in 1961 in dune country which covers the ancient city of Caesarea, is Israel's only course. The Club has about 400 golfers.

Italy One view of golfing origins in Italy is that it was played in Rome by officers who had followed Bonnie Prince Charlie into exile from Scotland (1766) but there are now 56 courses in widely contrasting settings. Acquasanta, near Rome, for instance, has the background of the Claudian aqueduct but the game remains largely a pursuit of the rich with many of the clubhouses designed on palatial lines.

Ivory Coast Two courses built very recently exist in a country which is beginning to develop a golfing consciousness.

Jamaica The oldest setting for golf in the West Indies; indeed, the Manchester Club at Mandeville, dating from 1868, is one of the oldest outside Scotland. The island now has eleven Clubs.

Japan Nowhere in the world in recent years has there been such a rapid golfing expansion than in Japan. Golf has become a prestige symbol but still supply nowhere near meets demand. Even the driving ranges are packed and, at some, you have to book a bay.

There are thought to be over seven million golfers although only 1 300 000 are members of around 850 Clubs—a far cry from the first 9-hole course built on the slopes of Mount Rokko near Kobe in 1901.

The game was started by a group of Englishmen who perhaps found judo a little too vigorous, the chief golfing pioneer being Arthur Groom, a tea merchant. However, the Japanese slowly took an interest and the 1920s and 1930s brought a significant growth in the number of Clubs.

SAMADEN
18 HOLE GOLF LINKS
ENGADIN ⁄ 1728 m ⁄ SCHWEIZ

(Plakatsammlung Kunstgewerbmuseum, Zürich)

The war took its toll of the courses and it was 1952 before the requisitioned ones were returned to Japanese owners; but the real spark that lit the flame was Japan's surprising victory in the 1957 Canada Cup tournament.

After that, everyone, it seemed, wanted to play golf and many new courses were created, quite literally, by moving mountains. A whole new generation of tournament professionals grew up and the commercialism and prize money surrounding today's tournament circuit is enormous.

Kenya As one might expect in British East Africa, or Kenya, as it is now, golf was an import of the British, dating from 1906 in Nairobi and a few years later in Mombasa.

Kenya is still the centre of golf in the country but there are more than 30 Clubs and the game attracts followers from all communities.

Korea In keeping with most countries in the Far East, Korea boasts an expanding golfing public. World War II and the Korean War limited expansion earlier but the game has been played for over 60 years although Seoul CC, the first 18-hole course, was not founded until 1931. There are now more than 20 courses and the Korean Open forms part of the Asia circuit with a first prize in 1980 of 10 000 US dollars.

Lebanon Golf has been played in Lebanon almost as long as in Egypt but, though the country has had its troubles in recent years, it has four courses and the game has a reasonable following.

Libya Has, or had, four courses although only two of 18 holes, both in Tripoli.

Luxembourg In the small Grand Duchy of Luxembourg, there is only one course, the Golf Club Grand-Ducal de Luxembourg, but there are 1000 golfers and the annual Amateur championships for ladies and men are well supported.

Malawi Since the days when Malawi was Nyasaland, the game has depended on a number of enthusiasts but it dates from 1911 in Blantyre. All seven courses are 9 holes, mostly with browns as greens.

Malaysia Real growth in golf in Malaysia has been confined to the last 30 years but, in keeping with so many countries in Asia, expansion is accelerating. There are 43 courses with more planned. The oldest Clubs, Perak at Taiping and Royal Selangor in Kuala Lumpur, date back to 1888 and 1893. The biggest incentive to the game, apart from the origins under British rule, has been the interest shown by Royal families and high ranking national and State government officials. The Malaysian Open is part of the thriving Asia circuit.

Mexico More than 40 courses form the nucleus of golf in Mexico which started with 9 holes in the Mexico City suburb of Puebla in 1897. The San Pedro Club became well known by having Willie Smith, a US Open champion, as professional but, in more recent times, Mexico has housed the Canada Cup and the world amateur team championships; and it has profited from the exploits of Mexican-born Lee Trevino.

Morocco Interest by King Hassan II, coupled with a developing tourist industry, has led to a dozen or more courses in Morocco including Royal Dar-es-Salaam near Rabat. Over 7000 yd long, it has 500 men to keep it in shape. It is irrigated by a pipe which had to be run out from the city but most of the other cities have courses as well.

New Zealand Another country in which the early beginnings of golf are vague but the father of the game in New Zealand is acknowledged as a Scotsman,

Charles Ritchie Howden, who later started the New Zealand Distillery Company. Golf and whisky are Scotland's two great exports.

The year 1871 is the first official date in New Zealand golfing history when the Dunedin Club, later called the Otago, was founded with Christchurch following in 1872. However, both Clubs ran into difficulties and the game lapsed for almost 20 years. It was revived again in Dunedin in 1892 and gradually the game grew to today's present strength of almost 400 courses.

Nigeria Nigeria has 17 Clubs, the oldest being Ikoyi in Lagos which was founded in 1933. It was at Ikoyi in 1981 during the Nigerian Open that Peter Tupling set the lowest recorded 72-hole total on a first class course of 255.

Norway One of those countries where the winter is long and the golfing season short. However, from the simple beginnings of a 9-hole course in Oslo in 1924, nine more have sprung up. The Oslo Golfklubb, now 18 holes, is still the hub of golf in Norway but interest is spreading.

Pakistan Before the days of Partition in 1947, the British had the main influence on golf in Pakistan but, though they experienced many difficulties, the Pakistanis themselves have kept the game going and founded their own Golf Union in 1960. There are about 16 courses although several are only 9 holes.

Peru Not one of the leading golfing countries of South America but Los Inkas CC in Lima is a fine course and there are some signs of an increase in popularity of the game at the other 14 Clubs.

Philippines Another country forming part of the thriving web of golfing development in the Far East. Manila GC originated around the turn of the century but today there are some 60 courses and around 80 000 golfers.

Portugal The development of the Algarve has led to the golfing boom in Portugal although it is visitors rather than the Portuguese who play.

The British port wine shippers started the game in Oporto but Estoril became the centre of Portuguese golf in 1929 and, despite an increase to 18 courses, remains a revered name.

Scotland The home of golf. The country where the game has been played, in one form or other, for more than 500 years. St Andrews and other regions of Fife, North Berwick, Dornoch, Prestwick and Musselburgh were the early nurseries of the game; and, ever since, it has been accepted as the game of the people.

With such deep traditions everyone, it seems, plays and plays without fuss or any of the luxurious clubhouse settings which golfers in other countries find so

Metropolitan GC, Cape Town (South African Tourist Corporation)

important. About a quarter of a million members belong to some 450 Clubs but many more play in one way, shape or form.

At least six Scottish Clubs have celebrated their bicentenary.

Singapore It is well served with golf courses for such a confined community; there are eleven Clubs and more than 10 000 official golfers. Singapore Island CC is the amalgamation of the former Royal Singapore and Royal Island, both of which were used during World War II by the Japanese for growing tapioca. However, golf slowly got back to normal and many new developments have been added to cater for the growing addiction to the game.

South Africa Another country indebted to the Scots for the introduction of the game. Its origins are traced back to 1882 when army officers built a 6-hole course adjoining their camp near Capetown.

The idea spread quickly and by the turn of the century, there were about 50 courses, mostly pretty rough; but to Royal Durban belongs the honour of the oldest permanent home (1902).

Nowadays, there are around 350 courses and the famous South African golfers have included Sid Brews, Bobby Locke and Gary Player.

Spain For years, the game in Spain has been the exclusive right of the prosperous families, but the opening up of so much of the country's coastline for tourism has led to a big increase in the number of courses—now standing at over 40.

The oldest on Spanish territory is Las Palmas in the Canary Islands which was founded in 1891, but Madrid established itself as the mainland centre although fine courses exist in Barcelona and Bilbao.

In recent years Spanish professionals, notably Severiano Ballesteros, have won great notoriety throughout the world but it has not yet produced any dramatic interest from the man in the street.

Sri Lanka Royal Colombo, the oldest Club in what was Ceylon, celebrates its centenary in 1882 but the game is limited to it and two other Clubs.

Sweden The most golf-minded of the Scandinavian countries, particularly in the last 20 years when the number of courses has risen to 150. After World War II, there were only about 3000 golfers; now about 80 000 play.

The little course at Carthage with its black-oiled sand greens. Prior to 1980, it was the only course in Tunisia but now there is one at Port El Kantaoui near Sousse and others are planned at Kantaoui, Hammamet and on the island of Jerba (Andy Gray)

Left: Mount Irvine Bay, Tobago

The Sager brothers introduced the game with 6 holes at Ryfors in 1888 but though an Anglican clergyman conceived the idea of golf in Gothenburg in the early 1890s, the real start of Swedish golf is regarded as 1904.

Switzerland At only a few of the 28 Clubs is play possible all the year round, but the game has grown in popularity since the Swiss Open Amateur and Ladies' Open Amateur championships were first held in 1907.

At the present time, the Swiss Open is one of the major European professional tournaments and has found a more or less permanent home at Crans-sur-Sierre. The first course at Crans was laid out in 1905 by Sir Arnold Lunn, one of the pioneers of international skiing, who also built the Palace Hotel at Montana.

Thailand The King of Siam, who had played a certain amount of golf in Europe, supported the influence of the British in introducing the game to Siam. Royal Bangkok was founded in 1890 but a team of British engineers, responsible for building the railway between Malaya and Siam, formed the Hua Hin Club at a seaside resort about 100 miles from the capital.

However, the most dramatic advance in the game's popularity followed long after Siam changed its name to Thailand in 1939. There are now almost 40 courses in the country, including two of the most recent, Rose Garden and Siam CC.

Lady caddies are a feature of golf in Thailand whose Open championship is an established part of the Asia circuit.

Trinidad Trinidad has nine courses, the most notable being Mount Irvine Bay which attracts many tourists each year.

Tunisia There have been several indications in recent years of the growth in the game although mainly as a tourist attraction. In 1982, a £60 000 Tunisian Open was introduced which attracted an international field.

Uganda A fairly thriving game before independence, the Uganda GC in Kampala celebrated its 50th anniversary in 1969. Most of the initiative came from members of the British Colonial service. The course at Jinja near the shores of Lake Victoria have the unusual local rule of allowing a free drop from hippos' footprints.

United States of America Far and away the biggest golfing nation both in the number of courses (12 350) and players (around 16½ million). They are also the leaders in terms of playing strength, amateur and professional.

In such a vast country, there is a wide variety of courses but, compared to Britain, the origins of the game are fairly recent; as, indeed, is their playing dominance at international level. There are records of golf being played in New York, South Carolina and Georgia around 200 years ago but there was no continuity. The accepted birth date of American golf is 1888 when the Apple Tree Gang founded the St Andrews Club in Yonkers, New York.

Development owed much to the early Scottish professionals and to the early golf course architects, notably Donald Ross. He was a professional from Dornoch who arrived in America with two dollars in his pocket in 1898 and became a much revered name.

The real explosion came in the 1920s and was helped by the beginnings of tournament golf which resulted in the US tour reaching such lucrative heights. The USPGA was formed in 1916 but the USGA, the governing body which runs the US Open and US Amateur championships, preceded it by 22 years.

Uruguay A small country in golfing terms, the Uruguay GC in Montevideo being the best known of the four courses.

USSR There has been much speculation in recent times about the construction of the first course in the Soviet Union. Despite plans being drawn up, nothing, as far as the outside world knows, has materialised.

Venezuela 21 courses in a country which runs a popular Open championship.

Wales With about 100 courses, Wales cannot match the golfing resources of England, Scotland and Ireland but there are more than 30 000 Welsh golfers and a good variety of fine courses.

Yugoslavia One course at Bled is the limit of Yugoslavia's golfing riches but there has been talk of more in the coastal resort areas.

Zaire A small but thriving golfing community with five courses.

Zambia The Zambian Open forms the highlight of Zambian golf each year in the country which was formerly Northern Rhodesia. The President, Kenneth Kaunda, is a keen supporter and a regular player himself.

The oldest Club is the Livingstone, founded in 1908.

Zimbabwe The golfing traditions of Rhodesia have been carried on under the Zimbabwean flag with many coloureds taking to the game for the first time.

Bulawayo GC was the first in 1895 followed by Royal Salisbury in 1899. Twelve courses, in fact, lie within a 20-mile radius of Salisbury but the total of 70 courses includes those at Leopard Rock near Umtali, Troutbeck in the Eastern Highlands, Chimanimani, and at the vast asbestos mine at Shabani.

Historical Milestones

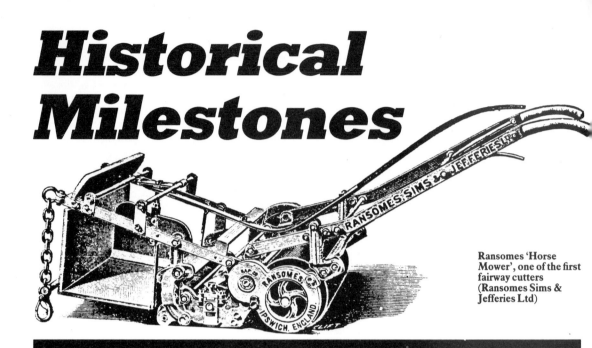

1340–50 A stained-glass window erected in Gloucester Cathedral showing a man swinging a club at a ball. It was commissioned by Sir Thomas Broadstone to commemorate his comrades who fell at Crécy.

1353 Reference to chole, a popular cross-country game in Flanders. It consisted of hitting balls with clubs towards a fixed mark, eg a church door. Two parties would play; one hitting the ball across country towards the goal, the other party on every fourth stroke hitting the ball into a hazard.

1457 First of three dates when 'gouf' was banned in Scotland by an Act of Parliament. It joined football which had been banned in 1424 by James I. Similar enactments were also made by James III in 1470 and James IV in 1491.

1502 King James IV buys clubs and balls from a bowmaker in Perth.

1504 James IV played golf with the Earl of Bothwell.

1527 Sir Robert Maule (1497–1560) was the first golfer mentioned by name after King James IV and the Earl of Bothwell. Sir Robert was described in the Panmure Register as 'ane man of comlie behaviour, of hie stature, sanguine in collure both of hyd and haire, colarique of nature and subject to suddane anger. . . . He had gryt delight in haukine and hountine. . . . Lykewakes he exercisit the gowf, and ofttimes past to Barry Links, quhan the wadsie [wager] was for drink.' Barry Links, where the Scots defeated the Danes in a great battle in 1010, is close to the modern Carnoustie.

1553 The Archbishop of St Andrews confirms the right of the community to play golf over the links of St Andrews.

1567 Mary Queen of Scots criticised for playing golf at Seton House within two weeks of her husband Darnley's death.

1589 Playing of golf forbidden in the Blackfriars Yard, Glasgow.

1592 Proclamation against the playing of golf at Leith on Sundays during the time of the 'sermonis'.

c **1600** Man injured playing golf on the links at Ayr.

c **1608** Prince of Wales played golf in the grounds of Royal Manor at Greenwich.

c **1620** First mention of the feathery ball. Before the introduction of the feathery ball, it is generally assumed that balls used for golf were of turned boxwood, similar to those used in the kindred games of chole and pall mall.

A monopoly of sale was granted to James Melvill, the price for each golf ball being fixed at fourpence.

1621 Golf played in King's Park, Stirling.

1629 The Marquis of Montrose was a golfer, as his

Bandy-Ball, a game from the Middle Ages with similarities to golf (Mary Evans Pic. Lib.)

father the Earl had been before him. Evidence of this is shown in his golfing expenses from visits to St Andrews and Leith as well as for his home course, Montrose. He may also have had something to do with the introduction of caddies. In the Marquis's accounts for 1628, there is record of the payment of four shillings 'to the boy who carried my clubs'.

1630 Dornoch described in glowing terms by Sir Robert Gordon, 'doe surpass the fields of Montrose or St Andrews'.

1641 News of the Irish rebellion conveyed to King Charles while he was playing golf at Leith.

1642 A golf-ball maker licensed by the Council of Aberdeen.

1658 First mention of golf in London, at 'Up Fields' (Vincent Square), Westminster.

1682 First International match. The Duke of York and a shoemaker defeating two English noblemen at Leith.

1721 Golf on Glasgow Green.

1724 Big crowds for a match at Leith.
The match was between Alexander Elphinstone, a younger son of Lord Balmerino, and Captain John Porteous of the Edinburgh City Guard. The stake was 20 guineas and, among the large crowd, were the Duke of Hamilton and the Earl of Morton.

1744 First meeting of the Honourable Company of Edinburgh Golfers; they competed for a silver club presented by the City of Edinburgh. Widely acclaimed as the first golf club in the world. John Rattray, a surgeon, was the first winner of the silver club.
First rules of the game (13) were drawn up.

1754 Date of the founding of the St Andrews Club, later the Royal and Ancient. Twenty-two noblemen and others of Fife held an open competition for the prize of a silver club. The first winner was Bailie William Landale, a merchant of St Andrews.
The Leith code of rules written in 1744 were adopted generally.

1759 First mention of strokeplay. Previously all golf consisted of matches.

1764 A round at St Andrews was reduced to 18 holes. Originally it had been 22.

1766 Silver driver donated for competition at Blackheath.

1773 Edinburgh Burgess Golfing Society formed.

1779 Golf played in New York by Scottish officers during the American Revolutionary War.

1780 Formation of (Royal) Aberdeen Golf Club.

1786 Crail Golfing Society formed. South Carolina Golf Association formed at Charleston, USA but no continuity.

1787 The Bruntsfield Links golfers formed themselves into a club.

1797 Burntisland Golf Club formed.

1810 First mention of a competition for ladies. It was

Chilean game of El Sueca (Mary Evans Pic. Lib.)

held for the fishwives of Musselburgh.

1818 Manchester golfers—Old Manchester Club—began playing on Kersal Moor.

1824 Perth Golfing Society formed.

1829 Calcutta Golf Club, India, founded, the first in the world outside Britain. Later became Royal Calcutta.

1832 North Berwick Golf Club formed.

1833 Perth Golfing Society became Royal Perth; it was created by William IV and was the first Royal club anywhere.

1834 William IV grants the Royal and Ancient Golf Club of St Andrews its name.

1836 The Honourable Company of Edinburgh Golfers move from Leith to Musselburgh.

1842 Bombay Golfing Society, India, formed, later Royal Bombay.

1848 Introduction of the gutta-percha ball, better known as the 'gutty'.

1851 Prestwick Golf Club founded.
Unofficial golf played in Sydney, Australia.

1856 Royal Curragh Golf Club founded in Kildare.
Pau Golf Club, France, formed; the first on the continent of Europe.

1857 First book on golf instruction published, *The Golfer's Manual*, by 'A Keen Hand' (H B Farnie).

1859 Death of the first great professional golfer, Allan Robertson (b 1815).

1860 The beginning of championship golf. The first Open at Prestwick; the winner: Willie Park, Sr. It was contested entirely by professionals, but in 1861 it was thrown open 'to all the world'.

1864 The (Royal) North Devon Club founded at Westward Ho!, the first seaside links in England.

1865 The London Scottish Golf Club founded at Wimbledon.

1867 First ladies' golf club founded at St Andrews.

1869 Birth of the (Royal) Liverpool Golf Club at Hoylake and the Alnmouth Golf Club, Northumberland.

1870 Formation of the (Royal) Adelaide Golf Club, the first in Australia.

1871 First organised golf in New Zealand. Dunedin Golf Club (later called the Otago) formed, followed a year later by the Christchurch Golf Club. However, both clubs lapsed and a new era did not dawn until 1891.

1872 Following Young Tom Morris winning the Open championship belt outright, the Prestwick and St Andrews clubs, together with the Honourable Company of Edinburgh Golfers, combined to provide a new Open championship trophy—a silver claret jug. It was won by Young Tom Morris, his fourth championship victory in succession.

1873 (Royal) Montreal Golf Club founded, the first club in Canada and the continent of North America.

1875 Oxford and Cambridge University Golf Clubs formed.

1878 Birth of the University Match (Oxford and Cambridge); the oldest club match in the world.

1880 The Tennant Cup founded by the Glasgow Club. It is the oldest surviving Open competition for amateurs.

1881 Royal Belfast Golf Club formed.

1884 Formation of the Oakhurst Golf Club. White Sulphur Springs, Virginia; but it did not last.

1885 Founding of South Africa's first club, the Royal Cape. The first recorded golf had been on a 6-hole course near the military camp at Wynberg.

The British Amateur championship founded at Hoylake, Cheshire. It is the oldest amateur championship in the world. First played on 20–23 April.

1888 Formation of the St Andrews Golf Club at Yonkers, New York; the real beginnings of golf in the United States.

Belgium's first course, Royal Antwerp; Malaysia's first course, Perak at Taiping.

1889 Hong Kong Golf Club founded, now Royal Hong Kong.

1890 Royal Bangkok Golf Club, Thailand, founded.

1891 Formation of Shinnecock Hills Golf Club on Long Island, New York, named after a tribe of Indians who once inhabited the far end of Long Island; its clubhouse is the oldest in the United States.

Las Palmas Golf Club, Canary Islands, founded.

Gothenburg Golf Club, Sweden, founded.

1892 First Indian Amateur championship.

Lomas Golf Club, Argentina, founded.

1893 Formation of the Ladies' Golf Union in Britain; also, the start of the British Ladies' championship.

Start of the New Zealand Amateur championship.

1894 The British Open taken to England for the first time and won by J H Taylor. He was the first English professional to win. John Ball (1890) and Harold Hilton (1892) had won as amateurs.

The United States Golf Association founded.

First Australian Men's Amateur and Ladies' championships. First Malaysian Amateur.

1895 First United States Open and Amateur championships played at Newport Golf Club, Rhode Island.

Canadian Amateur championship started.

Bulawayo Golf Club, Rhodesia, founded.

First two courses in Germany—Bad Homburg and Baden-Baden.

Argentinian Amateur championship started.

1897 Nine-hole course opened at Puebla, Mexico.

1898 Copenhagen Golf Club, Denmark, founded.

1901 First course in Japan, 9 holes on the slopes of Mount Rokko, near Kobe.

Ladies' course on Minchinhampton Common (Mary Evans Pic. Lib.)

Invention of the Haskell (USA) rubber-cored ball.
British Professional Golfers' Association formed—first in the world.
First course in Austria at Wien-Krieau.
1902 First amateur international match between England and Scotland.
1903 The Oxford and Cambridge Golfing Society toured the United States, the first overseas tour ever undertaken.
1904 First French Amateur championship at La Boulie.
First course in Czechoslovakia at Karlovy Vary.
First Australian and Canadian Open championships.
1905 First international golf match between Britain and the United States. The British ladies defeated the American ladies 6–1 at Cromer, England.
1906 First French Open championship started at La Boulie.
1907 The Frenchman, Arnaud Massy became the first overseas winner of the British Open.
Swiss Men's and Ladies' Open amateur championships first played at Interlaken.
First New Zealand Open championship.
1909 Austrian Amateur championship started.
1913 Francis Ouimet (1893–1967), a virtually unknown amateur, defeated the British professionals Harry Vardon and Ted Ray in a play-off for the US Open at the Country Club, Brookline, Boston. It marked the beginning of American dominance.
1916 United States Professional Golfers' Association formed. USPGA championship started.
1917 Golf started in Bogota, Colombia.
1919 Management of the British Open and Amateur championships taken over by the Royal and Ancient Golf Club.
Taiwan Golf and Country Club opened.
1921 The Royal and Ancient and the USPGA introduced the first limitation on the size and weight of the ball, and agreed that 'on and after May 1st, 1921, the weight of the ball shall not be greater than 1.62 ounces (45.88 g) and the size not less than 1.62 inches (41.15 mm)'.
First amateur international between Britain and the United States at Hoylake. The US won 9–3.
1922 The Prince of Wales, later King Edward VIII, Captain of the Royal and Ancient Golf Club.
Walker Cup matches started.
1925 Steel-shafted clubs legalised in the United States.
1926 First, semi-official, professional international match played at Wentworth between the United States and Britain. Britain won 13½–1½.
1927 Ryder Cup matches started.
1930 Grand Slam year for Bobby Jones. He won the British and American Open and Amateur championships.
Steel-shafted clubs legalised in Britain although Bobby Jones remained loyal to hickory throughout his

Arnaud Massy, first overseas winner of the British Open, 1907

career. He retired after the Grand Slam.
The Duke of York, later King George VI, became Captain of the Royal and Ancient Golf Club.
1932 Curtis Cup matches started at Wentworth. The United States ladies defeated the British 5½–3½.
1934 Start of the US Masters at Augusta, Georgia.
1937 European Golf Association founded.

An early gang mower (1923) manufactured by Ransomes (Ransomes Sims & Jefferies Ltd)

Radio broadcast, St Andrews, 1946 (BBC Hulton Pic. Lib.)

1951 Francis Ouimet (1893–1967) became the first American Captain of the Royal and Ancient.

1963 Asia Golf Confederation founded.

1964 Women's World Amateur team championship for Espirito Santo Trophy started in Paris.

1968 A women's team from continental Europe defeated a United States team 10½–7½ in Paris.

1971 First golf shot on the Moon (February). Captain Alan Shepard, Commander of the Apollo 14 spacecraft, hit two balls with an iron-headed club which he presented to the USGA Museum in 1974.

The Royal and Ancient Golf Club sent Shepard a telegram of congratulation and a reminder of the Rules of Golf section on etiquette, '. . . before leaving a bunker, a player should carefully fill up all holes made by him therein.'

1979 Spanish golfer, Severiano Ballesteros wins the British Open.

1981 German golfer, Bernhard Langer was runner-up in British Open.

First-day cover produced for the centenary of Royal Jersey GC (Courtesy of the Jersey Post Office)

The Supreme Champions

Bobby Jones's assertion that 'there are tournament winners and major tournament winners' was a neat way of stressing the difference between the good and the great.

He, for his part, was the supreme champion, and this section is concerned solely with those men whose achievements have enriched the history of competitive golf: the legends like Jones, Hogan and Nicklaus.

It has become customary to measure success by the number of victories in the major championships, but such a measurement is not entirely fair. Before the start of the US Masters in 1934 and the USPGA championship in 1916, the only major championships were the British and American Opens; and, until the start of the jet age, it was very much the exception for anyone to play in both in the same year.

As a result, Harry Vardon, say, had far fewer chances than Jack Nicklaus who has taken part in all four major championships since first appearing as a professional in 1962. Inspired and influenced by Jones, however, he has always set his standards by the major championships and, by this insistence, has guaranteed their pre-eminence.

They remain the most cherished titles in the world of golf largely because they act as some means of comparison between the generations. In modern times, they have also become a passport to fortune, but the stunning thought today is that Jones was an amateur. His total of championship victories is, therefore, based on the Open and Amateur championships of Britain and America.

Any parallel between him and Hogan or Sarazen or Snead cannot be exact. If one includes Jones's Amateur championship successes, one has to include the two by Nicklaus and one by Arnold Palmer but, while it is impossible to argue with figures, the accompanying charts and tables illustrate what it is, by any reckoning, that sets a few golfers apart from the others.

Champion of the year

It is commonly believed that a 36-hole competition is a better test of a golfer's ability than a single round, and a 72-hole competition better still.

Frequently, we see a first or even second round leader in a major championship fading completely from the scene long before the end.

The man who shoots 67 today takes 77 tomorrow. Sometimes it may be due to luck averaging out or to an attack of nerves but sometimes, too, it is because tomorrow's share of putts are holed today.

If 72 holes is a surer test of ability than 18 or 36, it follows that 288 holes must be an even better test; and, if the 288 holes are the aggregate of the four major championships, then the golfer with the lowest total for those 288 holes can fairly claim to be 'champion of the year'.

Until 1960, it was very rare for anyone to play in all four majors but since then it has become much more fashionable. The following is the roll of honour but it must be stressed that, in order to qualify, a player must have played in all four championships.

The name of Jack Nicklaus, as one would expect, features prominently, but in 1963 he was ineligible on account of failing to qualify in the US Open when defending champion although in the other three majors, he had two firsts and a third.

THE SUPREME CHAMPIONS

		British open	US open	Masters	PGA	Total
1960	Arnold Palmer	279(1)	280(1)	282(1)	286(7)	1127
1961	Arnold Palmer	284(1)	289(=14)	281(=2)	282(=5)	1136
1962	Arnold Palmer	276(1)	283(2)	280(1)	288(=17)	1127
1963	Gary Player	287(=7)	296(=8)	289(=5)	283(=13)	1155
1964	Jack Nicklaus	284(2)	295(=23)	282(=2)	274(=2)	1135
1965	Jack Nicklaus	294(=12)	299(=32)	271(1)	282(=2)	1146
1966	Arnold Palmer	288(=8)	278(2)	290(=4)	287(=6)	1143
1967	Doug Sanders	290(=18)	292(=34)	292(=16)	292(=28)	1166
1968	Billy Casper	292(4)	286(=9)	285(=16)	284(=6)	1147
1969	Miller Barber	288(10)	284(=6)	284(7)	280(=5)	1136
1970	Jack Nicklaus	283(1)	304(=51)	284(8)	283(6)	1154
1971	Jack Nicklaus	283(=5)	280(2)	281(=2)	281(1)	1125
1972	Jack Nicklaus	279(2)	290(1)	286(1)	287(=13)	1142
1973	Jack Nicklaus	280(4)	282(=4)	285(=3)	277(1)	1124
1974	Gary Player	282(1)	293(=8)	278(1)	280(7)	1133
1975	Jack Nicklaus	280(=3)	289(=7)	276(1)	276(1)	1121
1976	Raymond Floyd	286(4)	288(=13)	271(1)	282(=2)	1127
1977	Tom Watson	268(1)	284(=7)	278(1)	283(=6)	1114
1978	Tom Watson	287(=14)	289(=6)	278(=2)	276(=2)	1130
1979	Jack Nicklaus	286(=2)	291(=9)	281(4)	294(=65)	1152
1980	Jack Nicklaus	280(4)	272(1)	291(=33)	274(1)	1117
1981	Jack Nicklaus ⎱	290(=23)	281(=6)	282(=2)	279(=4)	1132 ⎱
	Bill Rogers ⎰	276(1)	276(=2)	295(=37)	285(=31)	1132 ⎰

Individual Victories in the Major Championships

(These include US and British Opens, US Masters, USPGA and US and British Amateurs.)

19—JACK WILLIAM NICKLAUS
US Open, 62–67–72–80
British Open, 66–70–78
US Masters, 63–65–66–72–75
USPGA, 63–71–73–75–80
US Amateur, 59–61

13—ROBERT TYRE (BOB—USA, BOBBY—GB) JONES, Jr
US Open, 23–26–29–30
British Open, 26–27–30
US Amateur, 24–25–27–28–30
British Amateur, 1930

11—WALTER CHARLES HAGEN
US Open, 14–19
British Open, 22–24–28–29
US Masters, None
USPGA, 21–24–25–26–27

9—BENJAMIN WILLIAM (BEN) HOGAN
US Open, 48–50–51–53
British Open, 1953
US Masters, 51–53
USPGA, 46–48

9—GARY PLAYER
US Open, 1965
British Open, 59–68–74
US Masters, 61–74–78
USPGA, 62–72

8—ARNOLD DANIEL PALMER
US Open, 1960
British Open, 61–62
US Masters, 58–60–62–64
USPGA, None
US Amateur, 1954

7—HARRY VARDON
British Open 1896–98–99–03–11–14
US Open, 1900

7—EUGENE (GENE) SARAZEN
US Open, 22–32
British Open, 1932
US Masters, 1935
USPGA, 22–23–33

7—SAMUEL JACKSON SNEAD
British Open, 1946
US Masters, 49–52–54
USPGA, 42–49–51

7—TOM WATSON
British Open, 1975–77–80–82
US Open, 1982
US Masters, 1977–81

Major Title Winners

US Open, British Open, US Masters, USPGA, US Amateur
In same year None
In different years Jack Nicklaus

US Open, British Open, US Masters, US Amateur
In same year None
In different years Arnold Palmer, Jack Nicklaus

British Open, US Open, US Masters, USPGA
In same year None
In different years Gene Sarazen, Ben Hogan, Gary Player and Jack Nicklaus

British Open, US Open, British Amateur, US Amateur
In same year R T Jones, Jr (1930)
In different years None

British Open, US Open, US Masters
In same year Ben Hogan (1953)
In different years Gene Sarazen, Arnold Palmer, Gary Player, Jack Nicklaus and Tom Watson

British Open, US Open, USPGA
In same year None
In different years Walter Hagen, Jim Barnes, Gene Sarazen, Tommy Armour, Ben Hogan, Gary Player, Jack Nicklaus and Lee Trevino.

British Open, USPGA, US Masters
In same year None
In different years Gene Sarazen, Ben Hogan, Sam Snead, Gary Player and Jack Nicklaus

US Open, USPGA, US Masters
In same year None
In different years Gene Sarazen, Byron Nelson, Ben Hogan, Gary Player and Jack Nicklaus

British Open, US Open, US Amateur
In same year R T Jones, Jr (1930)
In different years R T Jones, Jr, Jack Nicklaus, Arnold Palmer

British Open, British Amateur, US Amateur
In same year R T Jones, Jr (1930)
In different years Harold Hilton

British Open, US Open, British Amateur
In same year R T Jones, Jr (1930)
In different years None

US Open, US Amateur, British Amateur
In same year R T Jones, Jr (1930)
In different years W Lawson Little

British Open, US Open
In same year R T Jones, Jr (1926 and 1930), Gene Sarazen (1932), Ben Hogan (1953), Lee Trevino (1971), Tom Watson (1982)
In different years Ted Ray, Harry Vardon, Walter Hagen, Jim Barnes, R T Jones, Jr, Tommy Armour, Arnold Palmer, Gary Player, Jack Nicklaus, Tony Jacklin, Lee Trevino and Johnny Miller

British Amateur, US Amateur
In same year Harold Hilton (1911), R T Jones, Jr (1930), W Lawson Little (1934 and 1935), Bob Dickson (1967)
In different years Walter Travis, Jess Sweetser, Willie Turnesa, Dick Chapman, Harvie Ward, Deane Beman, Steve Melnyk and Marvin Giles III

US Open, US Amateur, US Masters
In same year None
In different years Arnold Palmer, Jack Nicklaus

US Open, US Amateur
In same year Charles Evans, Jr (1916), R T Jones, Jr (1930)
In different years Francis Ouimet, Jerome D Travers, R T Jones, Jr, John Goodman, W Lawson Little, Arnold Palmer, Gene Littler, Jack Nicklaus and Jerry Pate

British Open, British Amateur
In same year John Ball (1890), R T Jones, Jr (1930)
In different years Harold Hilton

US Open, USPGA
In same year Gene Sarazen (1922), Ben Hogan (1948), Jack Nicklaus (1980)

One of the few pictures of Bobby Jones taken after his retirement. A match for the Red Cross was played at Nassau, Bahamas between Jones and Tommy Armour (right) and Walter Hagen (putting) and Gene Sarazen. The Duke of Windsor is holding the flag (Keystone)

In different years Walter Hagen, Jim Barnes, Gene Sarazen, Tommy Armour, Olin Dutra, Byron Nelson, Ben Hogan, Gary Player, Jack Nicklaus, Julius Boros and Lee Trevino

British Open, USPGA
In same year Walter Hagen (1924)
In different years Jim Barnes, Jock Hutchison, Gene Sarazen, Walter Hagen, Tommy Armour, Densmore Shute, Sam Snead, Ben Hogan, Gary Player, Jack Nicklaus and Lee Trevino

US Open, US Masters
In same year Craig Wood (1941), Ben Hogan (1951 and 1953), Arnold Palmer (1960), Jack Nicklaus (1972)
In different years Gene Sarazen, Byron Nelson, Ralph Guldahl, Cary Middlecoff, Gary Player, Jack Nicklaus, Billy Casper, Tom Watson

British Open, US Masters
In same year Ben Hogan (1953), Arnold Palmer (1962), Jack Nicklaus (1966), Gary Player (1974) and Tom Watson (1977)
In different years Gene Sarazen, Sam Snead, Arnold Palmer, Gary Player, Jack Nicklaus, Tom Watson and Severiano Ballesteros

USPGA, US Masters
In same year Sam Snead (1949), Jack Burke (1956), Jack Nicklaus (1963 and 1975)
In different years Gene Sarazen, Byron Nelson, Henry Picard, Sam Snead, Ben Hogan, Doug Ford, Gary Player, Jack Nicklaus, Raymond Floyd

US Amateur, US Masters
Arnold Palmer, Jack Nicklaus, Craig Stadler

Young Tom Morris

b St Andrews, Fife, 20.4.1851;
d St Andrews, 25.12.1875

Sooner or later most of the early championship records have been broken, but three which Young Tom Morris established are never likely to succumb. Making allowances for 1871 when there was no Open, owing to the fact that he had won the championship belt outright, he scored four successive victories; and, when he won his first title in 1868, he succeeded his father, Old Tom, as champion. In 1869, they finished first and second.

Young Tom was the man who put championship golf on the map and though he had only a handful of challengers, there is no telling how many other records he would have set if he had not died at the tragically early age of 24.

His death came on Christmas Day 1875, only three months after that of his wife and newly born son. The tale, contradicted in the local St Andrews paper, was that he died of a broken heart. His memory is perpetuated by a plaque in St Andrews Cathedral which bears the inscription, 'Deeply regretted by numerous friends and all golfers, he thrice in succession won the championship belt and held it without rivalry and yet without envy, his many amiable qualities being no less acknowledged than his golfing achievements.'

Just how keen the rivalry was between father and son, is not recorded, but Old Tom once remarked in later years, 'I could cope wi' Allan [Robertson] mysel' but never wi' Tommy'; and nor could anyone else. At the age of 13, Young Tom won an exhibition match at Perth for a prize of £15; three years later, he won a professional tournament at Carnoustie, defeating Willie Park and Bob Andrew in a play-off, and in 1868 became the youngest Open champion.

Scores have inevitably improved over the years and it is no fairer to compare them than it is to measure success by the ever-increasing prize-money, but one achievement of Young Tom's is an undoubted measure of his ability.

In winning the 1870 Open by 12 strokes, only 1 stroke less than Old Tom's record-winning margin in 1862, he covered three rounds of Prestwick's 12-hole course in 149 strokes. It was a score never equalled even by Vardon, Taylor or Braid so long as the gutty ball was in use. Tom's last round of 49, 1 under fours, included a 3 at the 1st hole which measured considerably over 500 yd (450 m) and gained him custody of the championship belt which was later presented to the Royal and Ancient Golf Club.

There was thus a gap of a year while the championship trophy, still played for today, was presented; in 1872, he won that, too. He beat Davie Strath by 3 strokes and once thereafter beat the better ball of Strath and Jamie Anderson. On another occasion, he backed himself to beat 83 round the Old course for a whole week, winning every time and then lowering his target to 81 and 80.

He had some detractors; for instance it was said that his swing lacked classic grace, but the power of his broad shoulders gave him the ability to squeeze the ball out of the bad lies that abounded in those days.

THE GREAT TRIUMVIRATE
James Braid

b Earlsferry, Fife, 6.2.1870;
d London, 27.11.1950

John Henry Taylor

b Northam, North Devon, 19.3.1871;
d Northam, North Devon, 10.2.1963

Harry Vardon

b Grouville, Jersey, 9.5.1870;
d Totteridge, London, 20.3.1937

From 1894 until the outbreak of World War I in 1914 there were only five years in which the British Open

The Great Triumvirate who won 16 British Opens between them. James Braid (left), J H Taylor (centre), Harry Vardon (right)

championship was not won by one of the Great Triumvirate.

In that time, Harry Vardon won six times and J H Taylor and James Braid five times each. Three times they occupied the first three places and never once did one of them fail to finish in the first three. No major championship has ever been so dominated by three players over such a long period and they were the first to make the public conscious of golfing records.

Only Peter Thomson can rival them in terms of Open victories, but not even his tussle with Bobby Locke in the 1950s matched what was perhaps the most romantic period in golf.

Born within thirteen months of one another the Triumvirate did more than anyone to establish professional golf as an honourable trade.

Without their example, the recognition of professionals at clubs may have taken even longer than it did. Taylor, in particular, was a natural speaker and a natural leader who was largely responsible for the founding of the PGA and the development of artisan golf; but it was their contribution to the playing side of the game that undoubtedly left the biggest mark.

Although John Ball and Harold Hilton had both won the Open championship as amateurs, J H Taylor's first victory in 1894 halted the supremacy of the Scots professionals. It took place, too, at Sandwich, the first time the Open ventured into England, and highlighted Taylor's almost revolutionary new style of hitting boldly up to the pin.

His swing and follow-through were a little curtailed and his stance rigidly flat-footed, but there was an abundance of defiance and determination about his golf that made him such a redoubtable bad-weather player.

When Taylor pulled down his cap, stuck out his chin and embedded his large boots in the ground, he could hit straight through the wind, especially with his trusty mashie. His last and best victory came in just such conditions at Hoylake in 1913. He won by 8 strokes, showing a control on the last day that nobody could match. He was the only player to break 80 in the third and fourth rounds and confirmed his oft-quoted saying that the best way to win is to win easily. Though a highly strung and emotional man, he was a stern competitor who, at the age of 53, had the lowest score in the 1924 Open, taking into account the qualifying rounds as well.

That was as creditable a performance as any in a career that blossomed after his first success in the Open in 1894. He defended his title with another victory at St Andrews in 1895, but lost it to Vardon the following year at Muirfield in a play-off—the first play-off since the championship was decided over four rounds.

Vardon had started the final day 6 strokes behind

Taylor, but his ultimate victory was confirmation of his genius. In a career which saw him win his last Open 18 years after his first, he won a record six times. About the turn of the century when he went up and down the country, winning tournaments and breaking records, he raised the standards of those around him and had a great influence on methods of playing.

Until then, nobody had paid much attention to style, but suddenly people became aware that Vardon's upright swing was the essence of rhythm and grace. It was soon hailed as a perfect model for others to copy. Although he hit the ball a long way, he favoured light clubs and never carried more than ten.

Three of Vardon's six Opens were won after the advent of the rubber-cored ball, but it was with the gutty, before his serious illness in 1903, that he reigned supreme. Most of his success was attained in Britain, but he was also a pioneer of travel in days when it was long and laborious.

In 1900, he and Taylor finished first and second in the US Open at Chicago, the first time that either Open had been won by a traveller from overseas. Thirteen years later, he returned to Brookline for one of the most famous of all championships. It was the one in which he and Ted Ray lost a play-off to Francis Ouimet, an unknown local lad, who thus started the decline of British dominance.

Vardon's first tour of America took a lot out of him and it is said that he was never as brilliant again, although he was 44 years old when he won his last Open at Prestwick in 1914. After winning in 1903 with a total of 300, one of his proudest achievements, he contracted tuberculosis and had to go to a sanatorium for treatment but, by then, the third of the Trium- virate, James Braid, was in full swing.

The son of an Elie ploughman, he was a late starter compared to his great contemporaries. By the time he won his first Open in 1901, Taylor and Vardon had each won three times but, in a sudden golden era, Braid was the first of the three to win the champion- ship five times.

In the space of ten years, he won at St Andrews and Muirfield twice and at Prestwick once. He never suc- ceeded in England where he spent most of his life (first of all at the Army and Navy Stores in London, then at Romford and finally at Walton Heath) but, like Taylor and Vardon, he was seldom far away when not actually winning.

Until Jack Nicklaus finished second in 1979 for the seventh time, Taylor shared the title of champion runner-up with six, but Braid and Vardon were runners-up four times, Vardon once three years in succession.

Braid, who was said by Horace Hutchinson to drive with divine fury, was the winner of the first *News of the World* matchplay championship in 1903 and won money regularly in challenge and exhibition matches. In the 1904 Open at Sandwich, he played the last two rounds in a total of 140 strokes and was the first man to return a score under 70 in the championship. It came in his third round, Jack White, the winner, equalling it later in the day and Taylor, who finished third, beating it with 68.

Of the three, Braid's game was more liable to error, but his powers of recovery were immense, particularly in the now-familiar explosion shot from sand. It is just one more example of the way in which he, Taylor and Vardon set fashions over perhaps the most important 20 years in the whole history of championship golf.

	Harry Vardon	J H Taylor	James Braid
1894	=5	1	=10
1895	=9	1	DNP
1896	1	2 (lost play-off)	6
1897	6	=10	2
1898	1	4	11
1899	1	4	5
1900	2	1	3
1901	2	3	1
1902	=2	=6	=2
1903	1	=9	5
1904	5	=2	=2
1905	=9	=2	1
1906	3	2	1
1907	=7	2	=5
1908	=5	=7	1
1909	26	1	2
1910	=16	=14	1
1911	1	=5	=5
1912	2	=11	3
1913	=3	1	=18
1914	1	2	=10
1920	=14	12	=21
1921	=23	=26	=16
1922	=8	6	DNP
1924	DNP	5	=18

DNP Did not play.
=   Finished tied.

In addition, Vardon won the US Open in 1900 and was runner-up in 1913. He was also equal second when Ted Ray won in 1920. Taylor was second to Vardon in 1900.

Jack William Nicklaus

b Columbus, Ohio, 21.1.1940

To the question how good is Jack Nicklaus, the answer can only be: look at the record. The number of times his name appears in these pages is some guide, but statistics only scratch the surface. They deserve closer scrutiny.

From the time that he defeated Arnold Palmer in a play-off in his first US Open as a professional in 1962, he has started favourite in almost every tournament or

For most the game is easier without the ball but not Jack Nicklaus (Phil Sheldon)

championship in which he has taken part. Inevitably, he has had his bad days and his bad weeks, but what is bad for him is good for most others.

Fellow competitors still look over their shoulders even when Nicklaus is 7 or 8 strokes behind. He is always capable of a round that is beyond everyone else, and several have brought him victory in the major championships on which he concentrates his efforts.

To date, he has won 19—or 17 if one discounts his two US Amateur championships. These comprise four US Opens, three British Opens, five Masters and five USPGAs, but not the least impressive part of this roll of honour is the number of times that he has finished in the first ten. His consistency is phenomenal.

From 1962 to 1981 Nicklaus played 80 major championships. In only 20 of these did he finish outside the first ten; in only four did he fail to make the cut (the 1963 US Open, the 1967 Masters and the 1968 and 1978 USPGAs) and in no fewer than 42 was he in the first three.

In the 15 British Opens from 1966, he never finished worse than sixth. He has played 26 rounds under 70 (eleven more than anybody else) and he has been runner-up a record seven times. In addition, he has the highest number of rounds under 70 in the US Open, the record number of victories in the Masters and the highest number (14) of top five finishes.

Jack Nicklaus has been breaking records, in fact, ever since the Eisenhower Trophy in 1960 at Merion when he first dropped a hint of what was in store. Even making due allowance for the fact that the pins were positioned without the customary severity of an Open, 269 was an absurdly low score for a young amateur. The previous year, he had made his debut in the Walker Cup at Muirfield and went home to win the US Amateur, a title he captured again in 1961 at Pebble Beach. Coincidentally, he won the US Open at Pebble Beach eleven years later—the only person to win the US Amateur and US Open on the same course. In 1960, he also set the lowest US Open aggregate by an amateur (282).

Within a few months of turning professional, he won the US Open at Oakmont although his first appearance in the British Open, which Arnold Palmer won the same summer, was easily his worst (equal 34th). However, it is the only occasion in which Palmer has finished above Nicklaus in the British Open; and there have not been very many others elsewhere in major championships.

In retrospect, it seems inevitable that Nicklaus became a great golfer. In the Foreword to Nicklaus's book, *The Greatest Game of All*, Bobby Jones recalled that as early as the age of 15 when Nicklaus first appeared in the US Amateur, 'it was not difficult to see that a new talent of the first magnitude had arrived'.

With the adoption of Jones as his hero, Nicklaus set out on his path to the top, encouraged by his father, Charlie Nicklaus, a keen golfer and qualified pharmacist; and was taught from the beginning by Jack Grout to whom he still turns when he has a technical problem.

During his developmental years, Nicklaus attended high school and college but by 1961 he was known as 'the amateur the pros fear' and, in view of the opportunities which professional golf had to offer, it was inevitable that he should take the decision to join its ranks.

It was inevitable, too, that Palmer's reign as the world's leading golfer should have been ended by Nicklaus. Not that this was universally welcome in America where Palmer's popularity knew no limits. Many resented the fact that Nicklaus, little more than a young college boy, could play so well. They did not think it right that he should topple their great hero so soon. So life was not always easy for Nicklaus as a result.

Luckily, however, he had a warm regard for Palmer and understood the situation perfectly. Equally, the hysteria of his followers which Palmer experienced must have been an embarrassment to him at times, but Nicklaus quickly made himself a model champion; a champion with less of the identifiable emotion that Palmer displayed, but one whose golf was indisputably supreme.

There had been many signs of his rising genius notably in the 1960 Open when he finished second to Palmer, two strokes behind. It was the highest finish by an amateur since Johnny Goodman won in 1933 but there was still an element of suddenness about the way he became champion two years later within such a short time of turning professional.

It was the best first tournament any professional could have won, but Nicklaus enjoyed phenomenal success wherever he went. The first of the eight years (a record) that he has finished as leading money-winner in the United States was 1964, and he has won tournaments regularly ever since despite rationing his appearances and concentrating on the major championships. To date, he has won 66 tournaments which puts him in second place in the United States behind Sam Snead on 84.

A year after winning the US Open, he won the Masters and the PGA championship. He won the Masters again in 1965, breaking all records with a total of 271, 9 strokes ahead of Palmer and Player; and he became the only person to successfully defend his title the following April.

This came only after a play-off with Tommy Jacobs and Gay Brewer, but it was the start of a summer which saw his first success in the British Open at Muirfield, the course for which he already had great affection and after which he called his own course Muirfield Village several years later.

After an inauspicious beginning in the 1962 British Open, when he made the cut only by a single stroke, he had a chance in 1963 and followed Tony Lema home at St Andrews in 1964. On the last day, Nicklaus had the lowest aggregate (134) of any last day but with the fairways narrow and the rough deep at Muirfield, he squeezed home with 1 stroke in hand.

Nicklaus had gone on record as saying that he was not a good 'fast course' player, but he was prepared to accept the course's essential demand for accuracy rather than length, taking an iron from many of the tees.

He squandered a big lead on the last 9 holes of the third round and dropped strokes at the 11th, 13th and 14th in the last round, but he managed the four 4s he needed to win, one of them a birdie.

His triumph completed victory in the four major championships, enabling him to join Gene Sarazen, Ben Hogan and Gary Player, but by 1971 he became the first person to win them all a second time and now he has won them all three times. He passed Bobby Jones's total of 13 major championships and, on the professional tour front, joined the million dollar 'Club' in 1970. Since then he has become the founder member of the two and three million dollar 'Club', and sole member of the latter.

Yet the impressive part of this recital of superlatives are some of the individual records he holds. In the Masters, he is the most frequent winner, the youngest winner, the winner by the biggest margin and has the lowest number of top five finishes.

In the US Open, Nicklaus set a new record for the lowest aggregate with 272 in 1980 and has the highest number of rounds (21) under 70. This is a record he holds, too, in the British Open (26), as well as a share of the lowest fourth round—a 65. He has the lowest last round in the USPGA (64) and has the biggest span between his first and last victories in this (1963–80) and the US Open (1962–80).

By comparison with so many of his other great deeds, he has been least successful in the US Open even allowing for the fact that nobody has won it more often. For seven championships from 1973, he was never in the first three but at Baltusrol in 1980 his reaction was emphatic with a first round 63 and a sterling victory; and in 1982 he was, in some ways, unlucky to be thwarted by Tom Watson at Pebble Beach.

	British Open	US Open	US Masters	USPGA
1958	DNP	=41*		DNP
1959	DNP		F/Q*	DNP
1960	DNP	2*	=13*	DNP
1961	DNP	=4*	=7*	DNP
1962	=34	1	=15	=3
1963	3	F/Q	1	1
1964	2	=23	=2	=2
1965	=12	=32	1	=2
1966	1	3	1	=22
1967	2	1	F/Q	=3
1968	=2	2	=5	F/Q
1969	=6	=25	=24	=11
1970	1	=51	8	=6
1971	=5	2	=2	1
1972	2	1	1	=13
1973	4	=4	=3	1
1974	3	=10	=4	2
1975	=3	=7	1	1
1976	=2	=11	=3	=4
1977	2	=10	2	3
1978	1	=6	7	F/Q
1979	=2	=9	4	=65
1980	=4	1	=33	1
1981	=23	=6	=2	=4
1982	=10	2	=15	

United States Amateur champion 1959 and 1961.
DNP Did not play.
F/Q Failed to qualify for final 36 holes.
=   Finished tied.
*   As Amateur.

His 63 in 1981 equalled the lowest round in the history of the entire championship and *en route* to victory by 2 strokes over Isao Aoki, he lowered his own record aggregate to 272 and set a record for the lowest first 36 holes and the 54 holes (with Aoki) although this was beaten at Merion a year later.

Nor was that an end to his record breaking for 1980. In August, he won the USPGA championship by 7 strokes and equalled Walter Hagen's tally of five victories set in the 1920s.

At Sandwich the following summer, he created a record of a different sort for him—a first round of 83. On the second day he produced a 66 and so maintained the British Open as the only major in which he has never once missed the cut.

In addition he has six victories to his name in the Australian Open and has been a member of six winning World Cup teams, but he has accomplished this huge catalogue of success without allowing it to dictate his whole life and without spoiling him as a person.

He has always given straight answers and the golf

writers of the world have respected him for it but, early on, he could be a little abrasive. However, as the college boy image faded, he transformed his appearance and his weight and endeared himself to many by his good grace and generosity of mind.

Defeat can be harder to bear when somebody is as used to winning as he is but he accepts it calmly and philosophically and, at such moments, will continue interviews at length when some others grudge as much as a couple of minutes.

It is on these occasions that one is struck by his control, care, thoughtfulness and patience. But these are, after all, the same qualities that characterise his golf—the qualities that combine to make him unquestionably the best contemporary golfer and arguably the best that ever lived.

CAREER SUMMARY

(Professional Years: From 1962 to 1981 inclusive)
Official tour victories: 68
Second place or ties: 48
Third place or ties: 31
Total victories round the world: 86
Tops in career tour averages: 70·4 strokes per round
Tops in lowest scoring average: 8 times, 1976–75–74–73–72–71–65–64; runner-up 6 times
Top money-winner: 8 times, 1976–75–73–72–71–67–65–64; runner-up 4 times
Tops in career official tour earnings: $3 759 426
Most major championship titles: 19 (Masters 5; PGA Championship 5; United States Open 4; British Open 3; US Amateur 2)
PGA Player of the Year Award: 5 times, 1976–75–73–72–67
Play-off tour record: won 12, lost 9
Lowest tournament records: all 62s
Ohio Kings Island Open, 7 October 1973, third round
Sahara Invitational, 28 October 1967, third round
Australian Dunlop International, 5 November 1971, second round
(shot 59 in exhibition with three professionals 12 March 1973, at Palm Beach, Florida)

International and other victories

British Open (3): 1978–70–66 (runner-up 7 times)
Australian Open (6): 1978–76–75–71–68–64
World Series of Golf (5): 1976–70–67–63–62 (runner-up 6 times)
Ryder Cup: member of US teams that defeated Britain in 1981–77–75–73–71 and tied Britain 1969
World Matchplay Championship: 1970
World Cup: winner of individual championship a record three times (1971–64–63) and six times a partner on US winning teams

Scoring Average			
1962 – 70.80	1966 – 70.58	1970 – 70.75	1976 – 70.17
1963 – 70.42	1967 – 70.23	1971 – 70.08	1977 – 70.36
1964 – 69.96	1968 – 69.97	1972 – 70.23	1978 – 71.07
1965 – 70.09	1969 – 71.06	1973 – 69.81	1979 – 72.49
		1974 – 70.06	1980 – 70.86
		1975 – 69.87	1981 – 70.71

Robert Tyre Jones, JR

b Atlanta, Georgia 17.3.1902;
d Atlanta, 18.12.1971

The Impregnable Quadrilateral, so much nicer a term than the Grand Slam, is the most perfect achievement in golf. In the summer of 1930, Bobby Jones won the Open and Amateur championships of Britain and America.

Nowadays it is unthinkable for an amateur to win either Open and this is, therefore, a record that will almost certainly never be broken. It is the ultimate achievement and, though only 28 at the time, Jones understandably retired. For the previous eight years his consistency in the two Opens remains unsurpassed even by modern giants like Hogan and Nicklaus.

In his last nine US Opens, he was first four times and second four times. From 1923 to 1930, he was either US Open or Amateur champion although strangely he never won both in the same year until 1930. He won three of the four British Opens in which he took part and, after 1923, Walter Hagen, one of the leading golfers of the 1920s, only once finished above him in either championship.

In addition to winning the US Amateur a record five times, Jones was a finalist and semi-finalist twice and eventually succeeded in winning the British Amateur, a championship with its 18-hole matches which Jones always considered was the hardest of all to win.

In 36-hole matches, however, it was a different story. His successes in the Walker Cup and US Amateur were devastating. From 1923 to 1930, he lost only once over 36 holes—to George von Elm in the Amateur final of 1926.

At various other times, he defeated Chick Evans 7 and 6; von Elm 9 and 8; Roger Wethered 9 and 8, and 7 and 6; Cyril Tolley 12 and 11; Francis Ouimet 11 and 9; John Beck 14 and 13; and T P Perkins 13 and 12, and 10 and 9—both within 14 days.

No wonder Bernard Darwin wrote, 'Like the man in the song, many of Mr Jones's opponents are tired of living but feared of dying. However, their fears are rarely unduly protracted since they usually die very soon after lunch.'

In all, Jones won 13 major titles, a figure only beaten by Jack Nicklaus who, though not born until ten years after Jones retired, regarded Jones as his hero; but comparisons are worthless. Jones belonged to a leisured age when travel to Britain was a considerable undertaking. He played, too, with hickory-shafted clubs throughout his career but he had the style and technique to have played with a stair rod. He was as much loved in Britain as in America and did more than any overseas golfer to promote the importance of the British Open in the eyes of the world.

Although immensely considerate to others and later a model of behaviour, he often allowed youthful impetuosity to get the better of him if he failed to match his own high standards. It resulted in his tearing up his card in the third round of the 1921 Open at St Andrews and may have stemmed from the sort of frustration that the Old Course can invoke.

However, he made handsome amends, building up a genuine love of the Old course, extolling its virtues and when receiving the Freedom of the Burgh of St Andrews on 9 October 1958, paying it a unique compliment. He said he would choose St Andrews if he were allowed only one course in the world on which to play and added, 'I could take out of my life everything except my experiences at St Andrews and still have a rich, full life.'

Jones was only nine when he won the junior championship of his Club, East Lake, Atlanta, and was 14 when he won the Georgia State Amateur championship for the first time. A year later, he won the Southern Amateur and in 1919 was runner-up in the Canadian Open and US Amateur.

If Jones's father had not moved house from the city to the suburb of East Lake when the young Bobby was only five, he might not have taken to golf at all. His father cared little for sport but the fascination of looking through the gates of the East Lake Club had its effect. Jones clearly liked what he saw.

After being officially taken to the club by his mother, he was given the chance to try his hand and the game came easily to him. He needed few lessons but, like so many great players, he was a born imitator, basing his style on the professional at East Lake, Stewart Maiden, an emigrant Scot and friend to whom Jones always paid tribute. Without consciously trying Jones was a supreme stylist with a smooth, drowsy, rhythmic swing. His boyish good looks and sturdy, athletic build combined to give him a magnetic personality although it would be quite wrong to suggest that he did not suffer over his golf in the manner of humbler folk.

His great and trusted friend, O B Keeler, often wrote how Bobby could scarcely eat anything until a day's play was over; how, on occasions, he felt he could not even button his shirt collar for fear of the direst consequences; how he could lose a stone in weight during a championship and how he was capable of breaking down to the point of tears, not from any distress but from pure emotional overstrain.

Youthful good looks and the classic swing of Bobby Jones

Bernard Darwin recalled vividly, too, the close of the 1930 Open at Hoylake, the second leg of the Impregnable Quadrilateral. 'I was writing in the room where Bobby was waiting to see if he had won. He was utterly exhausted and had to hold his glass in two hands lest the good liquor be spilt. All he would say was that he would never, never do it again.'

Later that year he remained true to his word, but back in the days of his youth his career had not yet reached full flower.

Jones played in his first US Open at the age of 18, finishing in a tie for eighth place. As so often happens with young players, too much was probably expected of him too soon and for seven years from the age of 15 he played in ten major championships without success. The 1921 British Open was one example and the British Amateur the same year another.

Then, in 1923, the Bobby Jones era really opened with victory in the US Open at Inwood, New York, after a play-off with Bobby Cruickshank. In the last round, Cruickshank had finished with a birdie, but in the play-off Jones won with 76 to 78, the 2-stroke difference coming at the 18th hole.

Jones was second for the next two years but won the US Amateur in those years and in 1926 returned to Britain, the first time since his unfortunate baptism at St Andrews. After beating Cyril Tolley 12 and 11 in the Walker Cup and losing in the fifth round of the Amateur, he decided to stay on for the Open and had to qualify.

The fact that he qualified safely is only half the story. In so doing, he scored his famous 66 on the Old course at Sunningdale which was described as being as near flawless as any round of golf could be. He was only bunkered once, holed one long putt and hit every

The first great golfer with a commercial eye, Walter Hagen. Always looking to do something different like hitting a ball from the roof of the Savoy Hotel, London (BBC Hulton Pic. Lib.)

high living from his boyhood. His parents, of thrifty German stock, had to work hard to raise a family of five of which he was the only boy. His father made $18 a week as a blacksmith in the car shops of East Rochester and so the odd dollar from caddying came in very useful; but the urge to play could not be suppressed. He signed on as assistant at the Country Club of Rochester and quickly became a successful player—a player embarking on one of the most glamorous careers in the whole of professional sport.

Everyone knew Walter Hagen; everyone flocked to see him play. They admired his dashing style on the course and they were amused by the sometimes outrageous things that occupied him off it. But not all the countless stories of Hagen are true; nor was the image portrayed of him always accurate.

He drank only about half the drinks he accepted but he certainly never kept strict hours.

When told once that his opponent of the following day had been in bed for some time, he made the famous reply, 'Yeah, but he ain't sleeping.' The incident occurred in an Edinburgh night-club before the last day of the 1929 British Open at Muirfield where Hagen won. The opponent most feared to catch him, Leo Diegel, finished third.

There were other equally famous remarks, but all tended to emphasise the free and easy nature of a player who realised that golf was not necessarily a tight-lipped, solemn game; and that everyone has to cultivate his own way of relaxing. He could turn up on the first tee at the last minute, break his concentration between shots by chatting nonchalantly to spectators and still give of his best.

He was the first golfing showman and perhaps the first to indulge in any form of gamesmanship. Even in defeat, he seldom did anything by halves. In 1928, he lost a challenge match over 72 holes by 18 and 17 to Archie Compston, but a few days later, he won the Open championship at Sandwich.

He also gained the reputation of being a marvellous putter, but that sort of compliment is frequently used to hide a lack of other golfing virtues. In Hagen's case, that was not so. Before the days of the Masters, he won two US Opens, four British Opens and five USPGA championships, four of them in succession. One could not win all those simply with a putter.

What is more, his career covered a wide span. He first won the US Open in 1914 and finished third 21 years later. However, the 1920s were his best years. He was the first American-born winner of the British Open (1922) and the first American to win both the American and British titles.

His second British title was gained at Hoylake and he won for a third time at Sandwich in 1928. Although he only once finished in front of Bobby Jones in Jones's last eight US Opens, his second victory had come in 1919, but his most notable supremacy was in the USPGA championship. By winning from 1924 to when his chances of victory waned. He won the Spanish Open and the British PGA championship in 1975 in windy conditions at Sandwich which revived memories of Birkdale in 1961; and he has become highly successful on the seniors' tour in America.

In the modern golfing world, there is a natural search for players to idolise and respect not only as masters of their craft but as the personification of what heroes should be. Nobody has fitted that bill better than Palmer.

	US Open	British Open	Masters	USPGA
1958	=23	DNP	1	
1959	=5	DNP	3	=14
1960	1	2	1	7
1961	=14	1	=2	=5
1962	2	1	1	=17
1963	=2	=26	=9	=40
1964	=5	DNP	1	=2
1965		=13	=2	=33
1966	2	=8	=4	=6
1967	2	DNP	4	=14
1968	59	=10	F/Q	=2
1969	=6	DNP	27	F/Q
1970	=54	12	36	=2
1971	=24	F/Q	=18	=18
1972	3	=7	=33	=16
1973	=4	=14	=24	F/Q
1974	=5	DNP	=11	=28
1975	=9	=16	=13	=33
1976	=50	=55	F/Q	=14
1977	=19	7	=24	=19
1978		=34	=37	F/Q
1979	=56	DNP	F/Q	F/Q
1980	63	F/Q	=24	=72
1981		=23	F/Q	
1982	F/Q	=27		

DNP Did not play.
F/Q Failed to qualify.
=   Finished tied.
In 1962, 63 and 66 he lost a play-off in US Open.
He was United States Amateur champion in 1954.

Gene Sarazen

b Harrison, New York 27.2.1902

Of all the great winners of the major championships down the years, Gene Sarazen was undoubtedly the smallest in stature. In some ways, he came into golf by accident, but his playing career spanned more than half a century and is among the most distinguished in the history of the game.

Gene Sarazen pictured in later years with old friend and rival, Walter Hagen (International News Photos)

He is remembered for many things, but four feats of his must be recorded straightaway since they founded and preserved his reputation.

In the course of winning the British and American Opens in the same summer of 1932, he played 28 holes in 100 strokes at Fresh Meadow in the latter. Bobby Jones described it as 'the finest competitive exhibition on record'.

He became the first player to win all four major championships of the world, having been American champion for the first time at the age of 20; and he has to his credit two of the most famous single strokes ever played.

In only the second US Masters in 1935, he holed his second with a 4 wood at the 15th in the final round to turn a good chase into victory; and in the 1973 British Open at Troon, he holed in one at Troon's 8th, the celebrated Postage Stamp. To add piquancy to the tale, it was the 50th anniversary of his first appearance in the championship, also at Troon, and the shot was caught by the television cameras.

Sarazen was born in Harrison, New York, the son of a carpenter and christened Eugene Saraceni; the change of name came about because he felt he might be mistaken for a violinist. His father, who had studied for the priesthood back in Italy, was never in favour of his son becoming a golfer and it is possible that Gene might never have played at all if he had not contracted pleurisy while apprenticed to his father in Connecticut.

On medical advice, he found less strenuous work and, in the course of recuperation, tried his hand at golf. In a matter of months, he landed an assistant's post and before long he was Open champion. Having qualified for the championship in 1920 and 1921, his victory came at Skokie near Chicago where he was little known and spent the championship, so the story goes, sleeping in a dormitory of fellow professionals.

He practised extremely hard that week and had a premonition that he would win. He began with a 72 and 73 which put him in third place only to fall back with a moderate third round; but a 68, the first under 70 by a champion and the lowest last round until he beat it himself ten years later, gave him victory by a single stroke over John Black and Bobby Jones.

Golf has always been a full profession and a continuous business for Sarazen and, after the Open, he was inundated with invitations to take part in exhibition matches.

He won the PGA championship the same year and challenged Walter Hagen to a special match over 72 holes for the unofficial world championship. Not in the least daunted by the prospect, he beat 'The Haig' and then beat him again the following year at the 38th hole of the final of the PGA. They became good friends, dominated American professional golf for a number of years and, between them, put the professionals on the map, although Sarazen was always generous enough to give the lion's share of the credit to Hagen.

They became keen rivals and great contemporaries who, with Jones, set the tradition of supporting the British Open. Sarazen's first attempt in 1923 foundered even before he reached first base. He went to Troon, suitably hailed as the new star in the firmament, but failed to qualify in bad weather. With a humiliation that Hagen could understand after his experience in 1920, he vowed that he would be back even if he had to swim across the Atlantic.

As Herbert Warren Wind wrote of Hagen in *The Story of American Golf*, 'he had been press-agented as the golfer who would show British golf a thing or two' at Deal in 1920. 'Walter showed them four rounds in the eighties and finished a lurid fifty-fifth.'

Nobody doubted that Sarazen would be true to his word, but he had to wait until 1932 when the British Open was held at Prince's, Sandwich, for the first and only time. Accompanied by Daniels who had caddied for Hagen, Sarazen led from start to finish on a fast-running course, firmly obeying the advice of Daniels.

In 1928 over the fence at Royal St Georges, Sarazen took 7 on the 14th and lost to Hagen, but Daniels consoled him mightily by saying, 'I am going to win this championship for you if it is the last thing I do before I die.' Daniels kept his promise. Sarazen was never in danger and in the end had 5 strokes in hand over Macdonald Smith.

On the last day, in 1932, Daniels had been round the course early, checking the positions of the flags, showing that the modern propensity for pacing is nothing new but, in some ways, Sarazen's victory at Prince's was overshadowed by his second victory in the US Open a couple of weeks or so later.

In the previous months and years, he had not enjoyed the best of success and, for once in his life, he dabbled with technique.

He had always felt that his size had militated against him but, among other things, he experimented with the idea of a sand wedge with which he became a wizard; and, whether or not it was a big influence on his year of 1932, it gave him increased confidence.

Ironically, however, he started by playing cautiously and conservatively at Fresh Meadow in contrast to his normal approach of giving it everything he had. This seemed particularly misguided since the course encouraged players to attack from the tee and then to think about their second shots to well-bunkered greens.

With Sarazen's skill with his new bunker club, it seemed to further justify an attacking policy, but he decided otherwise and began with a 74 and a 76.

He persisted for a further 9 holes, but then was driven to return to his old ways. The results were as dramatic as could be. He played the last 28 holes in exactly 100 strokes, including a last round of 66. This was unheard of in those days and it remained the lowest last round by an American champion until Arnold Palmer returned 65 in 1960.

It was one of those almost fictional happenings that were such a feature of Sarazen's golfing life. His victory at the Masters and his hole in one at Troon are other examples, but 1932 marked the last of his victories in national championships although he came close more than once.

In his defence of the British Open at St Andrews in 1933, he finished 1 stroke away from a play-off with Densmore Shute and Craig Wood. Ironically, however, his trusty bunker club twice let him down. A lengthy argument with the Hill bunker cost him 6 at the short 11th in the second round and, in his final round, he failed to recover from Hell bunker on the 14th at his first attempt.

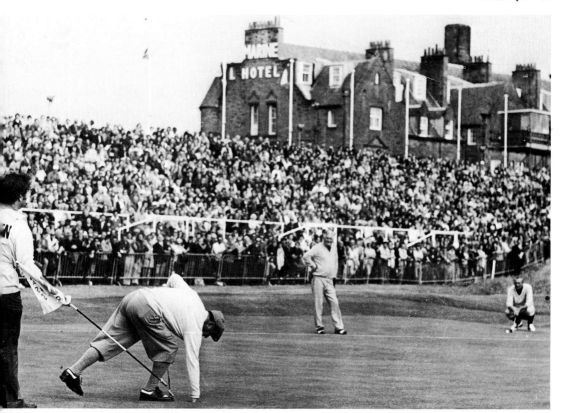

Sentimental return to Troon for Gene Sarazen in 1973, fifty years after his first appearance in the championship (United Press International)

Peter Thomson, 1958; Kel Nagle, 1960; Arnold Palmer, 1961; Arnold Palmer, 1962; Bob Charles, 1963; Tony Lema, 1964; Peter Thomson, 1965; Roberto de Vicenzo, 1967; Tony Jacklin, 1969; Lee Trevino, 1971; Lee Trevino, 1972; Tom Weiskopf, 1973; Gary Player, 1974; Tom Watson, 1977; Tom Watson, 1980; Bill Rogers, 1981

Longest course
Carnoustie, 1968, 7252 yd (6631 m)

Courses most often used (up to and including 1982)
Prestwick, 24 (but not since 1925); St Andrews, 22; Muirfield, 12; Hoylake and Sandwich, 10; Royal Lytham, 7; Musselburgh, 6; Royal Birkdale and Carnoustie, 5; Royal Troon, 5; Deal, 2; Royal Portrush, Prince's and Turnberry, 1

Lowest rounds on Open courses in an Open

Prestwick	**69,** Macdonald Smith, 1925
St Andrews	**65,** Neil Coles, 1970
Muirfield	**63,** Isao Aoki, 1980
Hoylake	**67,** Roberto de Vicenzo and Gary Player, 1967
Sandwich	**65,** Henry Cotton, 1934; Gordon Brand, 1981
Royal Lytham and St Annes	**65,** Eric Brown and Leopoldo Ruiz, 1958; Christy O'Connor, Sr, 1969; Bill
	Longmuir and Severiano Ballesteros, 1979
Prince's	**68,** Arthur Havers, 1932
Royal Birkdale	**66,** Peter Oosterhuis, 1971; Johnny Miller and Mark James, 1976
Carnoustie	**65,** Jack Newton, 1975
Royal Troon	**65,** Jack Nicklaus, 1973
Turnberry	**63,** Mark Hayes, 1977
Deal	**71,** George Duncan and Len Holland, 1920
Musselburgh	**77,** Willie Park, Jr, and Andrew Kirkaldy, 1889
Royal Portrush	**68,** Jimmy Adams, Charlie and Norman von Nida, 1951

PRIZE-MONEY		
Year	*Total £*	*First Prize £*
1920	225	75
1927	275	100
1930	400	100
1931	500	100
1946	1000	150
1949	1700	300
1953	2450	500
1954	3500	750
1955	3750	1000

Prize money continued

1958	4850	1000
1959	5000	1000
1960	7000	1250
1961	8500	1400
1963	8500	1500
1965	10 000	1750
1966	15 000	2100
1968	20 000	3000
1969	30 000	4250
1970	40 000	5250
1971	45 000	5500
1972	50 000	5500
1975	75 000	7500
1977	100 000	10 000
1978	125 000	12 500
1979	155 000	15 500
1980	200 000	25 000
1981	200 000	25 000
1982	250 000	32 000

ATTENDANCE AND GATE MONEY

Year	Attendance	Gate Money £
1962	37 098	15 207
1963	24 585	14 173
1964	35 954	14 704
1965	32 927	21 214
1966	40 182	23 075
1967	29 880	20 180
1968	51 819	31 907
1969	46 001	46 188
1970	81 593	62 744
1971	70 076	90 052
1972	84 746	98 925
1973	78 810	115 000
1974	92 796	158 729
1975	85 258	176 012
1976	92 021	243 793
1977	87 615	249 073
1978	125 271	421 474
1979	134 501	467 898
1980	131 610	538 288
1981	111 987	599 121

The largest single day attendance was 32 072 on the Friday of the 1979 championship.

The easiest hole at Royal St George's? Sam Torrance, the third person to hole-in-one at the 16th in the 1981 championship (Phil Sheldon)

RESULTS

1860 Prestwick

Willie Park, Musselburgh	174
Tom Morris Sr, Prestwick	176
Andrew Strath, St Andrews	180
Robert Andrew, Perth	191
George Brown, Blackheath	192
Charles Hunter, Prestwick St Nicholas	195

1861 Prestwick

Tom Morris Sr, Prestwick	163
Willie Park, Musselburgh	167
William Dow, Musselburgh	171
David Park, Musselburgh	172
Robert Andrew, Perth	175
Peter McEwan, Bruntsfield	178

1862 Prestwick

Tom Morris Sr, Prestwick	163
Willie Park, Musselburgh	176
Charles Hunter, Prestwick	178
William Dow, Musselburgh	181
*James Knight, Prestwick	186
*J F Johnston, Prestwick	208

1863 Prestwick

Willie Park, Musselburgh	168
Tom Morris Sr, Prestwick	170
David Park, Musselburgh	172
Andrew Strath, St Andrews	174
George Brown, St Andrews	176
Robert Andrew, Perth	178

*Amateur

1864 Prestwick

Tom Morris Sr, Prestwick	167
Andrew Strath, St Andrews	169
Robert Andrew, Perth	175
Willie Park, Musselburgh	177
William Dow, Musselburgh	181
William Strath, St Andrews	182

1865 Prestwick

Andrew Strath, St Andrews	162
Willie Park, Musselburgh	164
William Dow, Musselburgh	171
Robert Kirk, St Andrews	173
Tom Morris Sr, St Andrews	174
*William Doleman, Glasgow	178

1866 Prestwick

Willie Park, Musselburgh	169
David Park, Musselburgh	171
Robert Andrew, Perth	176
Tom Morris Sr, St Andrews	178
Robert Kirk, St Andrews	180
Andrew Strath, Prestwick	182
*William Doleman, Glasgow	182

1867 Prestwick

Tom Morris Sr, St Andrews	170
Willie Park, Musselburgh	172
Andrew Strath, St Andrews	174
Tom Morris Jr, St Andrews	175
Robert Kirk, St Andrews	177
William Doleman, Glasgow	178

1868 Prestwick

Tom Morris Jr, St Andrews	157
Robert Andrew, Perth	159
Willie Park, Musselburgh	162
Robert Kirk, St Andrews	171
John Allan, Westward Ho!	172
Tom Morris Sr, St Andrews	176

1869 Prestwick

Tom Morris Jr, St Andrews	154
Tom Morris Sr, St Andrews	157
*S Mure Fergusson, Royal and	
Ancient	165
Robert Kirk, St Andrews	168
David Strath, St Andrews	169
J Anderson, St Andrews	173

1870 Prestwick

Tom Morris Jr, St Andrews	149
Bob Kirk, Royal Blackheath	161
David Strath, St Andrews	161
Tom Morris Sr, St Andrews	162
*William Doleman, Musselburgh	171
Willie Park, Musselburgh	173

1871 No Competition

1872 Prestwick

Tom Morris Jr, St Andrews	166
David Strath, St Andrews	169
*William Doleman, Musselburgh	177
Tom Morris Sr, St Andrews	179
David Park, Musselburgh	179
Charlie Hunter, Prestwick	189

1873 St Andrews

Tom Kidd, St Andrews	179
Jamie Anderson, St Andrews	180
Tom Morris Jr, St Andrews	183
Bob Kirk, Royal Blackheath	183
Davie Strath, St Andrews	187
Walter Gourlay, St Andrews	188

1874 Musselburgh

Mungo Park, Musselburgh	159
Tom Morris Jr, St Andrews	161
George Paxton, Musselburgh	162
Bob Martin, St Andrews	164
Jamie Anderson, St Andrews	165
David Park, Musselburgh	166
W Thomson, Edinburgh	166

1875 Prestwick

Willie Park, Musselburgh	166
Bob Martin, St Andrews	168
Mungo Park, Musselburgh	171
Robert Ferguson, Musselburgh	172
James Rennie, St Andrews	177
David Strath, St Andrews	178

1876 St Andrews

Bob Martin, St Andrews	176
David Strath, North Berwick	176
(Martin was awarded the title	
when Strath refused to play-off)	
Willie Park, Musselburgh	183
Tom Morris Sr, St Andrews	185
W Thomson, Elie	185
Mungo Park, Musselburgh	185

1877 Musselburgh

Jamie Anderson, St Andrews	160
Bob Pringle, Musselburgh	162
Bob Ferguson, Musselburgh	164
William Cosegrove, Musselburgh	164
Davie Strath, North Berwick	166
William Brown, Musselburgh	166

1878 Prestwick

Jamie Anderson, St Andrews	157
Bob Kirk, St Andrews	159
J O F Morris, St Andrews	161
Bob Martin, St Andrews	165
John Ball, Hoylake	165
Willie Park, Musselburgh	166
William Cosegrove, Musselburgh	166

1879 St Andrews

Jamie Anderson, St Andrews	169
James Allan, Westward Ho!	172
Andrew Kirkaldy, St Andrews	172
George Paxton, Musselburgh	174
Tom Kidd, St Andrews	175
Bob Ferguson, Musselburgh	176

1880 Musselburgh

Bob Ferguson, Musselburgh	162
Peter Paxton, Musselburgh	167
Ned Cosgrove, Musselburgh	168
George Paxton, Musselburgh	169
Bob Pringle, Musselburgh	169
David Brown, Musselburgh	169

1881 Prestwick

Bob Ferguson, Musselburgh	170
Jamie Anderson, St Andrews	173
Ned Cosgrove, Musselburgh	177
Bob Martin, St Andrews	178
Tom Morris Sr, St Andrews	181
W Campbell, Musselburgh	181
Willie Park Jr, Musselburgh	181

1882 St Andrews

Bob Ferguson, Musselburgh	171
Willie Fernie, Dumfries	174
Jamie Anderson, St Andrews	175
John Kirkaldy, St Andrews	175
Bob Martin, St Andrews	175
*Fitz Boothby, St Andrews	175

1883 Musselburgh

Willie Fernie, Dumfries	159
Bob Ferguson, Musselburgh	159
(Fernie won play-off 158 to 159)	
W Brown, Musselburgh	160
Bob Pringle, Musselburgh	161
W Campbell, Musselburgh	163
George Paxton, Musselburgh	163

1884 Prestwick

Jack Simpson, Carnoustie	160
David Rollan, Elie	164
Willie Fernie, Felixstowe	164
Willie Campbell, Musselburgh	169
Willie Park Jr, Musselburgh	169
Ben Sayers, North Berwick	170

1885 St Andrews

Bob Martin, St Andrews	171
Archie Simpson, Carnoustie	172
David Ayton, St Andrews	173
Willie Fernie, Felixstowe	174
Willie Park Jr, Musselburgh	174
Bob Simpson, Carnoustie	174

1886 Musselburgh

David Brown, Musselburgh	157
Willie Campbell, Musselburgh	159
Ben Campbell, Musselburgh	160
Archie Simpson, Carnoustie	161
Willie Park Jr, Musselburgh	161
Thomas Gossett, Musselburgh	161
Bob Ferguson, Musselburgh	161

1887 Prestwick

Willie Park Jr, Musselburgh	161
Bob Martin, St Andrews	162
Willie Campbell, Prestwick	164
*Johnny Laidlay, Honourable	
Company	166
Ben Sayers, North Berwick	168
Archie Simpson, Carnoustie	168

1888 St Andrews

Jack Burns, Warwick	171
David Anderson Jr, St Andrews	172
Ben Sayers, North Berwick	172
Willie Campbell, Prestwick	174
*Leslie Balfour, Edinburgh	175
Andrew Kirkaldy, St Andrews	176
David Grant, North Berwick	176

*Amateur

1889 Musselburgh

Willie Park Jr, Musselburgh	155
Andrew Kirkaldy, St Andrews	155
(Play-off Park 158 to Kirkaldy 163)	
Ben Sayers, North Berwick	159
*Johnny Laidlay, Honourable	
Company	162
David Brown, Musselburgh	162
Willie Fernie, Troon	164

1890 Prestwick

*John Ball, Royal Liverpool	82	82	164
Willie Fernie, Troon	85	82	167
A Simpson, Carnoustie	85	82	167
Willie Park, Jr, Musselburgh	90	80	170
Andrew Kirkaldy, St Andrews	81	89	170
*Horace Hutchinson, Royal North Devon	87	85	172

1891 St Andrews

Hugh Kirkaldy, St Andrews	83	83	166
Willie Fernie, Troon	84	84	168
Andrew Kirkaldy, St Andrews	84	84	168
S Mure Fergusson, Royal and Ancient	86	84	170
W D More, Chester	84	87	171
Willie Park, Jr, Musselburgh	88	85	173

(From 1892 the competition was extended to 72 holes)

1892 Muirfield

*Harold Hilton, Royal Liverpool	78	81	72	74	305
*John Ball, Jr, Royal Liverpool	75	80	74	79	308
James Kirkaldy, St Andrews	77	83	73	75	308
Sandy Herd, Huddersfield	77	78	77	76	308
J Kay, Seaton Carew	82	78	74	78	312
Ben Sayers, North Berwick	80	76	81	75	312

1893 Prestwick

Willie Auchterlonie, St Andrews	78	81	81	82	322
*Johnny E Laidlay, Honourable					
Company	80	83	80	81	324
Sandy Herd, Huddersfield	82	81	78	84	325
Hugh Kirkaldy, St Andrews	83	79	82	82	326
Andrew Kirkaldy, St Andrews	85	82	82	77	326
J Kay, Seaton Carew	81	81	80	85	327
R Simpson, Carnoustie	81	81	80	85	327

1894 Sandwich

J H Taylor, Winchester	84	80	81	81	326
Douglas Rolland, Limpsfield	86	79	84	82	331
Andrew Kirkaldy, St Andrews	86	79	83	84	332
A Toogood, Eltham	84	85	82	82	333
Willie Fernie, Troon	84	84	86	80	334
Harry Vardon, Bury St Edmunds	86	86	82	80	334
Ben Sayers, North Berwick	85	81	84	84	334

1895 St Andrews

J H Taylor, Winchester	86	78	80	78	322
Sandy Herd, Huddersfield	82	77	82	85	326
Andrew Kirkaldy, St Andrews	81	83	84	84	332
G Pulford, Royal Liverpool	84	81	83	87	335
Archie Simpson, Aberdeen	88	85	78	85	336
Willie Fernie, Troon	86	79	86	86	337
David Brown, Malvern	81	89	83	84	337
David Anderson, Panmure	86	83	84	84	337

1896 Muirfield

Harry Vardon, Ganton	83	78	78	77	316
J H Taylor, Winchester	77	78	81	80	316
(Vardon won play-off 157 to 161)					
*Freddie G Tait, Black Watch	83	75	84	77	319
Willie Fernie, Troon	78	79	82	80	319
Sandy Herd, Huddersfield	72	84	79	85	320
James Braid, Romford	83	81	79	80	323

1897 Hoylake

*Harold H Hilton, Royal Liverpool	80	75	84	75	314
James Braid, Romford	80	74	82	79	315
*Freddie G Tait, Black Watch	79	79	80	79	317
G Pulford, Royal Liverpool	80	79	79	79	317
Sandy Herd, Huddersfield	78	81	79	80	318
Harry Vardon, Ganton	84	80	80	76	320

1898 Prestwick

Harry Vardon, Ganton	79	75	77	76	307
Willie Park, Musselburgh	76	75	78	79	308
*Harold H Hilton, Royal Liverpool	76	81	77	75	309
J H Taylor, Winchester	78	78	77	79	312
*Freddie G Tait, Black Watch	81	77	75	82	315
D Kinnell, Leven	80	77	79	80	316

1899 Sandwich

Harry Vardon, Ganton	76	76	81	77	310
Jack White, Seaford	79	79	82	75	315
Andrew Kirkaldy, St Andrews	81	79	82	77	319
J H Taylor, Mid-Surrey	77	76	83	84	320
James Braid, Romford	78	78	83	84	322
Willie Fernie, Troon	79	83	82	78	322

1900 St Andrews

J H Taylor, Mid-Surrey	79	77	78	75	309
Harry Vardon, Ganton	79	81	80	78	317
James Braid, Romford	82	81	80	79	322
Jack White, Seaford	80	81	82	80	323
Willie Auchterlonie, St Andrews	81	85	80	80	326
Willie Park, Jr, Musselburgh	80	83	81	84	328

1901 Muirfield

James Braid, Romford	79	76	74	80	309
Harry Vardon, Ganton	77	78	79	78	312
J H Taylor, Royal Mid-Surrey	79	83	74	77	313
*Harold H Hilton, Royal Liverpool	89	80	75	76	320
Sandy Herd, Huddersfield	87	81	81	76	325
Jack White, Seaford	82	82	80	82	326

1902 Hoylake

Sandy Herd, Huddersfield	77	76	73	81	307
Harry Vardon, South Herts	72	77	80	79	308
James Braid, Walton Heath	78	76	80	74	308
R Maxwell, Honourable Company	79	77	79	74	309
Tom Vardon, Ilkley	80	76	78	79	313
J H Taylor, Mid-Surrey	81	76	77	80	314
D Kinnell, Leven	78	80	79	77	314
*Harold Hilton, Royal Liverpool	79	76	81	78	314

1903 Prestwick

Harry Vardon, South Herts	73	77	72	78	300
Tom Vardon, Ilkley	76	81	75	74	306
Jack White, Sunningdale	77	78	74	79	308
Sandy Herd, Huddersfield	73	83	76	77	309
James Braid, Walton Heath	77	79	79	75	310
R Thompson, North Berwick	83	78	77	76	314
A H Scott, Elie	77	77	83	77	314

*Amateur

1904 Sandwich

Jack White, Sunningdale	80	75	72	69	296
James Braid, Walton Heath	77	80	69	71	297
J H Taylor, Mid-Surrey	77	78	74	68	297
Tom Vardon, Ilkley	77	77	75	72	301
Harry Vardon, South Herts	76	73	79	74	302
James Sherlock, Stoke Poges	83	71	78	77	309

1905 St Andrews

James Braid, Walton Heath	81	78	78	81	318
J H Taylor, Mid-Surrey	80	85	78	80	323
R Jones, Wimbledon	81	77	87	78	323
J Kinnell, Purley Downs	82	79	82	81	324
Arnaud Massy, La Boulie	81	80	82	82	325
E Gray, Littlehampton	82	81	84	78	325

1906 Muirfield

James Braid, Walton Heath	77	76	74	73	300
J H Taylor, Mid-Surrey	77	72	75	80	304
Harry Vardon, South Herts	77	73	77	78	305
J Graham, Jr, Royal Liverpool	71	79	78	78	306
R Jones, Wimbledon Park	74	78	73	83	308
Arnaud Massy, La Boulie	76	80	76	78	310

1907 Hoylake

Arnaud Massy, La Boulie	76	81	78	77	312
J H Taylor, Mid-Surrey	79	79	76	80	314
Tom Vardon, Sandwich	81	81	80	75	317
G Pulford, Royal Liverpool	81	78	80	78	317
Ted Ray, Ganton	83	80	79	76	318
James Braid, Walton Heath	82	85	75	76	318

1908 Prestwick

James Braid, Walton Heath	70	72	77	72	291
Tom Ball, West Lancashire	76	73	76	74	299
Ted Ray, Ganton	79	71	75	76	301
Sandy Herd, Huddersfield	74	74	79	75	302
Harry Vardon, South Herts	79	78	74	75	306
D Kinnell, Prestwick St Nicholas	75	73	80	78	306

1909 Deal

J H Taylor, Mid-Surrey	74	73	74	74	295
James Braid, Walton Heath	79	73	73	74	299
Tom Ball, West Lancashire	74	75	76	76	301
C Johns, Southdown	72	76	79	75	302
T G Renouf, Manchester	76	78	76	73	303
Ted Ray, Ganton	77	76	76	75	304

1910 St Andrews

James Braid, Walton Heath	76	73	74	76	299
Sandy Herd, Huddersfield	78	74	75	76	303
George Duncan, Hanger Hill	73	77	71	83	304
Laurie Ayton, Bishops Stortford	78	76	75	77	306
Ted Ray, Ganton	76	77	74	81	308
W Smith, Mexico	77	71	80	80	308
J Robson, West Surrey	75	80	77	76	308

1911 Sandwich

Harry Vardon, South Herts	74	74	75	80	303
Arnaud Massy, St Jean de Lux	75	78	74	76	303

(Play-off; Massy conceded at the 35th hole)

Harold Hilton, Royal Liverpool	76	74	78	76	304
Sandy Herd, Coombe Hill	77	73	76	78	304
Ted Ray, Ganton	76	72	79	78	305
James Braid, Walton Heath	78	75	74	78	305
J H Taylor, Mid-Surrey	72	76	78	79	305

Walter Hagen receiving the congratulations of his wife, 1924 (BBC Hulton Pic. Lib.)

1912 Muirfield

Ted Ray, Oxhey	71	73	76	75	295
Harry Vardon, South Herts	75	72	81	71	299
James Braid, Walton Heath	77	71	77	78	303
George Duncan, Hanger Hill	72	77	78	78	305
Laurie Ayton, Bishops Stortford	74	80	75	79	308
Sandy Herd, Coombe Hill	76	81	76	76	309

1913 Hoylake

J H Taylor, Mid-Surrey	73	75	77	79	304
Ted Ray, Oxhey	73	74	81	84	312
Harry Vardon, South Herts	79	75	79	80	313
M Moran, Dollymount	76	74	89	74	313
Johnny J McDermott, USA	75	80	77	83	315
T G Renouf, Manchester	75	78	84	78	315

1914 Prestwick

Harry Vardon, South Herts	73	77	78	78	306
J H Taylor, Mid-Surrey	74	78	74	83	309
H B Simpson, St Annes Old	77	80	78	75	310
Abe Mitchell, Sonning	76	78	79	79	312
Tom Williamson, Notts	75	79	79	79	312
R G Wilson, Croham Hurst	76	77	80	80	313

1920 Deal

George Duncan, Hanger Hill	80	80	71	72	303
Sandy Herd, Coombe Hill	72	81	77	75	305
Ted Ray, Oxhey	72	83	78	73	306
Abe Mitchell, North Foreland	74	73	84	76	307
Len Holland, Northampton	80	78	71	79	308
Jim Barnes, USA	79	74	77	79	309

1921 St Andrews

Jock Hutchison, USA	72	75	79	70	296
*Roger H Wethered, Royal and Ancient	78	75	72	71	296

(Hutchison won play-off 150 to 159)

T Kerrigan, USA	74	80	72	72	298
Arthur G Havers, West Lancs	76	74	77	72	299
George Duncan, Hanger Hill	74	75	78	74	301

1922 Sandwich

Walter Hagen, USA	76	73	79	72	300
George Duncan, Hanger Hill	76	75	81	69	301

*Amateur

1939 St Andrews
Dick Burton, Sale	70 72 77 71	290
Johnny Bulla, Chicago	77 71 71 73	292
Johnny Fallon, Huddersfield	71 73 71 79	294
Bill Shankland, Templenewsam	72 73 72 77	294
Alf Perry, Leatherhead	71 74 73 76	294
Reg A Whitcombe, Parkstone	71 75 74 74	294
Sam L King, Knole Park	74 72 75 73	294

1946 St Andrews
Sam Snead, USA	71 70 74 75	290
Bobby Locke, South Africa	69 74 75 76	294
Johnny Bulla, USA	71 72 72 79	294
Charlie H Ward, Little Aston	73 73 73 76	295
Henry Cotton, Royal Mid-Surrey	70 70 76 79	295
Dai J Rees, Hindhead	75 67 73 80	295
Norman von Nida, Australia	70 76 74 75	295

1947 Hoylake
Fred Daly, Balmoral, Belfast	73 70 78 72	293
Reg W Horne, Hendon	77 74 72 71	294
*Frank R Stranahan, USA	71 79 72 72	294
Bill Shankland, Templenewsam	76 74 75 70	295
Dick Burton, Coombe Hill	77 71 77 71	296
Charlie Ward, Little Aston	76 73 76 72	297
Sam L King, Wildernesse	75 72 77 73	297
Arthur Lees, Dore and Totley	75 74 72 76	297
Johnny Bulla, USA	80 72 74 71	297
Henry Cotton, Royal Mid-Surrey	69 78 74 76	297
Norman von Nida, Australia	74 76 71 76	297

1948 Muirfield
Henry Cotton, Royal Mid-Surrey	71 66 75 72	284
Fred Daly, Balmoral	72 71 73 73	289
Norman von Nida, Australia	71 72 76 71	290
Roberto de Vicenzo, Argentina	70 73 72 75	290
Jack Hargreaves, Sutton Coldfield	76 68 73 73	290
Charlie Ward, Little Aston	69 72 75 74	290

1949 Sandwich
Bobby Locke, South Africa	69 76 68 70	283
Harry Bradshaw, Kilcroney, Eire	68 77 68 70	283

(Locke won play-off 135 to 147; Locke's rounds were 67, 68)
Roberto de Vicenzo, Argentina	68 75 73 69	285
Sam King, Knole Park	71 69 74 72	286

Bobby Locke and Frank Stranahan pictured together during practice 1949 (Planet News Ltd.)

Charlie Ward, Little Aston	73 71 70 72	286
Arthur Lees, Dore and Totley	74 70 72 71	287
Max Faulkner, Royal Mid-Surrey	71 71 71 74	287

1950 Troon
Bobby Locke, South Africa	69 72 70 68	279
Roberto de Vicenzo, Argentina	72 71 68 70	281
Fred Daly, Balmoral, Belfast	75 72 69 66	282
Dai J Rees, South Herts	71 68 72 71	282
E Moore, South Africa	74 68 73 68	283
Max Faulkner, Royal Mid-Surrey	72 70 70 71	283

1951 Royal Portrush
Max Faulkner, Unattached	71 70 70 74	285
Tony Cerda, Argentina	74 72 71 70	287
Charlie Ward, Little Aston	75 73 74 68	290
Fred Daly, Balmoral	74 70 75 73	292
Jimmy Adams, Wentworth	68 77 75 72	292
Bobby Locke, South Africa	71 74 74 74	293
Bill Shankland, Templenewsam	73 76 72 72	293
Norman Sutton, Leigh	73 70 74 76	293
Harry Weetman, Croham Hurst	73 71 75 74	293
Peter W Thomson, Australia	70 75 73 75	293

1952 Royal Lytham
Bobby Locke, South Africa	69 71 74 73	287
Peter W Thomson, Australia	68 73 77 70	288
Fred Daly, Balmoral	67 69 77 76	289
Henry Cotton, Royal Mid-Surrey	75 74 74 71	294
Tony Cerda, Argentina	73 73 76 73	295
Sam L King, Knole Park	71 74 74 76	295

1953 Carnoustie
Ben Hogan, USA	73 71 70 68	282
*Frank R Stranahan, USA	70 74 73 69	286
Dai J Rees, South Herts	72 70 73 71	286
Peter W Thomson, Australia	72 72 71 71	286
Tony Cerda, Argentina	75 71 69 71	286
Roberto de Vicenzo, Argentina	72 71 71 73	287

1954 Royal Birkdale
Peter W Thomson, Australia	72 71 69 71	283
Sid S Scott, Carlisle City	76 67 69 72	284
Dai J Rees, South Herts	72 71 69 72	284
Bobby Locke, South Africa	74 71 69 70	284
Jimmy Adams, Royal Mid-Surrey	73 75 69 69	286
Tony Cerda, Argentina	71 71 73 71	286
J Turnesa, USA	72 72 71 71	286

1955 St Andrews
Peter W Thomson, Australia	71 68 70 72	281
Johnny Fallon, Huddersfield	73 67 73 70	283
Frank Jowle, Edgbaston	70 71 69 74	284
Bobby Locke, South Africa	74 69 70 72	285
Tony Cerda, Argentina	73 71 71 71	286
Ken Bousfield, Coombe Hill	71 75 70 70	286
Harry Weetman, Croham Hurst	71 71 70 74	286
Bernard J Hunt, Hartsbourne	70 71 74 71	286
Flory van Donck, Belgium	71 72 71 72	286

1956 Hoylake
Peter W Thomson, Australia	70 70 72 74	286
Flory van Donck, Belgium	71 74 70 74	289
Roberto de Vicenzo, Mexico	71 70 79 70	290
Gary Player, South Africa	71 76 73 71	291
John Panton, Glenbervie	74 76 72 70	292

*Amateur

Henry Cotton, Temple	72	76	71	74	293
E Bertolino, Argentina	69	72	76	76	293

1957 St Andrews

Bobby Locke, South Africa	69	72	68	70	279
Peter W Thomson, Australia	73	69	70	70	282
Eric C Brown, Buchanan Castle	67	72	73	71	283
Angel Miguel, Spain	72	72	69	72	285
David C Thomas, Sudbury	72	74	70	70	286
Tom B Haliburton, Wentworth	72	73	68	73	286
*W Dick Smith, Prestwick	71	72	72	71	286
Flory van Donck, Belgium	72	68	74	72	286

1958 Royal Lytham

Peter W Thomson, Australia	66	72	67	73	278
David C Thomas, Sudbury	70	68	69	71	278

(Thomson won play-off 139 to 143)

Eric C Brown, Buchanan Castle	73	70	65	71	279
Christy O'Connor, Killarney	67	68	73	71	279
Flory van Donck, Belgium	70	70	67	74	281
Leopoldo Ruiz, Argentina	71	65	72	73	281

1959 Muirfield

Gary Player, South Africa	75	71	70	68	284
Flory van Donck, Belgium	70	70	73	73	286
Fred Bullock, Prestwick St Ninians	68	70	74	74	286
Sid S Scott, Roehampton	73	70	73	71	287
Christy O'Connor, Royal Dublin	73	74	72	69	288
*Reid R Jack, Dullatur	71	75	68	74	288
Sam L King, Knole Park	70	74	68	76	288
John Panton, Glenbervie	72	72	71	73	288

1960 St Andrews

Kel D G Nagle, Australia	69	67	71	71	278
Arnold Palmer, USA	70	71	70	68	279
Bernard J Hunt, Hartsbourne	72	73	71	66	282
Harold R Henning, South Africa	72	72	69	69	282
Roberto de Vicenzo, Argentina	67	67	75	73	282
*Guy B Wolstenholme, Sunningdale	74	70	71	68	283

1961 Royal Birkdale

Arnold Palmer, USA	70	73	69	72	284
Dai J Rees, South Herts	68	74	71	72	285
Christy O'Connor, Royal Dublin	71	77	67	73	288
Neil C Coles, Coombe Hill	70	77	69	72	288
Eric C Brown, Unattached	73	76	70	70	289
Kel D G Nagle, Australia	68	75	75	71	289

1962 Troon

Arnold Palmer, USA	71	69	67	69	276
Kel D G Nagle, Australia	71	71	70	70	282
Brian Huggett, Romford	75	71	74	69	289
Phil Rodgers, USA	75	70	72	72	289
Bob Charles, NZ	75	70	70	75	290
Sam Snead, USA	76	73	72	71	292
Peter W Thomson, Australia	70	77	75	70	292

1963 Royal Lytham

Bob Charles, NZ	68	72	66	71	277
Phil Rodgers, USA	67	68	73	69	277

(Charles won play-off 140 to 148)

Jack Nicklaus, USA	71	67	70	70	278
Kel D G Nagle, Australia	69	70	73	71	283
Peter W Thomson, Australia	67	69	71	78	285
Christy O'Connor, Royal Dublin	74	68	76	68	286

1964 St Andrews

Tony Lema, USA	73	68	68	70	279
Jack Nicklaus, USA	76	74	66	68	284
Roberto de Vicenzo, Argentina	76	72	70	67	285
Bernard J Hunt, Hartsbourne	73	74	70	70	287
Bruce Devlin, Australia	72	72	73	73	290
Christy O'Connor, Royal Dublin	71	73	74	73	291
Harry Weetman, Selsdon Park	72	71	75	73	291

1965 Royal Birkdale

Peter W Thomson, Australia	74	68	72	71	285
Christy O'Connor, Royal Dublin	69	73	74	71	287
Brian Huggett, Romford	73	68	76	70	287
Roberto de Vicenzo, Argentina	74	69	73	72	288
Kel D G Nagle, Australia	74	70	73	72	289
Tony Lema, USA	68	72	75	74	289
Bernard J Hunt, Hartsbourne	74	74	70	71	289

1966 Muirfield

Jack Nicklaus, USA	70	67	75	70	282
David C Thomas, Dunham Forest	72	73	69	69	283
Doug Sanders, USA	71	70	72	70	283
Gary Player, South Africa	72	74	71	69	286
Bruce Devlin, Australia	73	69	74	70	286
Kel D G Nagle, Australia	72	68	76	70	286
Phil Rodgers, USA	74	66	70	76	286

1967 Hoylake

Roberto de Vicenzo, Argentina	70	71	67	70	278
Jack Nicklaus, USA	71	69	71	69	280
Clive A Clark, Sunningdale	70	73	69	72	284
Gary Player, South Africa	72	71	67	74	284
Tony Jacklin, Potters Bar	73	69	73	70	285
Sebastian Miguel, Spain	72	74	68	72	286
Harold Henning, South Africa	74	70	71	71	286

1968 Carnoustie

Gary Player, South Africa	74	71	71	73	289
Jack Nicklaus, USA	76	69	73	73	291
Bob J Charles, NZ	72	72	71	76	291
Billy Casper, USA	72	68	74	78	292
Maurice Bembridge, Little Aston	71	75	73	74	293
Brian Barnes, Burnham & Berrow	70	74	80	71	295
Neil C Coles, Coombe Hill	75	76	71	73	295
Gay Brewer, USA	74	73	72	76	295

1969 Royal Lytham

Tony Jacklin, Potters Bar	68	70	70	72	280
Bob J Charles, NZ	66	69	75	72	282
Peter W Thomson, Australia	71	70	70	72	283
Roberto de Vicenzo, Argentina	72	73	66	72	283
Christy O'Connor, Royal Dublin	71	65	74	74	284
Jack Nicklaus, USA	75	70	68	72	285
Denis M Love, Jr, USA	70	73	71	71	285

1970 St Andrews

Jack Nicklaus, USA	68	69	73	73	283
Doug Sanders, USA	68	71	71	73	283

(Nicklaus won play-off 72 to 73)

Harold Henning, South Africa	67	72	73	73	285
Lee Trevino, USA	68	68	72	77	285
Tony Jacklin, Potters Bar	67	70	73	76	286
Neil C Coles, Coombe Hill	65	74	72	76	287
Peter A Oosterhuis, Dulwich and Sydenham	73	69	69	76	287

*Amateur

The most coveted trophies in golf: British Open (left) and United States Open (right) (Phil Sheldon)

1972 Jack Nicklaus won his third US Open, leading or tying for the lead throughout. It was Pebble Beach's first Open. Nicklaus won the 1961 US Amateur, also at Pebble Beach.

Only 48 of the 150 starters broke 80 on both the first two days and only 40 rounds beat the par of 72 by the 70 contestants who played all four rounds.

Jerry McGee holed in one at the 8th on the third day, the first hole in one in the Open since 1956. Bobby Mitchell repeated the feat at the same hole next day.

Entry 4196. Prize-money $202 400.

1973 Johnny Miller broke the record for the lowest individual round and the lowest finishing round. His 63 gave him a total of 279, the lowest in five Opens at Oakmont, and victory by 1 stroke. Miller, starting his last round an hour ahead of the leaders, made up 4 strokes on John Schlee and then went ahead.

It was Sam Snead's third Open at Oakmont and he played through his 27th Open, breaking a record he shared with Gene Sarazen.

Entry 3580. Prize-money $219 400.

1974 On a Winged Foot course which proved very difficult Hale Irwin, the second bespectacled champion, beat Forrest Fezler by 2 strokes.

Only 23 out of 150 players scored lower than 75 on the first day.

Entry 3914. Prize-money $227 000.

1975 The 25th play-off in Open history brought victory for Lou Graham over John Mahaffey; a championship in which play in the second round was interrupted by an electrical storm.

Entry 4214. Attendance 97 345 plus 6246 for the play-off. Prize-money $235 700. First Prize $40 000.

1976 A championship at the Atlanta Athletic Club, the first to be held in the South, in which four players had a chance of victory on the 72nd hole. Jerry Pate, who birdied the hole by hitting a 5 iron across water to 3 ft (0.90 cm), was 1 stroke in front of John Mahaffey, Al Geiberger and Tom Weiskopf on the tee. His birdie was unanswerable as Mahaffey hit his second into the water and Weiskopf and Geiberger, having driven poorly, played short.

Attendance 113 084. Entry 4436.

1977 Hubert Green became champion at Southern Hills, Tulsa despite a threat to his life. This was conveyed to him by USGA officials during the last round, but he decided to play on and eventually holed from 3 ft (0.90 m) to beat Lou Graham.

A record seven players tied the first-round lead. Twelve players were within 2 strokes of the lead as the last round began.

Entry 4726. Prize-money $284 990.

1978 Andy North beat Dave Stockton and J C Snead by one stroke at Cherry Hills, but nobody beat par for the championship. North returned a 1 over par 285.

1979 Second victory for Hale Irwin. At Inverness, Toledo he won by 2 strokes with a final round of 75, the highest last round by a champion since 1949. Not since 1935 had there been anything higher, a 76.

Gary Player finished tied second with a final round of 68, his highest position since he won in 1965. Jack Nicklaus also finished with a 68, but only made the cut by 1 stroke. Tom Watson, the leading money-winner at the time, failed to make the cut.

Prize-money $330 400.

1980 A championship in which records galore were broken, beginning on the first day with Tom Weiskopf and Jack Nicklaus equalling Johnny Miller's record of 63 for the lowest individual round in the Open. Nicklaus, in fact, missed from about a yard on the 18th green for a 62.

A second round of 71 lowered the aggregate for 36 holes and a further 70 lowered the 54-hole record, but it was a record shared by Isao Aoki of Japan who began with three 68s and chased Nicklaus hard in the last round.

A final 68 by Nicklaus gave him victory by 2 strokes and enabled him to break the record aggregate which he held jointly with Lee Trevino. He also joined Willie Anderson, Bobby Jones and Ben Hogan as the only four-time winners. Aoki's second place was the best ever by an Asian golfer in the Open. Hubert Green's third round of 65 equalled the lowest third round and contained a record eight 3s in a row from the 9th.

Nicklaus's victory came 18 years after his first, a record span. It was the first time Nicklaus finished in the first six since 1973.

Tom Watson holed in one on the famous 4th on the first morning. Severiano Ballesteros was disqualified for being late on the first tee on the second day and Aoki and Nicklaus played together in all four rounds.

Attendance 102 000, the second largest in history.

1981 Victory for David Graham, the first by an Australian in the history of the event. He played the last 5 holes in 2 under par to come within 1 stroke of the record aggregate set by Jack Nicklaus the year before. He won by 3 strokes from Bill Rogers, who later in the year won the British Open, and George Burns who led for three rounds, setting the best total in history (203) for 54 holes. He was foiled by Graham's finish which was magnificent.

DETAILED RECORDS

Most victories
4, Willie Anderson, 1901–03–04–05
Bobby Jones, 1923–26–29–30
Ben Hogan, 1948–50–51–53
Jack Nicklaus, 1962–67–72–80

Most times runner-up or joint runner-up
4, Sam Snead, 1937–47–49–53
Bobby Jones, 1922–24–25–28
Arnold Palmer, 1962–63–66–67

Oldest winner
Ted Ray, 43 years 4 months 16 days, 1920
Julius Boros, 43 years 3 months 20 days, 1963
Ben Hogan, 40 years 10 months, 1953
Jack Nicklaus, 40 years 5 months 25 days, 1980

Youngest winner
John J McDermott, 19 years 10 months 14 days, 1911
Francis Ouimet, 20 years 4 months 11 days, 1913
Gene Sarazen, 20 years 4 months 16 days, 1922

Biggest margin of victory
11 strokes, Willie Smith, 1899
 9 strokes, Jim Barnes, 1921
 7 strokes, Fred Herd, 1898; Alex Smith, 1906;
Tony Jacklin, 1970

Lowest winning aggregate
272 (63, 71, 70, 68), Jack Nicklaus, Baltusrol, 1980
273 (68, 68, 70, 69), David Graham, Merion, 1981

Lowest aggregate by runner-up
274 (68, 68, 68, 70) Isao Aoki, Baltusrol, 1980

Lowest aggregate by an amateur
282 (71, 71, 69, 71), Jack Nicklaus, Cherry Hills, 1960

Lowest individual round
63, Johnny Miller, fourth round, Oakmont, 1973.
Tom Weiskopf, first round, Baltusrol, 1980.
Jack Nicklaus, first round, Baltusrol, 1980

Lowest individual round by an amateur
65, James B McHale, St Louis, 1947
65, Jim Simons, Merion, 1971

Lowest first round
63, Tom Weiskopf and Jack Nicklaus, Baltusrol, 1980

Lowest second round
64, Tommy Jacobs, Congressional CC, 1964;
Rives McBee, Olympic CC, 1966

Lowest third round
64, Ben Crenshaw, Merion, 1981

Lowest fourth round
63, Johnny Miller, Oakmont, 1973

Lowest first 36 holes
134 (63, 71) Jack Nicklaus, Baltusrol, 1980

Lowest second 36 holes
136 (70, 66), Gene Sarazen, Fresh Meadow, 1932
136 (68, 68), Cary Middlecoff, Inverness, 1957
136 (66, 70), Ken Venturi, Congressional CC, 1964
136 (68, 68), Tom Weiskopf, Atlanta Athletic Club, 1976
136 (68, 68), Lou Graham, Southern Hills, 1977

Lowest first 54 holes
203 (69, 66, 68), George Burns III, Merion, 1981
204 (63, 71, 70), Jack Nicklaus, and (68, 68, 68), Isao Aoki, Baltusrol, 1980

Lowest final 54 holes
204 (67, 72, 65), Jack Nicklaus, Baltusrol, 1967

Lowest 9 holes
30, James B McHale, first 9, third round, St Louis, 1947; Arnold Palmer, first 9, fourth round, Cherry Hills, 1960; Ken Venturi, first 9, third round, Congressional CC, 1964; Bob Charles, first 9, fourth round, Merion, 1971; Tom Shaw, first 9, first round, Merion, 1971, George Burns, first 9, second round, Pebble Beach, 1982

Biggest span between first and last victories
18 years, Jack Nicklaus, 1962–80
11 years, Julius Boros, 1952–63

Successive victories
3, Willie Anderson, 1903–05
2, J J McDermott, 1911–12; Bobby Jones, 1929–30; Ralph Guldahl, 1937–38; Ben Hogan, 1950–51

Victories by amateurs
4, Bobby Jones, 1923–26–29–30
1, Francis Ouimet, 1913; Jerome D Travers, 1915; Chick Evans, 1916; John G Goodman, 1933

Winner of US Open and Amateur on the same course
Jack Nicklaus, Pebble Beach, Amateur (1961); Open (1972)

The first Australian to win the US Open, David Graham, 1981 (Phil Sheldon)

Highest number of top ten finishes
17, Jack Nicklaus
16, Walter Hagen
15, Ben Hogan
13, Arnold Palmer
12, Sam Snead

First player to break 70
Dave Hunter, 68, first round, Englewood, New Jersey, 1909; Tom McNamara, 69, second round, Englewood, New Jersey, 1909

Highest number of rounds under 70
22, Jack Nicklaus
15, Arnold Palmer
14, Ben Hogan

Outright leader after every round
Walter Hagen, 1914; Jim Barnes, 1921; Ben Hogan, 1953; Tony Jacklin, 1970

Hot sequences
1922–30: Bobby Jones's finishes were =2nd, 1st, 2nd, 2nd, 1st, =11th, 2nd, 1st, 1st
In twelve successive appearances from 1940 to 1956 (he did not play in 1949), Ben Hogan's worst placing was tied for 6th place

1896 Shinnecock Hills GC, New York
James Foulis, Chicago	78	74	152
Horace Rawlins, Sadequada	79	76	155
G Douglas, Brookline	79	79	158
*A W Smith, Toronto	78	80	158
John Shippen, Shinnecock Hills	78	81	159
*H J Whigham, Onwentsia	82	77	159

1897 Chicago GC, Illinois
Joe Lloyd, Essex	83	79	162
Willie Anderson, Watch Hill	79	84	163
James Foulis, Chicago	80	88	168
Willie Dunn, New York	87	81	168
W T Hoare, Pittsburgh	82	87	169
A Ricketts, Albany	91	81	172
Bernard Nicholls, Lenox	87	85	172

1898 Myopia Hunt Club, Massachusetts
Fred Herd, Washington Park	84	85	75	84	328
Alex Smith, Washington Park	78	86	86	85	335
Willie Anderson, Baltusrol	81	82	87	86	336
Joe Lloyd, Essex County	87	80	86	86	339
Willie Smith, Shinnecock Hills	82	91	85	82	340
W V Hoare, Dayton	84	84	87	87	342

1899 Baltimore CC, Maryland
Willie Smith, Midlothian	77	82	79	77	315
George Low, Dyker Meadow	82	79	89	76	326
Val Fitzjohn, Otsego	85	80	79	82	326
W H Way, Detroit	80	85	80	81	326
Willie Anderson, New York	77	81	85	84	327
J Park, Essex County	88	80	75	85	328

1900 Chicago GC, Illinois
Harry Vardon, Ganton (England)	79	78	76	80	313
J H Taylor, Richmond (England)	76	82	79	78	315
David Bell, Midlothian	78	83	83	78	322
Laurie Auchterlonie, Glen View	84	82	80	81	327
Willie Smith, Midlothian	82	83	79	84	328
George Low, Dyker Meadow	84	80	85	82	331

1901 Myopia Hunt Club, Massachusetts
Willie Anderson, Pittsfield	84	83	83	81	331
Alex Smith, Washington Park	82	82	87	80	331
(Anderson won play-off 85 to 86)					
Willie Smith, Midlothian	84	86	82	81	333
Stewart Gardner, Garden City	86	82	81	85	334
Laurie Auchterlonie, Glen View	81	85	86	83	335
Bernard Nicholls, Boston	84	85	83	83	335

1902 Garden City GC, New York
Laurie Auchterlonie, Chicago	78	78	74	77	307
Stewart Gardner, Garden City	82	76	77	78	313
*Walter J Travis, Garden City	82	82	75	74	313
Willie Smith, Chicago	82	79	80	75	316
John Shippen, New York	83	81	75	79	318
Willie Anderson, Montclair	79	82	76	81	318

1903 Baltusrol GC, New Jersey
Willie Anderson, Apawamis		149	79	82	307
David Brown, Wollaston		156	75	76	307
(Anderson won play-off 82 to 84)					
Stewart Gardner, Garden City		154	82	79	315
Alex Smith, Nassau		154	81	81	316
Donald J Ross, Oakley		158	78	82	318
Jack Campbell, Brookline		159	83	77	319

1904 Glen View Club, Illinois
Willie Anderson, Apawamis	75	78	78	72	303
Gilbert Nicholls, St Louis	80	76	79	73	308
Fred Mackenzie, Onwentsia	76	79	74	80	309
Laurie Auchterlonie, Glen View	80	81	75	78	314
Bernard Nicholls, Elyria, Ohio	80	77	79	78	314
Robert Simpson, Riverside, Illinois	82	82	76	76	316
P F Barrett, Lambton, Ontario	78	79	79	80	316
Stewart Gardner, Garden City	75	76	80	85	316

1905 Myopia Hunt Club, Massachusetts
Willie Anderson, Apawamis	81	80	76	77	314
Alex Smith, Nassau	81	80	76	79	316
Peter Robertson, Oakmont	79	80	81	77	317
P F Barrett, Canada	81	80	77	79	317
Stewart Gardner, Garden City	78	78	85	77	318
Alex Campbell, The Country Club	82	76	80	81	319

1906 Onwentsia Club, Illinois
Alex Smith, Nassau	73	74	73	75	295
Willie Smith, Mexico	73	81	74	74	302
Laurie Auchterlonie, Glen View	76	78	75	76	305
James Maiden, Toledo	80	73	77	75	305
Willie Anderson, Onwentsia	73	76	74	84	307
Alec Ross, Brae Burn	76	79	75	80	310

1907 Philadelphia Cricket Club, Pennsylvania
Alec Ross, Brae Burn	76	74	76	76	302
Gilbert Nicholls, Woodland	80	73	72	79	304
Alex Campbell, The Country Club	78	74	78	75	305
John Hobens, Englewood	76	75	73	85	309
Peter Robertson, Oakmont	81	77	78	74	310
George Low, Baltusrol	78	76	79	77	310
Fred McLeod, Midlothian	79	77	79	75	310

1908 Myopia Hunt Club, Massachusetts
Fred McLeod, Midlothian	82	82	81	77	322
Willie Smith, Mexico	77	82	85	78	322
(McLeod won play-off 77 to 83)					
Alex Smith, Nassau	80	83	83	81	327
Willie Anderson, Onwentsia	85	86	80	79	330
John Jones, Myopia	81	81	87	82	331
Jack Hobens, Englewood	86	81	85	81	333
Peter Robertson, Oakmont	89	84	77	83	333

1909 Englewood GC, New Jersey
George Sargent, Hyde Manor	75	72	72	71	290
Tom McNamara, Wollaston	73	69	75	77	294
Alex Smith, Wykagyl	76	73	74	72	295
Isaac Mackie, Fox Hills	77	75	74	73	299
Willie Anderson, St Louis	79	74	76	70	299
Jack Hobens, Englewood	75	78	72	74	299

1910 Philadelphia Cricket Club, Pennsylvania
Alex Smith, Wykagyl	73	73	79	73	298
John J McDermott, Merchantville	74	74	75	75	298
Macdonald Smith, Claremont	74	78	75	71	298
(Alex Smith won play-off 71 to 75 to 77)					
Fred McLeod, St Louis	78	70	78	73	299
Tom McNamara, Boston	73	78	73	76	300
Gilbert Nicholls, Wilmington	73	75	77	75	300

1911 Chicago GC, Illinois
John McDermott, Atlantic City	81	72	75	79	307
Mike J Brady, Wollaston	76	77	79	75	307
George O Simpson, Wheaton	76	77	79	75	307

*Amateur

(McDermott won play-off 80 to 82 to 85)

Fred McLeod, St Louis	77	72	76	83	308
Gilbert Nicholls, Wilmington	76	78	74	81	309
Jock Hutchison, Allegheny	80	77	73	79	309

1912 Buffalo CC, New York

John J McDermott, Atlantic City	74	75	74	71	294
Tom McNamara, Boston	74	80	73	69	296
Alex Smith, Wykagyl	77	70	77	75	299
Mike J Brady, Wollaston	72	75	73	79	299
Alec Campbell, Brookline	74	77	80	71	302
George Sargent, Chevy Chase	72	78	76	77	303

1913 Brookline CC, Massachusetts

*Francis Ouimet, Woodland	77	74	74	79	304
Harry Vardon, England	75	72	78	79	304
Ted Ray, England	79	70	76	79	304

(Ouimet won play-off 72 to 77 to 78)

Walter Hagen, Rochester	73	78	76	80	307
Jim M Barnes, Tacoma	74	76	78	79	307
Macdonald Smith, Wykagyl	71	79	80	77	307
Louis Tellier, France	76	76	79	76	307

1914 Midlothian Country Club, Illinois

Walter C Hagen, Rochester	68	74	75	73	290
*Charles Evans, Jr, Edgewater	76	74	71	70	291
George Sargent, Chevy Chase	74	77	74	72	297
Fred McLeod, Columbia	78	73	75	71	297
*Francis Ouimet, Woodland	69	76	75	78	298
Mike J Brady, Wollaston	78	72	74	74	298
James A Donaldson, Glen View	72	79	74	73	298

1915 Baltusrol GC, New Jersey

*Jerome D Travers, Upper Montclair	148	73	76	297
Tom McNamara, Boston	149	74	75	298
Robert G MacDonald, Buffalo	149	73	78	300
Jim M Barnes, Whitemarsh Valley	146	76	79	301
Louis Tellier, Canoe Brook	146	76	79	301
Mike J Brady, Wollaston	147	75	80	302

1916 Minikahda Club, Minnesota

*Charles Evans, Jr, Edgewater	70	69	74	73	286
Jock Hutchison, Allegheny	73	75	72	68	288
Jim M Barnes, Whitemarsh Valley	71	74	71	74	290
Wilfrid Reid, Wilmington	70	72	79	72	293
Gilbert Nicholls, Great Neck	73	76	71	73	293
George Sargent, Interlachen	75	71	72	75	293

1919 Brae Burn CC, Massachusetts

Walter Hagen, Oakland Hills	78	73	75	75	301
Mike J Brady, Oakley	74	74	73	80	301

(Hagen won play-off 77 to 78)

Jock Hutchison, Glen View	78	76	76	76	306
Tom McNamara, New York	80	73	79	74	306
George McLean, Great Neck	81	75	76	76	308
Louis Tellier, Brae Burn	73	78	82	75	308

1920 Inverness Club, Ohio

Ted Ray, England	74	73	73	75	295
Harry Vardon, England	74	73	71	78	296
Jack Burke, Town and Country	75	77	72	72	296
Leo Diegel, Lake Shore	72	74	73	77	296
Jock Hutchison, Glen View	69	76	74	77	296
*Charles Evans, Jr, Edgewater	74	76	73	75	298
Jim M Barnes, Sunset Hills	76	70	76	76	298

1921 Columbia CC, Maryland

Jim M Barnes, Pelham	69	75	73	72	289
Walter Hagen, New York	79	73	72	74	298
Fred McLeod, Columbia	74	74	76	74	298
*Charles Evans, Jr, Edgewater	73	78	76	75	302
*Bob T Jones, Jr, Atlanta	78	71	77	77	303
Emmett French, Youngstown	75	77	74	77	303
Alex Smith, Shennecossett	75	75	79	74	303

1922 Skokie CC, Illinois

Gene Sarazen, Highland, Pittsburgh	72	73	75	68	288
John L Black, Oakland, California	71	71	75	72	289
*Bob T Jones, Jr, Atlanta	74	72	70	73	289
Bill E Mehlhorn, Shreveport	73	71	72	74	290
Walter Hagen, New York	68	77	74	72	291
George Duncan, England	76	73	75	72	296

1923 Inwood CC, New York

*Bob T Jones, Jr, Atlanta	71	73	76	76	296
Bobby A Cruickshank, Shackamaxon	73	72	78	73	296

(Jones won play-off 76 to 78)

Jock Hutchison, Glen View	70	72	82	78	302
Jack Forrester, Hollywood, New Jersey	75	73	77	78	303
Johnny J Farrell, Quaker Ridge	76	77	75	76	304
Francis Gallett, Port Washington	76	72	77	79	304
*W M Reekie, Upper Montclair	80	74	75	75	304

1924 Oakland Hills CC, Michigan

Cyril Walker, Englewood	74	74	74	75	297
*Bob T Jones, Jr, Atlanta	74	73	75	78	300
Bill E Mehlhorn, Normandy, Missouri	72	75	76	78	301
Bobby A Cruickshank, Shackamaxon	77	72	76	78	303
Walter Hagen, New York	75	75	76	77	303
Macdonald Smith, San Francisco	78	72	77	76	303

1925 Worcester CC, Massachusetts

Willie Macfarlane, Oak Ridge	74	67	72	78	291
*Bob T Jones, Jr, Atlanta	77	70	70	74	291

(Macfarlane won play-off 147 to 148)

Johnny Farrell, Quaker Ridge	71	74	69	78	292
*Francis Ouimet, Woodland	70	73	73	76	292
Gene Sarazen, Fresh Meadow	72	72	75	74	293
Walter Hagen, Pasadena, Florida	72	76	71	74	293

1926 Scioto CC, Ohio

*Bob T Jones, Jr, Atlanta	70	79	71	73	293
Joe Turnesa, Fairview	71	74	72	77	294
Bill E Mehlhorn, Chicago	68	75	76	78	297
Gene Sarazen, Fresh Meadow	78	77	72	70	297
Leo Diegel, Mountain View Farm	72	76	75	74	297
Johnny Farrell, Quaker Ridge	76	79	69	73	297

1927 Oakmont CC, Pennsylvania

Tommy Armour, Congressional	78	71	76	76	301
Harry Cooper, El Serreno	74	76	74	77	301

(Armour won play-off 76 to 79)

Gene Sarazen, Fresh Meadow	74	74	80	74	302
Emmett French, Southern Pines	75	79	77	73	304
Bill E Mehlhorn, New York	75	77	80	73	305
Walter Hagen, Pasadena, Florida	77	73	76	81	307

1928 Olympia Fields CC, Illinois

Johnny Farrell, Quaker Ridge	77	74	71	72	294
*Bob T Jones, Jr, Atlanta	73	71	73	77	294

(Farrell won play-off 143 to 144)

---

*Amateur

Ben Hogan, Fort Worth, Texas	72 68 72 70 282
Ed Furgol, Westwood, Missouri	71 70 73 71 285
Peter Thomson, Victoria (Australia)	70 69 75 71 285
Ted Kroll, Fort Lauderdale	72 70 70 73 285

1957 Inverness Club, Ohio

Dick Mayer, St Petersburg, Florida	70 68 74 70 282
Cary Middlecoff, Riverlake, Texas	71 75 68 68 282

(Mayer won play-off 72 to 79)

Jimmy Demaret, Concord International, New York	68 73 70 72 283
Juilus Boros, Mid Pines, North Carolina	69 75 70 70 284
Walter Burkemo, Franklin Hills, Michigan	74 73 72 65 284
Ken Venturi, California	69 71 75 71 286
Fred E Hawkins, El Paso, Texas	72 72 71 71 286

1958 Southern Hills CC, Oklahoma

Tommy Bolt, Paradise, Florida	71 71 69 72 283
Gary Player, Killarney (South Africa)	75 68 73 71 287
Julius Boros, Mid Pines, North Carolina	71 75 72 71 289
Gene Littler, Singing Hills, California	74 73 67 76 290
Walter Burkemo, Franklin Hills, Michigan	75 74 70 72 291
Bob R Rosburg, Silverado, California	75 74 72 70 291

1959 Winged Foot GC, New York

Billy Casper, Jr, Apple Valley	71 68 69 74 282
Bob R Rosburg, Palo Alto, California	75 70 67 71 283
Claude Harmon, Winged Foot, New York	72 71 70 71 284
Mike Souchak, Grossinger, New York	71 70 72 71 284
Doug Ford, Paradise, Florida	72 69 72 73 286
Ernie Vossier, Midland, Texas	72 70 72 72 286
Arnold Palmer, Laurel Valley, Pennsylvania	71 69 72 74 286

1960 Cherry Hills CC, Colorado

Arnold Palmer, Laurel Valley, Pennsylvania	72 71 72 65 280
*Jack Nicklaus, Scioto, Ohio	71 71 69 71 282
Dutch Harrison, Old Warson, Missouri	74 70 70 69 283
Julius Boros, Mid Pines, North Carolina	73 69 68 73 283
Mike Souchak, Grossinger, New York	68 67 73 75 283
Ted Kroll, De Soto Lakes, Florida	72 69 75 67 283
Jack Fleck, El Caballero, California	70 70 72 71 283
Dow Finsterwald, Tequesta, Florida	71 69 70 73 283

1961 Oakland Hills CC, Michigan

Gene Littler, Singing Hills, California	73 68 72 68 281
Bob Goalby, Paradise, Florida	70 72 69 71 282
Doug Sanders, Ojai, California	72 67 71 72 282
Mike Souchak, Grossinger, New York	73 70 68 73 284
*Jack Nicklaus, Scioti, Ohio	75 69 70 70 284
Dow Finsterwald, Tequesta, Florida	72 71 71 72 286
Eric Monti, Hillcrest, California	74 67 72 73 286
Doug Ford, Tuckahoe, New York	72 69 71 74 286

1962 Oakmont CC, Pennsylvania

Jack Nicklaus, Tucson National, Arizona	72 70 72 69 283

Arnold D Palmer, Miami	71 68 73 71 283

(Nicklaus won play-off 71 to 74)

Phil Rodgers, La Jolla, California	74 70 69 72 285
Bobby Nichols, Midland, Texas	70 72 70 73 285
Gay Brewer, Jr, Paradise, Florida	73 72 73 69 287
Tommy Jacobs, Bermuda Dunes, California	74 71 73 70 288
Gary Player, Ponte Vedra, Florida	71 71 72 74 288

1963 The Country Club, Brookline, Massachusetts

Julius Boros, Mid Pines, North Carolina	71 74 76 72 293
Jacky D Cupit, Mountain View, California	70 72 76 75 293
Arnold Palmer, Laurel Valley, Pennsylvania	73 69 77 74 293

(Boros won play-off 70 to 73 to 76)

Paul Harney, Sunset Oaks, California	78 70 73 73 294
Billy Maxwell, Tropicana, Nevada	73 73 75 74 295
Bruce Crampton, Sydney (Australia)	74 72 75 74 295
Tony Lema, San Leandro, California	71 74 74 76 295

1964 Congressional CC, Washington, D.C.

Ken Venturi, Paradise, Florida	72 70 66 70 278
Tommy Jacobs, Bermuda Dunes, California	72 64 70 76 282
Bob J Charles, De Soto Lakes, Florida	72 72 71 68 283
Billy Casper, Mountain View, California	71 74 69 71 285
Gay Brewer, Jr, Dallas	76 69 73 68 286
Arnold Palmer, Laurel Valley, Pennsylvania	68 69 75 74 286

1965 Bellerive CC, Missouri

Gary Player, Johannesburg (South Africa)	70 70 71 71 282
Kel Nagle, Pymble (Australia)	68 73 72 69 282

(Player won play-off 71 to 74)

Frank Beard, Seneca, Kentucky	74 69 70 71 284
Julius Boros, Mid Pines, North Carolina	72 75 70 70 287
Al Geiberger, Carlton Oaks, California	70 76 70 71 287
Raymond Floyd, St Andrews, Illinois	72 72 76 68 288
Bruce Devlin, Sydney (Australia)	72 73 72 71 288

1966 Olympic CC, California

Billy Casper, Jr, Peacock Gap, California	69 68 73 68 278
Arnold Palmer, Laurel Valley, Pennsylvania	71 66 70 71 278

(Casper won play-off 69 to 73)

Jack Nicklaus, Scioto, Ohio	71 71 69 74 285
Tony Lema, Marco Island, Florida	71 74 70 71 286
Dave Marr, Goodyear, Arizona	71 74 68 73 286
Paul Rodgers, La Jolla, California	70 70 73 74 287

1967 Baltusrol GC, New Jersey

Jack Nicklaus, Scioto, Ohio	71 67 72 65 275
Arnold Palmer, Laurel Valley, Pennsylvania	69 68 73 69 279
Don January, Dallas	69 72 70 70 281
Billy Casper, Jr, Bonita, California	69 70 71 72 282
Lee Trevino, Horizon Hills, Texas	72 70 71 70 283
Bob Goalby, Tamarisk, California	72 71 70 71 284
Deane R Beman, Bethesda, Maryland	69 71 71 73 284

*Amateur

Dead-eyed Dick, alias
Hubert Green (Phil Sheldon)

Don't throw it away; you
never know, it might come in
useful, Hale Irwin, twice a
US Open champion (Phil
Sheldon)

Gardner Dickinson, Jr, Lost Tree,
Florida   70 73 68 73 284

1968 Oak Hill CC, New York
Lee Trevino, Horizon Hills, Texas   69 68 69 69 275
Jack Nicklaus, Scioto, Ohio   72 70 70 67 279
Bert Yancey, Killearn, Florida   67 68 70 76 281
Bobby Nichols, Louisville, Kentucky   74 71 68 69 282
Don Bies, Seattle   70 70 75 69 284
Steve Spray, Cedar Rapids, Iowa   73 75 71 65 284

1969 Champions GC, Texas
Orville J Moody, Yukon, Oklahoma   71 70 68 72 281
Deane R Beman, Bethesda, Maryland   68 69 73 72 282
Al Geiberger, Santa Barbara, California 68 72 72 70 282
Bob R Rosburg, Westwood, Missouri   70 69 72 71 282
Bob Murphy, Jr, Bartow, Florida   66 72 74 71 283
Miller Barber, Woodlawn, Texas   67 71 68 78 284
Bruce Crampton, Bahama Reef   73 72 68 71 284
Arnold Palmer, Laurel Valley,
Pennsylvania   70 73 69 72 284

1970 Hazeltine GC, Minnesota
Tony Jacklin, The Cloisters, Georgia   71 70 70 70 281
Dave Hill, Evergreen, Colorado   75 69 71 73 288
Bob J Lunn, Haggin Oaks, California   77 72 70 70 289
Bob J Charles, Christchurch
(New Zealand)   76 71 75 67 289
Ken Still, Fircrest, Washington   78 71 71 71 291
Miller Barber, Woodlawn, Texas   75 75 72 70 292

1971 Merion GC, Pennsylvania
Lee Trevino, El Paso, Texas   70 72 69 69 280
Jack Nicklaus, Scioto, Ohio   69 72 68 71 280
(Trevino won play-off 68 to 71)
Bob R. Rosburg, French Lick, Indiana   71 72 70 69 282
Jim J Colbert, Jr, Prairie Creek,
Arkansas   69 69 73 71 282
*Jim Simons, Butler, Pennsylvania   71 71 65 76 283
Johnny L Miller, San Francisco GC   70 73 70 70 283
George Archer, Gilroy, California   71 70 70 72 283

1972 Pebble Beach, California
Jack Nicklaus, Scioto, Ohio   71 73 72 74 290
Bruce Crampton, Australia   74 70 73 76 293
Arnold Palmer, Laurel Valley,
Pennsylvania   77 68 73 76 294
Lee Trevino, El Paso, Texas   74 72 71 78 295
Homero Blancas, Houston, Texas   74 70 76 75 295
Kermit Zarley, Houston, Texas   71 73 73 79 296

1973 Oakmont CC, Pennsylvania
Johnny Miller, San Francisco GC   71 69 76 63 279
John Schlee, Preston Trails, Texas   73 70 67 70 280
Tom Weiskopf, Columbus, Ohio   73 69 69 70 281
Arnold Palmer, Laurel Valley,
Pennsylvania   71 71 68 72 282
Lee Trevino, El Paso, Texas   70 72 70 70 282
Jack Nicklaus, Scioto, Ohio   71 69 74 68 282

1974 Winged Foot GC, New York
Hale Irwin, Boulder CC, California   73 70 71 73 287
Forest Fezler, Indian Wells CC,
California   75 70 74 70 289
Lou Graham, Richland CC, Tennessee   71 75 74 70 290
Bert Yancey, Palm Aire CC, Florida   76 69 73 72 290

Arnold Palmer, Laurel Valley,
Pennsylvania   73 70 73 76 292
Jim Colbert, Overland Pk, Kansas   72 77 69 74 292
Tom Watson, Kansas City CC   73 71 69 79 292

1975 Medinah CC, Illinois
Lou Graham, Richland CC, Nashville   74 72 68 73 287
John D Mahaffey, Jr, Champions GC,
Houston, Texas   73 71 72 71 287
(Graham won play-off 71 to 73)
Bob Murphy, Delray Dunes, Florida   74 73 72 69 288
Hale Irwin, St Louis, Missouri   74 71 73 70 288
Ben Crenshaw, CC of Austin, Texas   70 68 76 74 288
Frank Beard, Hurstbourne CC   74 69 67 78 288

1976 Atlanta Athletic Club, Duluth, Georgia
Jerry Pate, Pensacola CC, Florida   71 69 69 68 277
Al Geiberger, Silver Lakes, California 70 69 71 69 279
Tom Weiskopf, Columbus, Ohio   73 70 68 68 279
Butch Baird, Miami Beach, Florida   71 71 71 67 280
John Mahaffey, Riverhill CC, Texas   70 68 69 73 280
Hubert Green, Bay Point CC, Florida   72 70 71 69 282

1977 Southern Hills CC, Tulsa, Oklahoma
Hubert M Green, Birmingham, Al.   69 67 72 70 278
Lou Graham, Richland CC, Nashville   72 71 68 68 279
Tom Weiskopf, Columbus, Ohio   71 71 68 71 281
Tom Purtzer, Moon Valley CC, Arizona   69 69 72 72 282
Jay Haas, St Clair CC, Belleville   72 68 71 72 283
Gary Jacobson, Minnetonka   73 70 67 73 283

1978 Cherry Hills, Denver, Colorado
Andy North, Gainesville, Florida   70 70 71 74 285
Jesse C Snead, Hot Springs, Virginia   70 72 72 72 286
Dave Stockton, Westlake GC,
Calfornia   71 73 70 72 286
Hale Irwin, St Louis, Missouri   69 74 75 70 288
Tom Weiskopf, Columbus, Ohio   77 73 70 68 288

1979 Inverness, Toledo, Ohio
Hale Irwin, St Louis, Missouri   74 68 67 75 284
Jerry Pate, Pensacola, Florida   71 74 69 72 286
Gary Player, South Africa   73 73 72 68 286
Larry Nelson, Kennesaw, Georgia   71 68 76 73 288
Bill Rogers, Texarkana, Texas   71 72 73 72 288
Tom Weiskopf, Columbus, Ohio   71 74 67 76 288

1980 Baltusrol GC, New Jersey
Jack Nicklaus, Muirfield Village GC,
Dublin, Ohio   63 71 70 68 272
Isao Aoki, Golf Kikaku, Tokyo, Japan   68 68 68 70 274
Keith Fergus, Sugar Creek CC, Texas   66 70 70 70 276
Tom Watson, Kansas City, Missouri   71 68 67 70 276
Lon Hinkle, Carrollton, Texas   66 70 69 71 276
Mike Reid, Riverside CC, Provo, Utah   69 67 75 69 280
Mark Hayes, Oak Tree GC, Edmond   66 71 69 74 280

1981 Merion GC, Pennsylvania
David Graham, Preston Trail GC,
Dallas, Texas   68 68 70 67 273
Bill Rogers, Northridge CC, Texas   70 68 69 69 276
George Burns III, Quail Ridge GC, Delray
Beach, Florida   69 66 68 73 276
John Cook, Muirfield Village GC,
Dublin, Ohio   68 70 71 70 279
John Schroeder, Delmar, California   71 68 69 71 279

*Amateur

US Masters

First played 1934

This is the youngest of the world's four major championships. Unlike the other three (the British Open, the US Open and the USPGA), it is always played on the same course, the Augusta National in Georgia, and is an invitation only tournament, invitations being based on a formula laid down in advance and reviewed from time to time.

Both the Augusta course and the Masters tournament were the brainchild of Bobby Jones whose influence always dominated the event even after his death. Although he retired as a player in 1930, he took part in the first tournament in 1934 because the Club was short of money and it needed someone to draw the local public.

Jones had invited some of his old rivals to what, by modern standards, was an informal gathering and he finished in a tie for 13th place. However, a start had been made and the following year it received maximum publicity from the famous double eagle at the 15th in the last round of the eventual winner, Gene Sarazen.

More recently, its fame has been spread by the televising of the event every April on a course, designed by Alister Mackenzie, which is spectacularly beautiful and always at its best in Masters week. Originally, it was a plantation that Baron Berckmans, a distinguished Belgian horticulturist, had developed into the South's first great nursery.

Another trend which the Masters set has been the advance booking of tickets and no admission on a casual daily basis. But the real difference between the Masters and other major tournaments is the absence of advertising or any form of commercialism.

Nowadays, the field comprises the leading American professionals and amateurs together with a few selected overseas players who meet prescribed qualifications. For many years, the Masters was guided by Jones and Clifford Roberts and, since their deaths, it continues to be run from within the Club. It consists of 72 holes of strokeplay.

MILESTONES

1934 First tournament in which Horton Smith finished birdie, par to beat Craig Wood by 1 stroke. First hole in one by Ross Somerville the Canadian amateur. There have been nine since. Full list:
4th hole: None
6th hole: Leland Gibson (1954), Billy Joe Patton (1954), Charles Coody (1972)

12th hole: Claude Harmon (1947), William Hyndman III (1959)
16th hole: Ross Somerville (1934), Willie Goggin (1935), Ray Billows (1940), John Dawson (1949), Clive Clark (1968)
1935 One of golf's most famous strokes was played by Gene Sarazen at the par-5 15th hole in the last round. He holed a 220 yd (200 m) 4 wood shot for a double eagle 2. Three behind Craig Wood on the 15th tee, he finished the last 3 holes in par, tied and won the play-off by 5 strokes. It was the only 36-hole play-off.
Frank Walsh took 12 on the 8th.
1936 Craig Wood shot 88 in the first round, 67 in the second. Horton Smith's second victory with a remarkable finish in extremely rainy conditions. He made up 6 strokes in the last two rounds on Harry Cooper; then went one ahead.
1937 Byron Nelson, the winner, picked up 6 strokes in the final round on Ralph Guldahl at the 12th and 13th. Nelson scored 2, 3 to Guldahl's 5, 6 and won by two. Nelson's first round 66 was the lowest to date.
1938 Henry Picard became the second winner by more than 1 stroke, winning by 2. A final 70 beat Ralph Guldahl and Harry Cooper who tied second on 287. Ben Hogan's first Masters.
1939 Sam Snead appeared to be the winner until Ralph Guldahl shot 33 on the back 9 to win by 1 stroke. In June of the same year, Snead took 8 on the final hole of the US Open at the Philadelphia Country Club.
1940 Two notable records. Jimmy Demaret won by 4 strokes, the biggest margin until 1948. In the first round, he covered the second 9 holes in 30 thus equalling the all-time record on a championship course. Lloyd Mangrum, who finished second, opened with a 64, the lowest score in any of the four major championships for many years. It was not matched at Augusta until 1965.
1941 Craig Wood's first major victory. The leader for three rounds, he was caught by Byron Nelson at the turn in the 4th, but came home in 34 to win by 3 strokes. Two months later, he also won the US Open.

The late Clifford Roberts, mastermind to the Masters (Phil Sheldon)

1942 The first 18-hole play-off. In it, Byron Nelson gained 5 strokes on his fellow Texan Ben Hogan in a stretch of 11 holes although Hogan played them in one under par.

1946 Another chance for Hogan who took 3 putts on the 72nd green to finish runner-up for the second year running. A little earlier, Herman Keiser, the winner, also took 3 putts on the last green. Keiser had started the final round 5 strokes ahead of Hogan.

1947 Jimmy Demaret emulated Horton Smith and Byron Nelson as two-time winners of the Masters. Tied for the first-round lead with Nelson, he then went into the lead and stayed there.

Gene Sarazen and George Fazio, first off in the final round, completed the course in 1 hr 57 min. Sarazen scored 70.

1948 Claude Harmon was better known as a club professional, but he won the Masters by 5 strokes and equalled the record aggregate of 279. He covered the 6th, 7th and 8th in the final round in 2, 3, 3—4 under par.

1949 After high winds on the first two days, Sam Snead had two marvellous 67s to finish on 282. His total for the last two rounds was 14 strokes better than that for the first two rounds. They remained the best two finishing rounds until Jack Nicklaus scored 64, 69 in 1965.

In Snead's last round, he had more birdies (8) than pars (7).

1950 A 7-stroke swing on the last 6 holes enabled Jimmy Demaret to catch Jim Ferrier and beat him by 2 strokes. He thus became the first three-time winner.

Herman Barron took 11 on the par-3 16th.

1951 Having been close several times, Ben Hogan finally won with a final-round 68 for 280 and victory by 2 strokes over Skee Riegel who, in turn, was 4 ahead of those tied for third place.

Dow Finsterwald took 11 on the par-3 12th.

1952 Sam Snead who triumphed in high winds in 1949, did so again. This time, the winds came in the last two rounds. After gaining a 3-stroke lead at half-way (70, 67), Snead added a 77 and a 72 for a 4-stroke victory over Jack Burke, the only player to break 70 on the last day.

1953 Part one of Ben Hogan's *annus mirabilis*. He became the first player to have three rounds under 70 in the Masters, his last three rounds being 69, 66, 69 for a total of 274, a new low and victory by 5 strokes.

The Masters record book states Hogan's belief that his play at Augusta was the finest of his career.

There were 13 eagles on the 13th hole.

1954 The year in which the two best-known professionals, Sam Snead and Ben Hogan, contested a play-off, but were nearly defeated before they got there by a virtually unknown amateur playing his first Masters, Billy Joe Patton from North Carolina.

Patton led the field after 36 holes, was 5 strokes behind after 54 and lead again as late as the 12th hole in the final round, having been helped by holing in one at the 6th. However, a 7 at the 13th and a 6 at the 15th saved the professionals' pride. Patton finished 1 stroke behind Snead and Hogan. In the play-off Snead scored 70 to Hogan's 71.

Patton, who had a birdie on all four days at the par-4 9th, had a remarkable haul of prizes. Gold and silver cup for best amateur score; gold medal for best amateur score; crystal vase for being the low scorer in the first round; crystal cup for a hole in one and a gold money clip for winning the pre-tournament long driving contest.

1955 Record 7-stroke victory for Dr Cary Middlecoff who

had a 65 in the second round which, though equalled by Frank Beard in 1968, was not bettered in any second round until 1979, when Miller Barber had a 64.

Ben Hogan and Sam Snead finished second and third.

1956 Jack Burke's winning score of 289 equalled the record highest, but he made up 8 strokes over the last 18 holes on the amateur Ken Venturi and beat him by one. Burke's final round was 71, Venturi's 80. Middlecoff, the holder, took 77 to finish third, 2 behind Burke. Gary Player's first Masters.

1957 A closing 66, the lowest final round at the time, brought victory for Doug Ford who holed out of a bunker at the 18th. He won by 3 strokes from Sam Snead who had started the last round 3 ahead.

1958 Arnold Palmer's first Masters victory. At 28, he was the youngest winner since Byron Nelson in 1937.

1959 Art Wall, the new champion, had 8 birdies in a final 66, 5 of them on the last 6 holes. He had started the final round 6 strokes behind Arnold Palmer, defending champion, and Canadian, Stan Leonard.

1960 Second of Arnold Palmer's victories. He led the field at the end of every round but in the final round he was 1 stroke behind Ken Venturi with 2 holes to play. Palmer birdied both to win by 1 stroke. It was the second time in five years that Venturi finished second.

George Bayer and Jack Fleck went round in 1 hr 52 min. Bayer scored 72 and Fleck 74.

1961 Gary Player, 25, became the first foreign winner of the Masters. He won by 1 stroke from the amateur Charles Coe and defending champion Arnold Palmer. In a dramatic finish, Player made a 4 from a bunker at the 18th; Palmer took 6 from the same bunker.

Coe's total of 281 is the lowest ever returned by an amateur at the Masters.

1962 Revenge for Palmer over Player in the first triple tie. In the play-off, Palmer scored 68 (the lowest in a play-off) to Player's 71 and Dow Finsterwald's 77. Palmer came home in 31.

1963 First victory for Jack Nicklaus, the youngest champion at 23. In rough weather, he won by 1 stroke from Tony Lema who was playing in his first Masters.

1964 Record fourth victory for Arnold Palmer in a span of only seven tournaments. He won by 6 strokes from Dave Marr and Jack Nicklaus, but it was his last victory in any of the world's four major championships.

The qualifying score was 148, equalled four times subsequently, but not bettered until 1979.

1965 Jack Nicklaus, second winner to have three rounds under 70, lowered the record aggregate to 271 and equalled Lloyd Mangrum's record individual round with a third-round 64.

Arnold Palmer and Gary Player tied second on 280, the only occasion on which the Big Three finished 1,2,3 in a major championship.

1966 Second triple tie but Jack Nicklaus (70) held off Tommy Jacobs (72) and Gay Brewer (78) in a play-off that only just beat darkness to become the first champion to successfully defend his title. It is one of the Masters oddest records that he remains so.

Twelve amateurs made the cut. The qualifying was the highest, 153, although a record number of 64 qualified. The 10-stroke rule was invoked for the first time.

1967 Gay Brewer who had taken 5 at the 72nd the year before, defeated his playing partner Bobby Nichols in an exciting

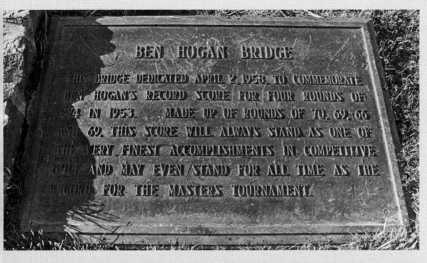

The commemorative bridges that record notable deeds at Augusta, Georgia (Phil Sheldon)

finish by 1 stroke.

Ben Hogan shot a third-round 66 at the age of 54, the lowest of the tournament.

Bobby Cole, 18, became the youngest player to survive the cut. He was still an amateur.

1968 The year Roberto de Vicenzo signed for a 4 on the 71st hole instead of a 3 and lost to Bob Goalby by 1 stroke.

Generally, the year of the best scores: 127 rounds of par or better were played during the four days compared with the next best of 94 in 1965.

During the final round, de Vicenzo, on his 45th birthday, played the first 3 holes in 4 under par, an all-time record. He began by holing his second at the par-4 1st hole, but little did anyone realise that the end would be so tragic.

1969 25 players led, or shared the lead, over the four days—a record—but George Archer (6 ft 6 in (1.98 m)), the tallest champion, triumphed in the end. Billy Casper, the joint runner-up 2 strokes behind, went out in 40 in the final round.

1970 Compensation for the year before as Casper became champion after a play-off with another Californian, Gene Littler.

1971 Charles Coody separated himself from some distinguished pursuers by playing the last 4 holes in 2 under par to become champion. After the 68th hole Johnny Miller had been 2 ahead of Coody and Jack Nicklaus. Coody's finish was in contrast to that in 1969 when he lost the title on the last 3 holes.

Art Wall, US Masters champion 1959, and the man who has had 41 holes-in-one (Phil Sheldon)

1972 Nicklaus joined Palmer as a four-time champion in a slightly disappointing Masters if there is such a thing. His total of 286 was the only one under par. Charles Coody, defending champion, holed in one at the 6th in the first round then took 7 at the par-4 7th.

1973 The Masters lost a day's play for the first time. Saturday was washed out by storms and the finish postponed until Monday when the first Georgian, Tommy Aaron, won the Green Jacket. In a close finish he won by 1 stroke from J C Snead.

At 24, Britain's Peter Oosterhuis became the youngest foreign player to lead the Masters at any point. He led after three rounds by 3 strokes, but he took a final 74 to finish in a triple tie for 3rd.

1974 Gary Player's second victory on a last day when six or seven others had a chance on the last 9 holes.

Sam Snead, 61 years 1 month and 8 days became the oldest player to make the cut.

Ralph Johnston became the first first-year player since Horton Smith in 1934 to complete four rounds of par or better.

Maurice Bembridge lowered the final round record with 64.

1975 Sometimes called the best Masters of all. Johnny Miller and Tom Weiskopf dominated the dramatic last day but could not prevent Jack Nicklaus from registering his record fifth victory. Weiskopf and Miller had chances of birdies at the 72nd hole to tie Nicklaus, but both failed. It was the fourth time Weiskopf finished second or joint second.

Hale Irwin had a final round of 64 to finish fourth, 5 strokes behind Weiskopf and Miller.

Miller had 6 birdies in a row from the 2nd in his record outward half of 30 in the third round.

1976 A championship dominated by Raymond Floyd. He led from start to finish; played the first 36 holes in a new record of 131 (65, 66); set another record for 54 holes (65, 66, 70), took an 8-stroke lead into the last round and equalled Jack Nicklaus's record aggregate of 271.

Floyd had a total of 21 birdies and 1 eagle.

Things are never as bad as they seem. Tom Watson carrying a worried look (Phil Sheldon)

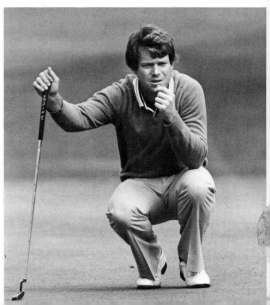

Above: Doing things in style (Mary Evans Pic. Lib.) and *below:* from the inside looking out. BBC television commentary team. Open championship 1981 (Phil Sheldon)

TEST YOUR KNOWLEDGE OF GOLFING TIES.

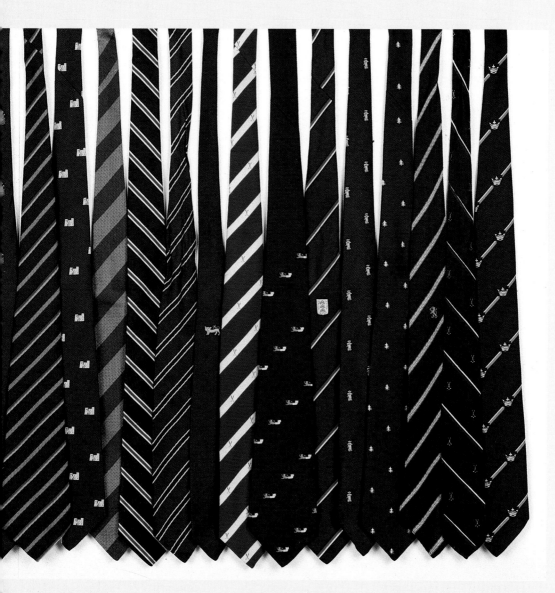

(*From the right*) Walton Heath; European Golf Association; Netherlands Golf Federation; Formby; Royal Troon; Danish Golf Union; Rye; Professional Golfers Association (Officials); Great Britain and Ireland Eisenhower Trophy; Oxford and Cambridge Golfing Society; United States Golf Association Executive Committee; The Leatherjackets; Wentworth; Royal Cinque Ports; Spanish Golf Federation; Royal Guernsey; French Golf Federation; USGA/R and A; Noordvijk; Honourable Company of Edinburgh Golfers; Royal St George's; Great Britain and Ireland Walker Cup; Haagsche (The Hague); Royal Porthcawl; Czechoslovak Golf Federation; Ganton; Royal Ashdown Forest; Royal Liverpool; Royal Porthcawl; Royal Lytham and St Annes.

(From the right) The League; Turnberry; Royal Mid-Surrey; National Golf Links of America; Royal County Down; The Hittites; Pine Valley; Royal and Ancient; The Country Club, Brookline; Sunningdale; The Windcheaters; Welsh International; Scottish International; English International; Irish International; Royal St David's; Royal Worlington and Newmarket; The Moles; Royal Birkdale; United States International teams; Singapore Island; Golf Union of Ireland Executive; Woodhall Spa; The 32 Club; Muirfield Village; Shinnecock Hills; The Fanlingerers; South African International; Council of National Golf Unions; Royal Dornoch.

WILL'S CIGARETTES.

TROON.
18th Green.

WILL'S CIGARETTES.

RICHMOND PARK.
Approach to 10th Green.

WILL'S CIGARETTES.

HOYLAKE.
11th Green.

WILL'S CIGARETTES.

ROYAL CROMER.

WILL'S CIGARETTES.

WESTWARD HO!
Bunkers in front of 4th Tee.

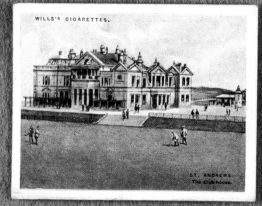

WILL'S CIGARETTES.

ST. ANDREWS.
The Club house.

WILL'S CIGARETTES.

MUIRFIELD.
18th Green.

WILL'S CIGARETTES.

BURNHAM AND BERROW.
5th Green.

WILL'S CIGARETTES.

NORTH BERWICK,
Point Garry Green.

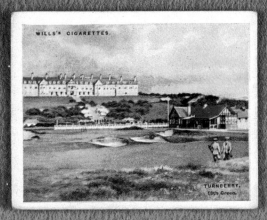

WILL'S CIGARETTES.

TURNBERRY.
18th Green.

WILL'S CIGARETTES.

NEWCASTLE.
Co. Down, Ireland.

WILL'S CIGARETTES.

PORTHCAWL.

Above: Bob Charles, prince of left-handers (Dunlop Sports) *Left:* Gene Sarazen, the ageless Master (Phil Sheldon) *Below:* The end of one of the greatest final rounds in the US Open. David Graham, Merion, 1981 (Phil Sheldon)

START	LEADERS	PAR	1	2	3	4	5	6	7	8	9	10	11	12	13	14	15	16	17	18	MESSAGES
	HOLE		4	5	3	5	4	4	4	4	3	4	4	4	3	4	4	4	3	4	
7	BURNS		7	7	7	6	6	6	6	6	6	5	5	5	5	5	5	4	5		
4	GRAHAM D		5	6	6	6	5	5	5	5	5	5	5	5	5	5	6	7	7		
3	ROGERS		3	3	3	3	3	2	2	3	4	3	3	4	4	4	3	3	4		
2	RODRIGUEZ		2	2	2	3	2	1	0	1	1	1	0	1	0	0	0	1	0	0	
1	THORPE		1	1	1	1	0	0	0	1	1	1	2	2	2	2	2	1	0	1	
2	NICKLAUS		2	2	1	1	2	3	2	2	3	3	3	2	2	2	2	2	1	0	
	CRENSHAW		2	2	2	2	2		2	1		2			0	0	0	1			
	CONNER		1	0	0	0			0	0						0					
	COOK J																				
	SCHROEDER																				

1977 Tom Watson got the better of a terrific final day duel with Jack Nicklaus, who was playing just in front of him. A 67 for 276 gave Watson his second major championship victory, one he repeated in July over Nicklaus in the British Open.

Severiano Ballesteros, who celebrated his 20th birthday on the third day, became the youngest professional to take part in the Masters.

1978 Gary Player's third victory, 17 years after his first—a record span. Starting the last day 7 strokes behind the leader, Hubert Green, he had 7 birdies on the last 10 holes to win by 1 stroke. He came back in 30 to hoist a record last-round 64 by a winner.

Wally Armstrong finished equal 5th with 280, the lowest score ever by a player in his first Masters until Fuzzy Zoeller's win a year later.

Tsuneyuki Nakajima of Japan took 13 at the 13th. Three months later, he took 9 at the 17th in the British Open at St Andrews.

1979 Victory after the first sudden-death play-off in the Masters for Fuzzy Zoeller, the first player to win on his first Masters appearance (1934 and 1935 excluded). He beat Ed Sneed and Tom Watson with a birdie 3 at the 11th (the play-off started at the 10th) after all three had missed birdie chances at the 10th. It was a Masters which Sneed lost. Having started poorly and then held his challenge together stoutly on the 11th, 12th, 13th, 14th and 15th, he dropped strokes on each of the last 3 holes. At the 18th, his 6 ft (1.8 m) winning putt hung on the lip.

Jack Nicklaus maintained his incredible run of consistency, but overran the 17th green downwind in the final round and took 5.

Raymond Floyd, getting down to business (Phil Sheldon)

Earlier in the tournament, Miller Barber had equalled the lowest score with a second round of 64. Owing to the edge of a tornado hitting Augusta, it was a round which began on Friday and ended on Saturday morning.

The 36-hole cut was 145, the lowest ever.

First prize of $50 000.

1980 A Masters in which Severiano Ballesteros stole the show. Three strokes ahead after 36 holes and 7 ahead after 54, he was 10 strokes clear with 9 holes to play. Then 3 putts on the 10th, 5 at the par-3 12th and a 6 on the 13th gave Gibby Gilbert and Jack Newton a chance. It also meant that Ballesteros would not break the record winning margin, the record aggregate or become the first champion with four rounds under 70.

However, Ballesteros played the last 5 holes in 1 under par to become the youngest winner and the first European to win. With Jack Newton finishing equal 2nd, it was the first time two overseas players had finished so well. A third overseas player, David Graham, was 5th.

Tom Weiskopf took 13 on the par-3 12th in the first round and 7 on the same hole in the second round.

1981 Tom Watson's second victory, and once again it was Jack Nicklaus who chased him home. Nicklaus, in fact, held a fairly healthy halfway lead after a second round of 65—the lowest of the week. However, Nicklaus suffered the unusual experience of going from 4 ahead to 4 behind in the space of 12 holes of the third round. Nicklaus then played the 15th and 16th brilliantly and with Watson hitting his second with a wedge into the front bunker at the 17th and following with 3 putts, the two were level again.

Nicklaus fell one behind by taking 3 putts at the 18th and, though the last round had its ups and downs, Watson held his lead despite putting his second in the Creek at the 13th.

1982 Craig Stadler beat Dan Pohl at the first hole (the 10th) of a sudden-death play-off to take his first major title, having been 6 strokes ahead with 7 holes to play. Unseasonably cold weather and fast greens, allied to a storm which caused the first round to be completed on the second day, produced unusually high scores early on.

Tom Weiskopf, four times runner-up (Phil Sheldon)

1955
Cary Middlecoff 72 65 72 70 279
Ben Hogan 73 68 72 73 286
Sam Snead 72 71 74 70 287

1956
Jack Burke, Jr 72 71 75 71 289
Ken Venturi 66 69 75 80 290
Cary Middlecoff 67 72 75 77 291

1957
Doug Ford 72 73 72 66 283
Sam Snead 72 68 74 72 286
Jimmy Demaret 72 70 75 70 287

1958
Arnold Palmer 70 73 68 73 284
Doug Ford 74 71 70 70 285
Fred Hawkins 71 75 68 71 285

1959
Art Wall, Jr 73 74 71 66 284
Cary Middlecoff 74 71 68 72 285
Arnold Palmer 71 70 71 74 286

1960
Arnold Palmer 67 73 72 70 282
Ken Venturi 73 69 71 70 283
Dow Finsterwald 71 70 72 71 284

1961
Gary Player 69 68 69 74 280
Arnold Palmer 68 69 73 71 281
Charlie Coe 72 71 69 69 281

1962
Arnold Palmer 70 66 69 75 280
Gary Player 67 71 71 71 280
Dow Finsterwald 74 68 65 73 280
(Palmer won play-off 68 to 71 to 77)

1963
Jack Nicklaus 74 66 74 72 286
Tony Lema 74 69 74 70 287

Julius Boros 76 69 71 72 288
Sam Snead 70 73 74 71 288

1964
Arnold Palmer 69 68 69 70 276
Dave Marr 70 73 69 70 282
Jack Nicklaus 71 73 71 67 282

1965
Jack Nicklaus 67 71 64 69 271
Arnold Palmer 70 68 72 70 280
Gary Player 65 73 69 73 280

1966
Jack Nicklaus 68 76 72 72 288
Tommy Jacobs 75 71 70 72 288
Gay Brewer 74 72 72 70 288
(Nicklaus won play-off 70 to 72 to 78)

1967
Gay Brewer 73 68 72 67 280
Bobby Nichols 72 69 70 70 281
Bert Yancey 67 73 71 73 284

1968
Bob Goalby 70 70 71 66 277
Roberto de Vincenzo
  69 73 70 66 278
Bert Yancey 71 71 72 65 279

1969
George Archer 67 73 69 72 281
Tom Weiskopf 71 71 69 71 282
George Knudson 70 73 69 70 282
Billy Casper 66 71 71 74 282

1970
Billy Casper 72 68 68 71 279
Gene Littler 69 70 70 70 279
(Casper won play-off 69 to 74)
Gary Player 74 68 68 70 280

1971
Charles Coody 66 73 70 70 279
Johnny Miller 72 73 68 68 281

Jack Nicklaus 70 71 68 72 281

1972
Jack Nicklaus 68 71 73 74 286
Tom Weiskopf 74 71 70 74 289
Bruce Crampton 72 75 69 73 289
Bobby Mitchell 73 72 71 73 289

1973
Tommy Aaron 68 73 74 68 283
Jesse C Snead 70 71 73 70 284
Peter Oosterhuis 73 70 68 74 285
Jim Jamieson 73 71 70 71 285
Jack Nicklaus 69 77 73 66 285

1974
Gary Player 71 71 66 70 278
Dave Stockton 71 66 70 73 280
Tom Weiskopf 71 69 70 70 280

1975
Jack Nicklaus 68 67 73 68 276
Johnny Miller 75 71 65 66 277
Tom Weiskopf 69 72 66 70 277

1976
Ray Floyd 65 66 70 70 271
Ben Crenshaw 70 70 72 67 279
Jack Nicklaus 67 69 73 73 282
Larry Ziegler 67 71 72 72 282

1977
Tom Watson 70 69 70 67 276
Jack Nicklaus 72 70 70 66 278
Tom Kite 70 73 70 67 280
Rik Massengale 70 73 67 70 280

1978
Gary Player 72 72 69 64 277
Rod Funseth 73 66 70 69 278
Hubert Green 72 69 65 72 278
Tom Watson 73 68 68 69 278

1979
Fuzzy Zoeller 70 71 69 70 280
Tom Watson 68 71 70 71 280
Ed Sneed 68 67 69 76 280
(Zoeller won play-off at 2nd extra hole)

1980
Severiano Ballesteros
  66 69 68 72 275
Gibby Gilbert 70 74 68 67 279
Jack Newton 68 74 69 68 279

1981
Tom Watson 71 68 70 71 280
Jack Nicklaus 70 65 75 72 282
Johnny Miller 69 72 73 68 282

1982
Craig Stadler 75 69 67 73 284
Dan Pohl 75 75 67 67 284
(Stadler won play-off at 1st extra hole)
Severiano Ballesteros 73 73 68 71 285
Jerry Pate 74 73 67 71 285

Now hear this. Jack Nicklaus making a point to two other Masters champions, Severiano Ballesteros and Gary Player (Phil Sheldon)

USPGA

First played 1916

The PGA championship is the oldest and most important of the events which make up the US professional tour. It has become known as one of the four championships comprising the modern Grand Slam, but is less publicised than the US and British Opens and the Masters.

This is because its emphasis is more domestic and entry to the championship as a player is based on qualification from events in America. Full membership of the American PGA is an essential. Life exemption from pre-qualifying for any PGA event is one of the benefits to the winner and it has now assumed a settled date in the calendar. For some time it was played opposite the British Open or in the week immediately following it. In 1953, Ben Hogan was prevented from playing in it after winning the Masters, US Open and British Open.

From the year of its inception until 1958, it was traditionally a matchplay event with a distinguished list of early champions including Jim Barnes, Walter Hagen, Gene Sarazen and Tommy Armour. Hagen won it five times, including four in a row. Starting in 1924, he won 22 consecutive matches against the best professional golfers in America.

As the modern dislike for matchplay among professionals grew in America, the championship fell victim to the supporters of strokeplay and the influence of television. Two rounds a day were also going out of fashion and in 1958 it became 72 holes of strokeplay just like all the other tournaments.

After Sam Snead won his third victory in 1951, nobody won more than once until Jack Nicklaus won his second victory in 1971, when the event was held in February, and Gary Player followed suit a year later. Nicklaus later won thrice more, but it remains a championship which Arnold Palmer never won.

Jock Hutchison, USPGA champion 1920 (G M Cowie)

MILESTONES

1916 First title won by Jim Barnes, an Englishman from Lelant in Cornwall, later both British and American Open champion. He defeated Jock Hutchison a 32-year-old Scotsman from St Andrews by 1 hole. Both Barnes and Hutchison lived in America.
1919 Second title for Barnes. In the final, he beat another Scottish-born professional, Fred McLeod, by 6 and 5. McLeod was US Open champion in 1908.
1920 Jock Hutchison (runner-up in 1916) beat J Douglas Edgar by 1 hole in the final. Edgar, Canadian Open Champion in 1919 and 1920, was killed some months later.

1921 Walter Hagen became the first American-born champion and began a remarkable period of dominance with Gene Sarazen. Between them they won from 1921 to 1927. In the final, Hagen beat Jim Barnes 3 and 2.
1922 Hagen did not defend and in his absence Sarazen, later to become his great rival, beat Emmet French 4 and 3 in the final at Oakmont, Pennsylvania. He is the youngest winner of the title.
1923 The only final involving Sarazen and Hagen produced the first extra hole victory for Sarazen. He won on the 38th, his second title in a row.
1924 First of an historic run of four victories for Walter Hagen. He scored his second victory in a final against Jim Barnes.
1925 Hagen needed 39 holes to beat Al Watrous and 40 to shake off Leo Diegel but, starting his final at Olympia Fields with an eagle, he beat Bill Mehlhorn by 6 and 5.
1926 Hagen won for the third time in a row. Having accounted for Johnny Farrell by 6 and 5 in the semi-final, he beat Leo Diegel by 5 and 3. At the 1st hole after lunch, Diegel's ball finished under Hagen's parked car.
1927 Hagen's record run extended to a fourth successive victory at Cedar Crest CC, Dallas, although he was behind for most of the final against Joe Turnesa. He finally squared at the 29th and went ahead at the 31st.
1928 Hagen took his run of victorious matches to 22 before he lost in the third round, but Leo Diegel, finalist in 1926, crowned a great week at Five Farms, Baltimore. It was he who beat Hagen; he then beat Gene Sarazen 9 and 8 and finally defeated Al Espinosa 6 and 5.
1929 Second successive victory for Leo Diegel. He won the final against Johnny Farrell, US Open champion, by 6 and 4. However, Diegel was only 1 up after 27 holes. Twice, subsequently, Farrell, set a stymie, putted Diegel's ball into the hole.

Byron Nelson congratulates Henry Picard at the end of the 1939 USPGA championship. Picard won at the 37th (New York Times)

1930 In a great final, Tommy Armour beat Gene Sarazen by 1 hole with a putt of 14 ft (4.3 m) on the 36th green. Sarazen was 1 up after 9, Armour 1 up after 18 holes and the match all square after 27 holes.

1931 Tom Creavy, one-time caddie for Gene Sarazen and Johnny Farrell, scored a surprise victory, the second winner aged 20. On his way to the final Creavy beat Jock Collins, Peter O'Hara, Cyril Walker and Sarazen; in the final, he beat Densmore Shute by 2 and 1. Illness later curtailed his tournament career.

1932 Olin Dutra caused something of a surprise on his way to the final where he beat Frank Walsh. In the semi-final, Walsh beat Bobby Cruickshank who, in an earlier round, beat Al Watrous after being 9 down with 12 to play. On the 24th green, Watrous conceded a 6 ft (1.8 m) putt for a half. In this same championship Johnny Golden beat Walter Hagen at the 43rd hole, the longest match in the history of the USPGA.

1933 Sarazen's third and last victory, eleven years after his first. He beat Willie Goggin by 5 and 4 in the final at Blue Mound CC, Milwaukee.

1934 Paul Runyan won the championship, beating his old teacher Craig Wood at the 38th, equalling the longest match played in the final.

1935 Johnny Revolta, a former caddie with the reputation of being a fine bunker player and putter, beat Tommy Armour by 5 and 4 to win the championship. In the final, he displayed a phenomenal short game, having beaten Walter Hagen in the first round.

1936 Densmore Shute, though heavily out-hit, beat Jimmy Thomson in the final.

1937 Shute became the last man to win the PGA title twice in succession. He won an extra-hole final at the 37th after Harold 'Jug' McSpaden had missed a shortish putt to win on the 36th, but McSpaden had led a bit of a charmed life. He won at the 38th in the first round and at the 39th in the 4th.

1938 After a welter of low scoring, Paul Runyan recorded his second victory. His margin of 8 and 7 over Sam Snead was the biggest in a final. Runyan had a first round of 67 and a 5-up lead.

1939 One of Byron Nelson's few defeats at this time. Having looked likely to beat Henry Picard in the final at Pomonok CC, New York, he lost at the 37th.

1940 Nelson soon atoned for his defeat in the previous final. Snead, despite going 1 up on the 32nd, lost by 1 hole. It was his second losing final in three years.

1941 Three down on the 28th tee, Vic Ghezzi came from behind in the final against Byron Nelson at Cherry Hills. It was Nelson's third final in a row.

1942 Sam Snead's first national championship. At Seaview CC, Atlantic City, he beat Jim Turnesa in the final by 2 and 1. Turnesa's victims included Hogan, McSpaden and Nelson.

1944 Nelson's third defeat in the final in five years. Bob Hamilton, his surprising conqueror, halved the 36th with a birdie when 1 up.

1945 Byron Nelson's fifth final in six years produced a clear-cut victory over Sam Byrd by 4 and 3 at Morraine CC, Dayton, Ohio. It was one of the peaks of his career.

1946 At Portland GC, Oregon, Ben Hogan won his first PGA title, virtually deciding his final with Ed 'Porky' Oliver by covering the first 9 holes after lunch in 30. It took him from 3 down to 2 up.

1947 Deadly putting and the odd stroke of luck enabled Australian-born Jim Ferrier to beat Chick Harbert by 2 and 1 in the final at Plum Hollow CC, Detroit.

1948 In the year in which he won his first US Open, Ben Hogan won his second PGA. After some devastating scoring in the earlier rounds, he beat Mike Turnesa by 7 and 6 despite being heavily outdriven.

Dick Burton and Jimmy Demaret watch Byron Nelson drive off, Winged Foot, 1946

1949 Sam Snead scored his second victory on a course, the Hermitage, Richmond, Virginia in his own home territory. Well supported by the crowd, he beat Johnny Palmer in the final.

1950 Having beaten Lloyd Mangrum and Jimmy Demaret, Chandler Harper defeated Henry Williams by 4 and 3 in the final to record his only national success.

1951 Sam Snead followed Walter Hagen and Gene Sarazen by winning a third title; at 39, he was also the oldest winner at that time. In a one-sided final against Walter Burkemo at Oakmont, he won 5 of the first 6 holes.

1952 Jim Turnesa was also 39 when he won his title at the Big Spring CC, Louisville. Although the famous Turnesa family had many achievements—brother Joe was runner-up to Hagen in 1927—this was the best. In the final, Jim beat Chick Harbert having been 3 down at lunch.

1953 Walter Burkemo, beaten by Sam Snead in the final of 1951, won his greatest honour in golf in his home state of Michigan. He beat Felice Torza by 2 and 1 and completed an amazing recovery as Torza was 7 up at lunch. Burkemo had originally thought of becoming a professional boxer.

Six former champions fell in the first two rounds, a bad blow for those wedded to matchplay.

1954 Burkemo reached the final in defence of his title and won 3 of the first 4 holes but Chick Harbert, twice runner-up, was 8 under par for the remaining holes. He won 4 and 3.

1955 Doug Ford, noted for his great putting, scored a good victory in the final over Cary Middlecoff at Meadowbrook CC.

1956 The penultimate championship to be decided by matchplay produced the biggest field, 128. The new champion was Jack Burke who, showing great touch with his putter throughout, came from behind in the semi-final and final. In the final, he beat Ted Kroll.

1957 The end of an era. The last major professional matchplay event in America. Held at Miami Valley GC, Dayton, Ohio, it saw Lionel Hebert crowned as champion. It was his first tournament victory. His victim in the final was Dow Finsterwald.

1958 As frequently happens, the runner-up one year becomes champion the next and Finsterwald maintained the tradition in the first PGA championship to be decided by strokeplay. At Llanerch CC, Pennsylvania, he was ahead with a 67 on the first day but behind with a round to play. However, he went out in 31 in the final round, returned another 67 and beat Billy Casper by 2 strokes.

1959 Bob Rosburg, a graduate at Stanford, achieved his most outstanding success at Minneapolis. Amazingly enough, nine players shared the first round lead on 69, but it was Rosburg's final round of 66 which settled things. It enabled him to beat Doug Sanders and Jerry Barber, 6 and 7 strokes more in the last round, by 1 stroke. Barber's 36-hole total of 134 (69,65) has never been beaten in the PGA championship, nor has his 30 for the front 9 in his 65.

1960 The PGA is well known as the one major championship which Arnold Palmer never won. The year 1960 was as good a chance as he had. As the new Open champion, he opened with a 67, but he followed with 74 and 75 and the winner was Jay Hebert. He followed his brother, Lionel, champion in 1957.

1961 Jerry Barber rivalled Gene Sarazen as the smallest champion. At 5 ft 5 in (1.65 m) and the wearer of spectacles, he was not long, but he was deadly on the greens, as he

Not some FBI agents attending the burial of a dead colleague but some of the American Ryder Cup team paying homage at the grave of Harry Vardon, 1961

showed over the last three holes. He holed from 6, 12 and 20 yd (5.5, 11 and 18 m) at Olympia Fields to earn a play-off with Don January. This he won with 67 to 68, was voted Player of the Year and captained the Ryder Cup team in England.

1962 Gary Player, having already won the British Open and the Masters, registered his third major victory at Aronimink. He defeated Bob Goalby by 1 stroke with Jack Nicklaus, the new Open champion playing in his first PGA, equal third.

1963 Nicklaus, though he failed to qualify in defence of his Open title, won the Masters and did not have to wait long to add a third major title. In fierce heat in Dallas, he started the final round 3 strokes behind Bruce Crampton who had a third round 65, but a final 68 gave him victory by 2 strokes from Dave Ragan. By his victory, Nicklaus joined the company of Ben Hogan, Gene Sarazen and Byron Nelson as winner of the US Open, Masters and PGA; and Nicklaus had been a professional for less than two years.

1964 Bobby Nichols's greatest hour. He started with a 64 at the Firestone CC, Akron, Ohio, and led after every round. He held off Arnold Palmer and Jack Nicklaus who were second and third but for Palmer, the only player to break 70 in all four rounds (68,68,69,69), it was another disappointment. Nichols's total of 271 is the lowest recorded in any PGA championship.

1965 Victory for Dave Marr at Laurel Valley was the highlight of his career. Four even rounds (70,69,70,71) gave him victory over Billy Casper and Jack Nicklaus by 2 strokes after he had driven into a bunker at the final hole but saved his 4. Arnold Palmer could not sustain a challenge on his own front door, but Nicklaus's share of second place meant that in his first four PGAs, he finished third, first, equal second and equal second.

1966 Al Geiberger recorded the biggest victory to date; 4

strokes from Dudley Wysong at Firestone CC. Wysong lost to Jack Nicklaus in the final of the 1961 US Amateur at Pebble Beach.

1967 Don January, the eventual winner, and Don Massengale tied with 281 at the Columbine CC, Denver. In 1961, January had lost a play-off to Jerry Barber and so was due a major win.

1968 The 50th championship produced the oldest winner in Julius Boros, 48, and another close call for Arnold Palmer at the Pecan Valley CC, Texas. At the final hole, Boros got up and down in two from a long way to beat Palmer and Bob Charles by 1 stroke.

1969 Gary Player, the target of some unruly local demonstrators who broke on to the course, just failed to deny the new champion, Raymond Floyd at the NCR course, Dayton, Ohio. He took a 5-stroke lead into the last round, but it was whittled down to one in a close finish.

1970 Dave Stockton, having lifted himself with a third-round 66 to take a 3-stroke lead, ended with 73 for a 2-stroke victory. Bob Murphy finished with a 66 to share second place with Arnold Palmer. It was Palmer's third second-place finish. He never came as close again.

1971 The first championship to be held in February and the first to be housed on the PGA National course at Palm Beach Gardens, Florida. It was appropriate, therefore, that a near neighbour, Jack Nicklaus, should record his second PGA success when he had 2 strokes to spare over Billy Casper. His victory meant that he was the first player to win the US and British Opens, the PGA and the Masters twice.

1972 A championship won by a remarkable recovery stroke. At the 16th at Oakland Hills in the final round Gary Player, having dropped strokes at the 14th and 15th, pushed his drive, but hit a daring 9 iron over a host of trouble to within 4 ft (1.2 m) of the flag. He holed for a birdie and went on to his second title.

1973 Remembered not as the best PGA championship, but the one in which Nicklaus won his 14th major victory and went ahead of Bobby Jones. At Canterbury GC, Cleveland, he won by 4 strokes from Bruce Crampton, thus equalling the biggest margin of victory since the championship moved to strokeplay.

1974 Gary Player had a 64 in his second round at Tanglewood GC, one off the PGA record set the following year, but in a week of heavy rain the new champion was Lee Trevino. Nicklaus was second and Bobby Cole of South Africa, who went into the lead at the start of the last round, was third. Trevino's win followed his victories in the US and British Opens.

1975 Jack Nicklaus crept within one of Walter Hagen's record with his fourth win. It was his 16th major victory, but he had to contend with a brilliant spell from Bruce Crampton. On the long and demanding Firestone CC South course, Crampton had a second-round 63. This is the lowest round ever played in the PGA and his total of 134 equalled that held by Jerry Barber for 36 holes.

However, playing together in the third round, Nicklaus had a 67 to Crampton's 75 and though Crampton finished strongly in the last round, nobody could catch Nicklaus.

1976 A championship in which thunderstorms made a Monday finish necessary, brought a second victory for Dave Stockton. His total of 281 at Congressional equalled the highest winning aggregate at that time, but Stockton had to get down in 2 from off the last green holing from 10 ft (3 m) to prevent a play-off with Don January and Ray Floyd. 282 was the highest winning total.

Gil Morgan's 36-hole total of 134 (66, 68) equalled the lowest in a PGA championship.

1977 Pebble Beach's first PGA seemed to be destined for Gene Littler. He led from the first round, was still 5 ahead with 9 holes to play and was only headed on the 3rd hole of the sudden-death play-off. Lanny Wadkins, having won no event for almost four years, had two eagles on the front 9 of the final round and profited when Littler dropped strokes on 5 of the first 6 holes on the back 9. Jack Nicklaus led after 15 holes, but he bogeyed the par-3 17th while Wadkins had a birdie at the par-5 18th.

Having had to hole from 20 ft (6 m) to stay in the play-off at the 1st hole, Wadkins won with a 4 to a 5 on the 3rd. It was the first time a sudden-death play-off had decided a major championship.

1978 A three-way tie resulting in the first major victory for John Mahaffey at Oakmont. It was the second sudden-death play-off in two years. Mahaffey won with a birdie on the 2nd extra hole from Tom Watson and Jerry Pate. Pate missed a short putt to win the championship on the 72nd hole, but Watson had been 4 ahead of Pate and 5 ahead of Mahaffey with 9 holes to play. However, after many setbacks, nobody begrudged Mahaffey his success.

1979 For the third year running, it needed a sudden-death play-off to decide the championship at Oakland Hills. David Graham and Ben Crenshaw were those involved and Graham holed from 6 yd (5.5 m) and 10 ft (3 m) on the first two sudden-death holes before winning on the 3rd with a 2 to a 4. He thus became the first Australian winner since Jim Ferrier in 1947, but there was drama on the 72nd hole. Needing a 4 for a 2-stroke victory which would have set a new 72-hole record aggregate and equalled the lowest single round in the USPGA (63), he took 6. His drive was way right, his second through the green and he needed 2 chips and 2 putts.

Crenshaw who was down in 2 from a bunker at the 17th and from the back of the 18th, got into a play-off but, after the British Open a few weeks previously, he again suffered a disappointment when in sight of his first major championship win.

He was unluckily thwarted by Graham's 2 saving putts, but Graham's last round 65 was remarkable despite taking 6 at the last. His total of 272 (69, 68, 70, 65) earned first prize of $30 000. Sam Snead finished 40th on 288, level fours, at the age of 67.

Crenshaw became only the second man to break 70 in all four rounds (69, 67, 69, 67). The first was Arnold Palmer at Columbus in 1964 (68, 68, 69, 69) but, like Crenshaw, he was second. Bobby Nichols won a record 271.

1980 After victory in the US Open, Jack Nicklaus won his fifth PGA title, breaking or equalling more records in the process. His 7-stroke victory was the biggest since the championship was decided by strokeplay and he equalled Walter Hagen's tally of five victories.

There had been changes to the Oak Hill course since the 1968 Open but they failed to limit Nicklaus's scoring powers. One stroke behind Gil Morgan at halfway, a third-round 66 gave him a 3-stroke lead and there was no holding him on the final day. First prize was $60 000 and the total purse $375 000.

1981 Larry Nelson's victory which also assured him of a place in the Ryder Cup team, was his first in a major championship but it was decisive enough. Second and third rounds of 66 gave him a lead of four going into the last round and he won by four. Lee Trevino was disqualified for not signing his card and Tom Watson failed to qualify.

DETAILED RECORDS

Held by matchplay 1916 to 1957.
Since 1958 held as strokeplay

Most victories
5, Walter Hagen, 1921–24–25–26–27; Jack Nicklaus, 1963–71–73–75–80
3, Gene Sarazen, 1922–23–33; Sam Snead, 1942–49–51

Most times runner-up or joint runner-up
4, Byron Nelson, 1939–41–44; Arnold Palmer, 1964–68–70; Billy Casper, 1958–65–71; Jack Nicklaus, 1964–65–74

Oldest winner
Julius Boros, 48 years 4 months 18 days, 1968

Youngest winner
Gene Sarazen, 20 years 5 months 20 days, 1922
Tom Creavy, 20 years 7 months 11 days, 1931

Biggest margin of victory
Matchplay (final): 8 and 7, Paul Runyan beat Sam Snead, 1938
Strokeplay: 7 strokes, Jack Nicklaus, 1980; 4 strokes, Al Geiberger, 1966, Jack Nicklaus, 1973

Lowest winning aggregate
271 (64, 71, 69, 67), Bobby Nichols, Columbus CC, Ohio, 1964
272 (69, 68, 70, 65), David Graham, Oakland Hills, 1979

Highest winning aggregate
282 (69, 71, 72, 70), Lanny Wadkins, Pebble Beach, 1977; after a play-off with Gene Littler

Lowest individual round
63, Bruce Crampton, second round, Firestone CC, Akron, 1975
64, Bobby Nichols, first round, Columbus CC, 1964; Jack Nicklaus, fourth round, Columbus CC, 1964; Gary Player, second round, Tanglewood GC, 1974

Lowest first round
64, Bobby Nichols, Columbus CC, 1964

Lowest second round
63, Bruce Crampton, Firestone CC, Akron, 1975

Lowest third round
65, Bruce Crampton, DAC CC, Dallas, 1963

Lowest fourth round
64, Jack Nicklaus, Columbus CC, 1964

Lowest 36-hole total
134 (69, 65), Jerry Barber, Minneapolis GC, 1959
134 (71, 63), Bruce Crampton, Firestone CC, 1975
134 (66, 68), Gil Morgan, Congressional CC, 1976

Lowest 54-hole total
202 (69, 66, 67), Raymond Floyd, NCR CC, Dayton, 1969

Lowest 9 holes
30, Art Wall, Jr, second 9, third round, Llanerch CC, 1958; Jerry Barber, first 9, second round, Minneapolis GC, 1959; Bob Rosburg, first 9, fourth round, Minneapolis GC, 1959; Jim Colbert, second 9, second round, Firestone CC, 1975

Biggest span between first and last victories
17 years, Jack Nicklaus, 1963–80

Successive victories
4, Walter Hagen, 1924–25–26–27
2, Jim Barnes, 1916–19; Gene Sarazen, 1922–23; Leo Diegel, 1928–29; Densmore Shute, 1936–37

Matchplay—most times in final
6, Walter Hagen, 1921–23–24–25–26–27
5, Sam Snead, 1938–40–42–49–51; Byron Nelson, 1939–40–41–44–45

Most consecutive finals
5, Walter Hagen, 1923–27

Most matches won
51, Gene Sarazen
42, Walter Hagen

Most consecutive matches won
22, Walter Hagen
14, Densmore Shute
13, Gene Sarazen

Longest final
38 holes: Gene Sarazen beat Walter Hagen, 1923; Paul Runyan beat Craig Wood, 1934; Vic Ghezzi beat Byron Nelson, 1941

Longest match
43 holes: Johnny Golden beat Walter Hagen, 1932

Best comeback
In a 36-hole match at Keller GC, St Paul, Minnesota, in 1932, Bobby Cruickshank beat Al Watrous at the 41st hole, having been 9 down with 12 holes to play. In the next round, Cruickshank lost to Frank Walsh who lost in the final to Olin Dutra.

Most extra hole matches in one championship
In 1937, Harold 'Jug' McSpaden won on the 38th in the first round, on the 39th in the fourth round and lost the final to Densmore Shute on the 37th.
In 1953, Dave Douglas won on the 20th in the first round, on the 19th in the second round and on the 37th in the third round. His opponents were Lew Worsham, Sam Snead and Jackson Bradley.

RESULTS

1916 Siwanoy CC, New York
Jim M Barnes beat Jock Hutchison 1 up

1919 Engineers CC, New York
Jim M Barnes beat Freddy McLeod 6 and 5

1920 Flossmoor CC, Illinois
Jock Hutchison beat J D Edgar 1 up

1921 Inwood CC, New York
Walter Hagen beat Jim M Barnes 3 and 2

1922 Oakmont CC, Pennsylvania
Gene Sarazen beat Emmet French 4 and 3

1923 Pelham CC, New York
Gene Sarazen beat Walter Hagen at 38th

1924 French Lick CC, Indiana
Walter Hagen beat Jim M Barnes 2 up

1925 Olympia Fields CC, Illinois
Walter Hagen beat Bill Mehlhorn 6 and 5

1926 Salisbury GC, New York
Walter Hagen beat Leo Diegel 5 and 3

The Major Open Championships

Australian Open Championship

First played 1904

Most victories
7, Gary Player, 1958–62–63–65–69–70–74
6, Jack Nicklaus, 1964–68–71–75–76–78
5, Ivo Whitton, 1912–13–26–29–31

Oldest winner
Peter Thomson, 43 years, 1972

Youngest winner
Ivo Whitton, 19 years, 1912

Lowest aggregate
264 (62, 71, 62, 69), Gary Player, Kooyonga GC, Adelaide, 1965

Lowest individual round
62 (twice), Gary Player, Kooyonga GC, Adelaide, 1965

Biggest margin of victory
8 strokes, Jack Nicklaus, Royal Hobart, 1971
7 strokes, Gary Player, Royal Melbourne, 1968

Amateur winners
Hon Michael Scott, 1904–07; C Pearce, 1908; C Felstead, 1909; I Whitton, 1912–13–26–29–31; A Russell, 1924; M Ryan, 1932; J Ferrier, 1938–39; B Devlin, 1960

Biggest span between victories
19 years, Ivo Whitton, 1912–31

Prize-money
1948, $500; 1978, $220 000; 1981, $150 000

One of the greatest and most popular touring professionals, Kel Nagle (Bill Cox)

RESULTS

Year	Winner	Venue	Score
1904	*Hon Michael Scott	The Australian (Botany)	315
1905	D Soutar	Royal Melbourne	330
1906	Carnegie Clark	Royal Sydney	322
1907	*Hon Michael Scott	Royal Melbourne	318
1908	*Clyde Pearce	The Australian	311
1909	*C Felstead	Royal Melbourne	316
1910	Carnegie Clark	Royal Adelaide	306
1911	Carnegie Clark	Royal Sydney	321
1912	*Ivo Whitton	Royal Melbourne	321
1913	*Ivo Whitton	Royal Melbourne	302
1920	Joe Kirkwood	The Australian	290
1921	A Le Fevre	Royal Melbourne	295
1922	C Campbell	Royal Sydney	307
1923	T Howard	Royal Adelaide	301
1924	*A Russell	Royal Melbourne	303
1925	F Popplewell	The Australian	299
1926	*Ivo Whitton	Royal Adelaide	297
1927	R Stewart	Royal Melbourne	297
1928	F Popplewell	Royal Sydney	295
1929	*Ivo Whitton	Royal Adelaide	309
1930	F Eyre	Metropolitan	306
1931	*Ivo Whitton	The Australian	301
1932	*M J Ryan	Royal Adelaide	296
1933	M L Kelly	Royal Melbourne	302
1934	W J Bolger	Royal Sydney	283
1935	F McMahon	Royal Adelaide	293

1936	Gene Sarazen	Metropolitan	282
1937	G Naismith	The Australian	299
1938	*Jim Ferrier	Royal Adelaide	283
1939	*Jim Ferrier	Royal Melbourne	285
1946	Ossie Pickworth	Royal Sydney	289
1947	Ossie Pickworth	Royal Queensland	285
1948	Ossie Pickworth	Kingston Heath	289
1949	Eric Cremin	The Australian	287
1950	Norman von Nida	Kooyonga	286
1951	Peter Thomson	Metropolitan	283
1952	Norman von Nida	Lake Karrinyup	278
1953	Norman von Nida	Royal Melbourne	278
1954	Ossie Pickworth	Kooyonga	280
1955	Bobby Locke	Gailes	290
1956	Bruce Crampton	Royal Sydney	289
1957	Frank Phillips	Kingston Heath	287
1958	Gary Player	Kooyonga	271
1959	Kel Nagle	The Australian	284
1960	*Bruce Devlin	Lake Karrinyup	282
1961	Frank Phillips	Victoria	275
1962	Gary Player	Royal Adelaide	281
1963	Gary Player	Royal Melbourne	278
1964	Jack Nicklaus	The Lakes	287
1965	Gary Player	Kooyonga	264
1966	Arnold Palmer	Royal Queensland	276
1967	Peter Thomson	Commonwealth	281
1968	Jack Nicklaus	Lake Karrinyup	270
1969	Gary Player	Royal Sydney	288
1970	Gary Player	Kingston Heath	280
1971	Jack Nicklaus	Royal Hobart	269
1972	Peter Thomson	Kooyonga	281
1973	Jesse Snead	Royal Queensland	280
1974	Gary Player	Lake Karrinyup	279
1975	Jack Nicklaus	Australian	279
1976	Jack Nicklaus	Australian	286
1977	David Graham	Australian	284
1978	Jack Nicklaus	Australian	284
1979	Jack Newton	Metropolitan	288
1980	Greg Norman	The Lakes	284
1981	Bill Rogers	Victoria	282

*Amateur

Canadian Open Championship

First played 1904

Most victories
4, Leo Diegel, 1924–25–28–29

Oldest winner
Kel Nagle, 43 years, Pinegrove, Quebec, 1964

Youngest winner
Albert H Murray, 20 years 10 months, Montreal, 1908

Lowest 72-hole aggregate
263, John Palmer (USA), St Charles CC, Winnipeg, 1952

Lowest individual round
63, Jerry Pate (USA) fourth round, Windsor, Essex, 1976
64, Jack Nicklaus (USA) fourth round, Windsor, Essex, 1976

Amateur winner
Doug Sanders, Beaconsfield GC, Montreal, 1956

Biggest margin of victory
16 strokes, John Douglas Edgar, Hamilton, 1919.
He defeated Bobby Jones and Karl Keffer with a total of 278. Edgar won again in 1920, but was killed in 1921, it was said in a street gang fight in Atlanta before he could try for three in a row.

Brothers as champion
Charles and Albert both won the title twice. Charles in 1906 and 1911 and Albert, the elder by 7 years in 1908 and 1913.

Sponsorship
Seagram's began sponsorship in 1936 with a purse of $3000. It reached $25 000 in 1957; $100 000 in 1965 and in 1967; for one year only, it went to $200 000 ($100 000 of which came from the City of Montreal).
In 1971 Peter Jackson, a division of Imperial Tobacco, took over at $150 000. By 1979, it was $350 000, both Peter Jackson and the Royal Canadian Golf Association contributing to the purse.

RESULTS

Year	Winner	Venue	Score
1904	J H Oke	Montreal	156
1905	George Cumming	Toronto	146
1906	Charles R Murray	Ottawa	170
Increased to 72 holes from 1907			
1907	Percy Barrett	Toronto	300
1908	Albert Murray	Montreal	300
1909	Karl Keffer	Toronto	309
1910	D Kenny	Toronto	303
1911	Charles R Murray	Ottawa	314
1912	George Sargent	Toronto	299
1913	Albert Murray	Montreal	295
1914	Karl Keffer	Toronto	300
1919	J Douglas Edgar	Hamilton	278
1920	J Douglas Edgar	Ottawa	298
1921	William Trovinger	Toronto	293
1922	Al Watrous	Montreal	303
1923	Clarence Hackney	Toronto	295
1924	Leo Diegel	Montreal	285
1925	Leo Diegel	Toronto	295
1926	Macdonald Smith	Montreal	283
1927	Tommy Armour	Toronto	288
1928	Leo Diegel	Toronto	282
1929	Leo Diegel	Montreal	274
1930	Tommy Armour	Hamilton	277
1931	Walter Hagen	Toronto	292
1932	Harry Cooper	Ottawa	290
1933	Joe Kirkwood	Toronto	282
1934	Tommy Armour	Toronto	287
1935	G Kunes	Montreal	280
1936	Lawson Little	Toronto	271
1937	Harry Cooper	Toronto	285
1938	Sam Snead	Toronto	277
1939	Jug McSpaden	Saint John, New Brunswick	282
1940	Sam Snead	Toronto	281
1941	Sam Snead	Toronto	274
1942	Craig Wood	Toronto	275

Lannie Wadkins and Billy Casper; Casper was Canadian open champion in 1967 (Action Photos)

1943–44	No championship.		
1945	Byron Nelson	Toronto	280
1946	George Fazio	Montreal	278
1947	Bobby Locke	Toronto	268
1948	C Congdon	Vancouver, British Columbia	280
1949	Dutch Harrison	Toronto	271
1950	Jim Ferrier	Montreal	271
1951	Jim Ferrier	Toronto	273
1952	Johnny Palmer	Winnipeg	263
1953	Dave Douglas	Toronto	273
1954	Pat Fletcher	Vancouver	280
1955	Arnold Palmer	Toronto	265
1956	*Doug Sanders	Montreal	273

1957	George Bayer	Kitchener	271
1958	Wes Ellis, Jr	Edmonton	267
1959	Doug Ford	Montreal	276
1960	Art Wall	Toronto	269
1961	Jack Cupit	Winnipeg	270
1962	Ted Kroll	Montreal	278
1963	Doug Ford	Toronto	280
1964	Kel D G Nagle	Montreal	277
1965	Gene Littler	Toronto	273
1966	Don Massengale	Vancouver	280
1967	Billy Casper	Montreal	279
1968	Bob Charles	Toronto	274
1969	Tommy Aaron	Montreal	275
1970	Kermit Zarley	London, Ontario	279
1971	Lee Trevino	Montreal	275
1972	Gay Brewer	Ridgeway, Ontario	275
1973	Tom Weiskopf	Quebec	278
1974	Bobby Nichols	Mississauga, Toronto	270
1975	Tom Weiskopf	Royal Montreal	274
1976	Jerry Pate	Essex, Windsor	267
1977	Lee Trevino	Glen Abbey, Oakville, Ontario	280
1978	Bruce Lietzke	Glen Abbey, Oakville, Ontario	283
1979	Lee Trevino	Glen Abbey Oakville, Ontario	281
1980	Bob Gilder	Royal Montreal	274
1981	Peter Oosterhuis	Glen Abbey, Oakville, Ontario	280

*Amateur

Japanese Open Championship

First played 1927

Most victories
6, Tomekichi Miyamoto, 1929–30–32–35–36–40

Oldest winner
Tomekichi Miyamoto, 39 years, 1940

Youngest winner
Severiano Ballesteros, 20 years 6 months, 1977

Lowest winning score
278, Takashi Murakami, Kasugai CC, 1975

Lowest individual round
66, Takashi Murakami, Kasugai CC, 1975

Overseas winners
Hang Chang Sang (Korea) 1972; Ben Arda (Philippines) 1973; Severiano Ballesteros (Spain) 1977 and 1978; Kuo Chie Hsiung (Taiwan) 1979.

First non-Asian winner
Severiano Ballesteros (Spain) 1977

Amateur winner
Rokuro Akaboshi, **309**, Hodogaya, 1927

Total prize-money
1981: 50 000 000 yen (approximately US $254 412)
There were no championships between 1942 and 1950

RESULTS

Year	Winner	Venue	Score
1927	*R Akahoshi	Hodogaya	309
1928	R Asami	Tokio	301
1929	T Miyamoto	Ibaraki	298
1930	T Miyamoto	Ibaraki	287
1931	R Asami	Hodogaya	281
1932	T Miyamoto	Ibaraki	298
1933	K Nakamura	Kasumigaseki	294
1934	No championship owing to typhoon disaster.		
1935	T Miyamoto	Asaka	293
1936	T Miyamoto	Inagawa	296
1937	Chin Sei Sui	Sagami	284
1938	R M Fuku	Fujisawa	294
1939	T Toda	Hirono	287
1940	T Miyamoto	Asaka	285
1941	En Toku Shun	Hodogaya	290
1942–49	No competition.		
1950	Y Hayashi	Abiko	288
1951	Son Shi Kin	Inagawa	284
1952	T Nakamura	Kawana	278
1953	Son Shi Kin	Takarazuka	299
1954	Y Hayashi	Tokio	291
1955	K Ono	Hirono	293
1956	T Nakamura	Kasumigaseki	281
1957	H Kobari	Aichi	285
1958	T Nakumura	Takanodai	288
1959	Chen Ching-Po	Sagamihara	298
1960	H Kobari	Hirono	296
1961	K Hosoishi	Takanodai	289
1962	T Sugihara	Chiba	287
1963	T Toda	Yokkaichi	283
1964	H Sugimoto	Tokio	288
1965	T Kitta	Miyoshi	284
1966	S Sato	Sodegaura	285
1967	T Kitta	Hirono	282
1968	T Kono	Sobu	284
1969	H Sugimoto	Ono	284
1970	M Kitta	Musashi	282
1971	Y Fujii	Aichi	282
1972	H Chang Sang	Iwai City	278
1973	B Arda	Osaka	278
1974	M Ozaki	Central	279
1975	T Murakami	Kasugai	278
1976	K Shimada	Central	288
1977	S Ballesteros	Narashino	284
1978	S Ballesteros	Yokohama	281
1979	Kuo Chie-Hsiung	Hino GC, Kyoto	285
1980	Katsuji Kikuchi	Sagamihara	296
1981	Yutaka Hagawa	Nihon Rhine	280

*Amateur

Right: 'Jumbo' Ozaki quite literally gritting his teeth (Phil Sheldon)

Japanese PGA Records

LEADING MONEY-WINNERS

Year	Winner	Yen
1969	Takaaki Kono	7 980 000
1970	Takaaki Kono	11 800 000
1971	Masashi Ozaki	17 143 906
1972	Masashi Ozaki	27 519 618
1973	Masashi Ozaki	48 859 000
1974	Masashi Ozaki	49 024 108
1975	Takashi Murakami	44 173 550
1976	Isao Aoki	41 960 801
1977	Masashi Ozaki	35 932 608
1978	Isao Aoki	79 258 200
1979	Isao Aoki	61 348 211

Over-all leading money-winner
Isao Aoki, 326 345 140 Yen at December 1979

Record official prize-money for one calendar year
62 987 200 Yen, Isao Aoki, 1978 (unofficial)
79 258 200 Yen, 1978

Most tournaments won in one year
10, Masashi Ozaki, 1972

Lowest aggregates
72 holes:
265 (23 under par), Masashi Ozaki, Seto-Naikai Circuit (Hiroshima CC, Happongi, Club), 1971

54 holes:
197 (19 under par), Isao Aoki, Kanto District Professional championship (Isogo CC), 1972
36 holes:
129 (13 under par), Lu Liang Huan, Sanpo Classic (Chiba Asahi CC), 1976
18 holes:
61 (7 under par), Takashi Murakami, Kanto Professional championship (Isogo CC), 1972
9 holes:
28 (7 under par), Takashi Murakami, Kanto Professional championship (Isogo CC), second 9, third round, 1972

Biggest margin of victory
11 strokes, C H Kuo, Dunlop International, 1979. Winning score 265

Most over-all victories
38, Masashi Ozaki

New Zealand Open

First played 1907 (since 1959 sponsored by BP New Zealand Ltd)
No championships 1915–18 and 1940–45

Most victories
9, Peter Thomson (Australia) 1950–51–53–55–59–60–61–65–71
7, Kel Nagle (Australia) 1957–58–62–64–67–68–69; A J Shaw 1926–29–30–31–32–34–36

Oldest winner
Kel Nagle, 48 years 11 months, 1969

Youngest winner
Bob Charles, 18 years 7 months (then an amateur), 1954

Lowest aggregate
266, Kel Nagle, Christchurch GC, 1964. (1907 championship played over 36 holes.)

Biggest margin of victory
18 strokes, A J Shaw, Manawatu GC, Palmerston North, 1930

Amateur winners
H W Berwick (Australia), 1956
R J Charles, 1954
A D S Duncan, 1907–10–11
R H Glading, 1946–47
J P Hornabrook, 1937–39
E M Macfarlane, 1925
S Morpeth, 1928

Lowest individual round
63, Peter Thomson, Wanganui, 1963

Consecutive victories
4, A J Shaw, 1929–30–31–32
3, E S Douglas, 1913–14–19; Peter Thomson, 1959–60–61; Kel Nagle, 1967–68–69
2, J A Clements, 1908–09; A D S Duncan, 1910–11; A Brooks, 1922–23; R H Glading, 1946–47; Peter Thomson, 1950–51; Kel Nagle, 1957–58

Unusual records
In 1930, Andy Shaw led by 15 strokes after 36 holes. He won by 18 strokes. His aggregate was 10 strokes better than the previous best. He achieved all this despite rain and strong winds. He was born near Troon, Scotland in 1898.
The first champion in 1907, A D S Duncan, finished leading amateur 28 years later at the age of 60.
In 1954, competing in his second championship, Bob Charles led after every round. Peter Thomson finished third, 4 months after winning his first British Open title.
B M Silk finished leading amateur in 1934 and did so again (for the fourth time) in 1963, aged 53

TOTAL PRIZE-MONEY

Year	
1907	£25 for the winner, £10 for the runner-up or the two leading professionals
	$
1953	470
1958	800
1963	2000
1968	5000
1973	16 000
1978	50 000

The spectacular increase in recent years is attributable to the sponsorship of BP New Zealand Ltd, who took over in 1969

RESULTS

Year	Winner	Venue	Scor
1907	*Mr A D S Duncan	Napier	15
1908	J A Clements	Otago	33
1909	J A Clements	Auckland	32
1910	*Mr A D S Duncan	Christchurch	29
1911	*Mr A D S Duncan	Wanganui	31
1912	J A Clements	Wellington	32
1913	E S Douglas	Otago	30
1914	E S Douglas	Auckland	31
1919	E S Douglas	Napier	32
1920	J H Kirkwood	Hamilton	30
1921	E S Douglas	Christchurch	30
1922	A Brooks	Manawatu	30
1923	A Brooks	Wanganui	31
1924	E J Moss	Auckland	30
1925	*E M Macfarlane	Christchurch	30
1926	A J Shaw	Miramar	30
1927	E J Moss	Hamilton	30
1928	*S Morpeth	Otago	30
1929	A J Shaw	Wanganui	29
1930	A J Shaw	Manawatu	28
1931	A J Shaw	Christchurch	28
1932	A J Shaw	Wellington	28
1933	E J Moss	Titirangi	30
1934	A J Shaw	Wanganui	28
1935	A Murray	Christchurch	28
1936	A J Shaw	New Plymouth	29
1937	*J P Hornabrook	Hamilton	29
1938	Bobby Locke	Otago	28

Bob Shearer, New Zealand Open winner, 1981 (Phil Sheldon)

1939	*J P Hornabrook	Miramar	291
1946	*R H Glading	Manawatu	306
1947	*R H Glading	New Plymouth	291
1948	A Murray	Otago	294
1949	James Galloway	Hastings	283
1950	Peter Thomson	Christchurch	280
1951	Peter Thomson	Titirangi	288
1952	A Murray	Wanganui	293
1953	Peter Thomson	Otago	295
1954	*Bob Charles	Wellington	280
1955	Peter Thomson	Auckland	280
1956	*H W Berwick	Christchurch	292
1957	Kel Nagle	Manawatu	294
1958	Kel Nagle	Hamilton	278
1959	Peter Thomson	Paraparaumu	287
1960	Peter Thomson	Invercargill	281
1961	Peter Thomson	New Plymouth	267
1962	Kel Nagle	Titirangi	281
1963	Bruce Devlin	Wanganui	273
1964	Kel Nagle	Christchurch	266
1965	Peter Thomson	Auckland	278
1966	Bob Charles	Paraparaumu	273
1967	Kel Nagle	Hamilton	275
1968	Kel Nagle	Christchurch	272
1969	Kel Nagle	Wanganui	273
1970	Bob Charles	Auckland	271
1971	Peter Thomson	Dunedin	276
1972	Bill Dunk	Paraparaumu	279
1973	Bob Charles	Palmerston North	288
1974	R Gilder	Christchurch	283
1975	Bill Dunk	Hamilton	272
1976	Simon Owen	Wellington	284
1977	Bob Byman	Auckland	290
1978	Bob Shearer	Wanganui	277
1979	Stuart Ginn	Dunedin	278
1980	Buddy Allin	New Plymouth	274
1981	Bob Shearer	Wellington	285

*Amateur

South African Open

First played 1909

Most victories
13, Gary Player, 1956–60–65–66–67–68–69–72–75–76–77–79–81
9, Bobby Locke, 1935–37–38–39–40–46–50–51–55

Youngest winner
Bobby Locke, 17 years, 1935

Oldest winner
Sid Brews, 53 years, 1952

Lowest aggregate
272, Bobby Cole, Royal Johannesburg, 1974

Lowest individual round
63, Gary Player, Royal Johannesburg, 1977 (This was accomplished five months after Mark Hayes lowered British Open record to 63)

Amateur winners (since 1930)
Bobby Locke, 1935 and 1937
C E Olander, 1936
R W Glennie, 1947
M Janks, 1948
J R Boyd, 1953
R C Taylor, 1954
A A Stewart, 1958
D Hutchinson, 1959

Total prize-money
1978 R45 000
1981 R55 000

Unusual records
At the age of 15, Wayne Player, Gary Player's son, led the pre-qualifying round with a 65. Then, at the 1st hole of the championship proper at Royal Johannesburg in 1977, he holed a 3-iron shot for an albatross 2

1981
Sponsored by Datsun

RESULTS

After 1908—72 holes played
1899, Walter Day (Kimberley); 1902, Professional match (3 competitors)—Final: W Day (Kimberley) beat J Johnson (Port Elizabeth); 1903, L B Waters (Johannesburg); 1904, L B Waters (Johannesburg); 1905, A Gray (Port Elizabeth); 1906, A Gray (Port Elizabeth)

Year	Winner	Venue	Score
1907	Lawrence Waters	Kimberley	147
1908	George Fotheringham	Johannesburg	163
1909	John Fotheringham	Potchefstroom	306
1910	George Fotheringham	Wynberg	315
1911	George Fotheringham	Durban	301

Lowest 54 holes

194, John Lister, Gallaher, Ulster Open, Shandon Park, Belfast, 1970

194, Vicente Fernandez, Benson and Hedges, Fulford, 1975

195, Kel Nagle, Irish Hospitals, Woodbrook, 1961

195, Bernard Hunt, Piccadilly Tournament, Wentworth (East course), 1966

Fewest putts in 18 holes

22, Bill Large, qualifying round for Benson and Hedges matchplay championship, Moor Park, 1972

Most consecutive birdies

11, José Maria Canizares, Swiss Open, Crans sur Sierre, 1978. He had 5 to finish his second round and 6 to begin his third round

7, Peter Thomson, Dunlop, Wentworth, 1958

7, Bernard Hunt, Daks, Wentworth, 1958

7, Angel Miguel, Daks, Wentworth, 1960

7, Peter Butler, Benson and Hedges, Fulford, 1971

7, Peter Townsend, Viyella PGA, Wentworth, 1974

7, Brian Waites, Bob Hope Classic, RAC Club, 1980

LEADING PGA MONEY-WINNERS 1964–81

Year	Winner	£
1964	Neil Coles	7 890
1965	Peter Thomson	7 011
1966	Bruce Devlin	13 205
1967	Gay Brewer	20 235
1968	Gay Brewer	23 107
1969	Billy Casper	23 483
1970	Christy O'Connor	31 532
1971	Gary Player	11 281
1972	Bob Charles	18 538
1973	Tony Jacklin	24 839
1974	Peter Oosterhuis	32 127
1975	Dale Hayes	20 507
1976	Severiano Ballesteros	39 504
1977	Severiano Ballesteros	46 436
1978	Severiano Ballesteros	54 348
1979	Sandy Lyle	49 232
1980	Greg Norman	74 828
1981	Bernhard Langer	81 036

EUROPEAN CAREER MONEY-WINNING LEADERS *(AT 1.1.82)*

(positions at 1.1.81 in brackets)

		Seasons	£
1	Severiano Ballesteros (Sp) *(1)*	8	313 625
2	Neil Coles (GB) *(2)*	25	262 997
3	Brian Barnes (GB) *(3)*	17	228 804
4	Tony Jacklin (GB) *(4)*	18	185 399
5	Nick Faldo (GB) *(13)*	6	180 070
6	Bernard Gallacher (GB) *(6)*	14	175 097
7	Graham Marsh (Aus) *(7)*	12	174 451
8	Sandy Lyle (GB) *(15)*	4	172 090
9	Greg Norman (Aus) *(18)*	5	164 278
10	Manuel Pinero (Sp) *(14)*	10	164 047
11	Dale Hayes (SA) *(5)*	9	159 977
12	Tommy Horton (GB) *(10)*	18	149 330
13	Bernhard Langer (Ger) *(–)*	6	146 183
14	Hugh Baiocchi (SA) *(12)*	10	145 843
15	Mark James (GB) *(16)*	6	144 188
16	Gary Player (SA) *(8)*	26	144 044
17	Sam Torrance (GB) *(21)*	10	143 977
18	Bob Charles (NZ) *(9)*	19	136 654
19	Christy O'Connor (Ire) *(11)*	27	130 987
20	Eddie Polland (GB) *(20)*	14	129 560
21	Peter Oosterhuis (GB) *(17)*	13	123 777
22	Ken Brown (GB) *(24)*	6	122 520
23	Howard Clark (GB) *(–)*	8	119 531
24	Eamonn Darcy (Ire) *(–)*	9	118 749

HARRY VARDON TROPHY

The Harry Vardon Trophy is awarded annually by the PGA to the leading player in the Order of Merit.

Year	Winner	Club/Country
1937	Charles Whitcombe	Crews Hill
1938	Henry Cotton	Royal Mid-Surrey
1939	Reg Whitcombe	Parkstone
1940–45	*in abeyance*	
1946	Bobby Locke	South Africa
1947	Norman von Nida	Australia
1948	Charlie Ward	Little Aston
1949	Charlie Ward	Little Aston
1950	Bobby Locke	South Africa
1951	John Panton	Glenbervie

MOST BIRDIES AND EAGLES IN A ROUND: EUROPE

1 Eagle, 11 Birdies	Jimmy Martin (63)	Swallow Penfold	*Stoneham*	**1961**
1 Eagle, 9 Birdies	Eric Brown (64)	Dunlop Masters	*Hollinwell*	**1957**
1 Eagle, 8 Birdies	José Maria Canizares (64)	Swiss Open	*Crans sur Sierre*	**1978**

1952	Harry Weetman	Croham Hurst
1953	Flory van Donck	Belgium
1954	Bobby Locke	South Africa
1955	Dai Rees	South Herts
1956	Harry Weetman	Croham Hurst
1957	Eric Brown	Buchanan Castle
1958	Bernard Hunt	Hartsbourne
1959	Dai Rees	South Herts
1960	Bernard Hunt	Hartsbourne
1961	Christy O'Connor	Royal Dublin
1962	Christy O'Connor	Royal Dublin
1963	Neil Coles	Coombe Hill
1964	Peter Alliss	Parkstone
1965	Bernard Hunt	Hartsbourne
1966	Peter Alliss	Parkstone
1967	Malcolm Gregson	Dyrham Park
1968	Brian Huggett	Betchworth Park
1969	Bernard Gallacher	Ifield
1970	Neil Coles	Coombe Hill
1971	Peter Oosterhuis	Dulwich & Sydenham
1972	Peter Oosterhuis	Pacific Harbour, Fiji
1973	Peter Oosterhuis	Pacific Harbour, Fiji
1974	Peter Oosterhuis	Pacific Harbour, Fiji
1975	Dale Hayes	St Pierre and South Africa
1976	Severiano Ballesteros	Spain
1977	Severiano Ballesteros	Spain
1978	Severiano Ballesteros	Spain

Precision driving in the final of the Suntory world matchplay championship. It was very much a case of head to head and toe to toe (Phil Sheldon)

1979	Sandy Lyle	Hawkstone Park
1980	Sandy Lyle	Hawkstone Park
1981	Bernhard Langer	W Germany

Finalists in the first matchplay championship, sponsored by the News of the World, shake hands with the 1937 finalists at Stoke Poges. On the left, Percy Alliss and Ted Ray. On the right, James Braid and Jimmy Adams (Topical Press)

Brotherly love, or did he get paid? Baldomero caddying for Severiano Ballesteros (Phil Sheldon)

BRAID TAYLOR MEMORIAL MEDAL

This award is made to the PGA member, resident in Britain, who finishes highest in the Open Championship.

1966 David Thomas *2nd*
1967 Clive Clark *3rd*
1968 Maurice Bembridge *5th*
1969 Tony Jacklin *1st*
1970 Tony Jacklin *5th*
1971 Tony Jacklin *3rd*
1972 Tony Jacklin *3rd*
1973 Neil Coles *2nd*
1974 Peter Oosterhuis *2nd*
1975 Neil Coles
Peter Oosterhuis *7th*
1976 Tommy Horton
Mark James
Christy O'Connor, Jr *5th*
1977 Tommy Horton *9th*
1978 Peter Oosterhuis *6th*
1979 Mark James *4th*
1980 Carl Mason *4th*
1981 Mark James *=3rd*

THE TOOTING BEC CUP

Presented to the PGA in 1901, the Tooting Bec Cup is now awarded to the member, resident in Great Britain and Ireland, who returns the lowest round in the Open Championship.

Year	Winner	Venue	Score
1924	Ernest Whitcombe	Royal Liverpool	70
1925	Ted Ray	Prestwick	73
1926	Held in abeyance		
1927	Fred Robson	St Andrews	69
1928	Held in abeyance		
1929	Percy Alliss	Muirfield	69
1930	Archie Compston	Royal Liverpool	68
1931	Held in abeyance		
1932	Arthur Havers	Prince's	68
1933	Abe Mitchell	St Andrews	68
1934	William Davis	Royal St George's	68
1935	Alf Perry	Muirfield	67
1936	William Branch	Royal Liverpool	68
1937	Reg Whitcombe	Carnoustie	70
1938	Dick Burton	Royal St George's	69
	Jack Busson		
1946	Dai Rees	St Andrews	67
1947	Laurie Ayton	Royal Liverpool	69
	Henry Cotton		
1948	Henry Cotton	Muirfield	66
1949	Jimmy Adams	Royal St George's	67
	Ken Bousfield		
1950	Fred Daly	Troon	66
1951	Jimmy Adams	Royal Portrush	68
	Charlie Ward		
1952	Fred Daly	Royal Lytham	67
1953	Eric Lester	Carnoustie	70
	Dai Rees		
1954	Jack Hargreaves	Royal Birkdale	67
	Sid Scott		
1955	Johnny Fallon	St Andrews	67
1956	Dennis Smalldon	Royal Liverpool	68
1957	Laurie Ayton	St Andrews	67
	Eric Brown		
	Johnny Fallon		
1958	Eric Brown	Royal Lytham	65
1959	Peter Alliss	Muirfield	67
1960	Bernard Hunt	St Andrews	66
1961	Christy O'Connor	Royal Birkdale	67
1962	Sid Scott	Troon	68
1963	Tom Haliburton	Royal Lytham	68
	Christy O'Connor		
1964	Malcolm Gregson	St Andrews	67
	Bernard Hunt		
1965	Brian Huggett	Royal Birkdale	68
1966	Peter Butler	Muirfield	65
1967	Hugh Boyle	Royal Liverpool	68
	Lionel Platts		
1968	Brian Barnes	Carnoustie	70
	Gordon Cunningham		
1969	Christy O'Connor	Royal Lytham	65
1970	Neil Coles	St Andrews	65
1971	Peter Oosterhuis	Royal Birkdale	66
1972	Harry Bannerman	Muirfield	67
	Tony Jacklin		
	Guy Hunt		
1973	Neil Coles	Troon	66
1974	John Garner	Royal Lytham	69
	John Morgan		
	Peter Townsend		
1975	Maurice Bembridge	Carnoustie	67
	Neil Coles		
	Bernard Gallacher		

1976	Mark James	*Royal Birkdale*	66
1977	Tommy Horton	*Turnberry*	65
1978	Garry Cullen	*St Andrews*	67
1979	Bill Longmuir	*Royal Lytham*	65
1980	Ken Brown	*Muirfield*	68
	Eamonn Darcy		
	Bill McColl		
1981	Gordon Brand	*Sandwich*	65

Ryder Cup

'*The Ryder Cup is not only about winning, but also about goodwill. There is too little tradition left in the game as it is.*'

Dave Marr
Captain US team 1981

MILESTONES

The Ryder Cup came into being slightly by chance. If Samuel Ryder, a boy from Manchester, had not persuaded his father, a seed merchant, to sell flower seeds in penny packets, he would never have moved south to start his own business at St Albans in Hertfordshire.

There, late in life, he took up golf under the skilled and watchful eye of Abe Mitchell and, whether at Mitchell's suggestion or not, presented a cup for competition between the professionals of America and Britain.

In an earlier unofficial match Britain won 13½–1½ at Wentworth, but in the first official match in 1927, five years after the start of the Walker Cup, Britain quickly learned the lesson about the formidable nature of American golfers.

1927 Britain, captained by Ted Ray, travelled to Worcester, Massachusetts where America, under Walter Hagen, captured the trophy 9½–2½. America won three of the four 36-hole foursomes and then took six of the singles. Charles Whitcombe won a notable half with Gene Sarazen while George Duncan won Britain's only single against Joe Turnesa, runner-up the same year to Hagen in the USPGA championship. It was Hagen's fourth victory in succession. In the Ryder Cup, Hagen won his foursome with Johnny Golden and his single against Arthur Havers.

1929 Immediate revenge for Britain at Moortown and defeat for Walter Hagen in the singles battle of the captains. He lost 10 and 8 to George Duncan, a victory that helped to turn the tables after America had again won the foursomes. It is the biggest 36-hole singles margin in the history of the event. The victory of Charles Whitcombe by 8 and 6 over Johnny Farrell, 1928 US Open champion, was followed by wins for Archie Compston, Aubrey Boomer and a youthful Henry Cotton.

1931 The Americans underlined their supremacy in their own country. At Scioto, Ohio, they lost only one foursome and two singles. They had five victories by 7 and 6 or more.

1933 One of the more famous matches which Britain won at Southport and Ainsdale, victory coming in the last match on the course. It was the most exciting finish to a team match seen up until then and one watched by enormous crowds.

The British, captained by J H Taylor, went for a run on the sands at 6.30 each morning and underwent other forms of physical training unheard of before or since.

How much it contributed to their victory was never known but, for the first time, Britain gained a foursomes lead and hung on in the singles. Eventually, everything depended on Syd Easterbrook and Densmore Shute, the 1933 British Open champion. They came to the last all square. Easterbrook putted almost dead for his four but Shute, characteristically for an American, knocked his winning putt past the hole and then, uncharacteristically for an American, missed the return.

Britain, without Henry Cotton who had gone to Brussels, had won but the match very nearly did not take place. Hagen did not keep the appointed meeting with Taylor to exchange orders beforehand—or a second appointed meeting. A third hour was named with Taylor issuing an ultimatum that, if Hagen defaulted again, he would call the match off and the world should know why. This time, Hagen kept his appointment and all was well.

1935 Under Hagen's captaincy of America for the fifth time, Britain never recovered from their defeat in the foursomes at Ridgewood, New Jersey. All they gained were two victories by 1 hole and two halves.

1937 History did not repeat itself at Southport and Ainsdale. The British pairing of Henry Cotton and Alf Padgham was very much a case of putting the two best eggs in the same basket. Byron Nelson and Ed Dudley cracked them and America never looked back. Cotton won his single, but the outstanding achievement was the victory of Dai Rees over Nelson. It was the first of many appearances by Rees, but the last as American Captain by Hagen.

Samuel Ryder, the donor, presents the Ryder Cup to George Duncan, 1929

Southampton Docks, first sight of Britain for the 1949 American Ryder Cup team. They are seen on the deck of the Queen Elizabeth. From left to right: Bob Hamilton, Sam Snead, Chick Harbert, Jimmy Demaret, Ben Hogan, Lloyd Mangrum, Dutch Harrison, Clayton Heafner, Johnny Palmer and Ed Dudley (Planet News Ltd.)

1939 The match did not take place although the Americans picked a side.

1947 Britain went to Portland, Oregon, although the fact that the Ryder Cup was resumed so soon after the war owed a great deal to Robert Hudson, a Portland businessman who more or less financed the expedition and played host to the British.

The benevolence, however, was centred off the course. The Americans won the first eleven matches, a whitewash being prevented by Sam King winning the final single against Herman Keiser.

It was the biggest victory margin in the history of the event. Porky Oliver and Lew Worsham equalled the biggest 36-hole foursome win, by 10 and 9, in the history of the event.

1949 America, captained by Ben Hogan who was still recovering from his terrible car accident, lost the foursomes 3–1. However, they staged a typical comeback in the singles. Dutch Harrison set the example by leading off in the singles with five straight 3s against Max Faulkner and his victory was followed by five others. The match was played at Ganton and the score was 7–5.

1951 Another heavy defeat for the British who won only one foursome and one single, although both involved Arthur Lees.

Played at Pinehurst, North Carolina, with Ben Hogan, Sam Snead (Captain), Jimmy Demaret and Lloyd Mangrum in the American side. All four won their singles. It was Demaret's sixth and last game.

The American side included Clayton Heafner whose son, Vance, played in the Walker Cup match in 1977. They are the only father and son to play in the Ryder and Walker Cup.

1953 One of the best matches of the series at Wentworth, the result hinging on the missing of two shortish putts by the youngest British players in the singles. It was, nevertheless, a fine recovery by the British to get that close. They lost the foursomes 3–1, but had the edge in the singles. Harry Weetman beat Sam Snead after being 4 down with 6 to play.

1955 The match ventured into the Californian desert for the first time. The margin of the American victory was 8–4, but it was closer than that scoreline suggests. Most notable for two victories by John Jacobs in his only Ryder Cup match.

1957 First British victory for 34 years and, as it proved, the last. At Lindrick before huge crowds, Britain came back after losing the foursomes 3–1. They won six singles by convincing margins and lost only one. Dai Rees who captained the side won both his matches as did Ken Bousfield. It was the first time since 1933 that no American won twice. In 1933, Ed Dudley and Billy Burke won the only American point in the foursomes but did not play in the singles.

The first European side to play in the Ryder Cup, Greenbrier, 1979. Standing (left to right): Mark James, Sandy Lyle, Nick Faldo, Peter Oosterhuis, Antonio Garrido, Bernard Gallacher. Seated (left to right): Des Smyth, Ken Brown, Tony Jacklin, John Jacobs (non-playing captain), Severiano Ballesteros, Brian Barnes, Michael King (Phil Sheldon)

1959 The year in which the British party had a narrow escape when their plane met a storm while travelling from Los Angeles to Palm Desert. After that, the Americans won 8½–3½ but Eric Brown, the only British singles winner, preserved his 100 per cent singles record in his fourth and final match. He won all four singles and lost all four foursomes.

1961 Change to four series of 18-hole matches, foursomes the first day at Royal Lytham and singles the next. America, with Arnold Palmer in the team for the first time, won the four-somes 6–2, but there was only one point in the singles. It was also the first appearance of Billy Casper who set a record for the number of individual matches played. He was helped by the change of format.

1963 Introduction of fourballs, play being extended over three days. It was done to try and further interest in the matches in America, but served merely to emphasise American superiority. They won easily in Atlanta. Britain managed only one fourball victory out of eight.

1965 A closer match at Royal Birkdale although the day of fourballs ended in the dark. The first day of foursomes was halved, America winning the fourballs 4–2 and the singles 10–5. Peter Alliss won both his singles for Britain against Billy Casper and Ken Venturi.

1967 America's biggest win in Houston, 23½–8½, since the

match was contested over six rounds. Britain scored no victories in the eight fourballs.

1969 After Tony Jacklin's victory in the Open championship earlier in the summer, the most exciting match of the whole series ended in a half.

The last day began with the scores even and ended the same way. Jacklin scored a 4 and 3 victory over Nicklaus on the last morning and was involved in the deciding game, again against Nicklaus, in the afternoon. Just ahead of them, Brian Huggett got a courageous half against Billy Casper. At the time that Huggett holed from 5 ft (1.5 m) on the 18th, Jacklin holed a huge putt on the 17th to get back to square.

Huggett thought that his putt might be to win the whole contest, but not so. Jacklin and Nicklaus, all square with one to play, halved the 18th in 4, although Nicklaus generously conceded Jacklin's final putt of about two and a half feet after he had holed an awkward one himself.

To underline the closeness of the three days, 18 of the 32 matches finished on the 18th green. The teams became 12 a side.

1971 After the excitement of Birkdale, 1971 produced the best performance by a British side in America. This score was 18½–13½ at St Louis, the five-point difference coming in the fourballs in which the British rarely fare well. It was an encouraging match for some of the young British players including Peter Oosterhuis, Peter Townsend, Harry Bannerman, Bernard Gallacher, Maurice Bembridge and Brian Barnes. The final two days consisted of a foursome and fourball not a day of each.

1973 In the first match to be played in Scotland, Britain led at lunchtime on the second day at Muirfield, but America won the singles 11–5, although four were halved and six went to the 17th green or beyond.

1975 Played in Arnold Palmer country at Laurel Valley, Pennsylvania, America won 21–11, a result that was always assured after winning all four foursomes on the first morning. The singles were, for the most part, close and Brian Barnes beat Jack Nicklaus twice on the last day.

1977 At Royal Lytham, only 18 holes were played each day; it was an experiment that was not a success and not popular among the players. There were five foursomes on the first day, five fourballs on the second day and ten singles on the third.

America led 7½–2½ after two days, but Hale Irwin, Tom Watson and Jack Nicklaus all lost their singles. Nicklaus's defeat meant that he had won only one of his last five singles in the Ryder Cup.

1979 For the first time, a European side was selected to play the Americans at the Greenbrier Club at White Sulphur Springs. Antonio Garrido and Severiano Ballesteros, British Open champion, won their places, although they only won one match.

The form of play was altered yet again. There were two days when eight foursomes and eight fourballs were played, the final day being devoted to twelve singles matches. However, Gil Morgan and Mark James were not fit enough to play in the singles, it being agreed by the captains to call it a half to both sides. It was the first time this had happened.

The European team, captained by John Jacobs, came back well on the second day after trailing 5½–2½ on the first. They entered the final day trailing by one, but they lost the singles 8½–3½, although four matches which they lost finished on the last green.

For the Americans, captained by Billy Casper, Larry Nelson had a 100 per cent record from five games.

Tom Watson withdrew from the American side a few days before the match to be with his wife and newly born child. His place went to Mark Hayes.

Peter Oosterhuis's singles defeat by Hubert Green was his first in eight games.

Lee Elder became the first black golfer to take part in the Ryder Cup.

1981 After Europe had taken a one point lead at the end of the first day, the Americans exercised their dominance to win 18½–9½ at Walton Heath, the first time the Ryder Cup had been played in the South of England since 1953.

As has happened many times, the result was closer than the score suggests, but the outstanding player on either side was Larry Nelson who won all four of his matches—making his tally in two Ryder Cups nine out of nine.

Tom Kite, America's leading money winner for 1981, was 10 under par for his singles match against Sandy Lyle.

DETAILED RECORDS

Most appearances
10, Christy O'Connor, Sr (Great Britain and Ireland), 1955–73
9, Sam Snead (US), 1937–59, excluding 1957. No matches were played in 1939 and 1941, but the United States picked a team and Snead's total includes these two occasions

Most consecutive appearances
10, Christy O'Connor, Sr

Biggest margin of victory in individual matches
Over 36 holes (1927–59)
Foursomes: **10 and 9,** Ed Oliver and Lew Worsham (United States), 1947. Walter Hagen and Densmore Shute (United States), 1931
Singles: **10 and 8,** George Duncan (Great Britain), 1929
Over 18 holes (from 1961)
Foursomes: **6 and 5,** David Thomas and George Will (Great Britain and Ireland), 1965; Dave Marr and Arnold Palmer (United States), 1965; Bobby Nichols and Johnny Pott (United States), 1967; Jack Nicklaus and Arnold Palmer (United States), 1973
Singles: **7 and 6,** Miller Barber (United States), 1969; Lee Trevino (United States), 1971
Fourball: **7 and 6,** Tom Kite and Hale Irwin (United States), 1979; **7 and 5,** Lee Trevino and Jerry Pate (United States), 1981; **5 and 4,** Arnold Palmer and Dow Finsterwald (United States), 1963; Dave Marr and Arnold Palmer (United States), 1965; Arnold Palmer and Gardner Dickinson (United States), 1971; Brian W Barnes and Bernard Gallacher (Great Britain and Ireland), 1973

Largest winning margin by team
36-hole matches, 1947: the United States won 11–1
18-hole matches (3 days), 1967: the United States won 23½–8½

Best team recovery
In 1957, Great Britain and Ireland lost the foursomes 3–1, but won the singles 6½–1½ for over-all victory

Most consecutive team victories
7 by the United States, 1935–55

Course most often used
Britain: Southport and Ainsdale, Royal Lytham and Royal Birkdale, twice each
USA: No course has been used more than once

Oldest competitors
Britain: Ted Ray, 50 years 2 months 5 days, 1927
Christy O'Connor, Sr, 49 years 8 months 30 days, 1973
USA: Don January, 47 years 9 months 26 days, 1977
Julius Boros, 47 years 7 months 17 days, 1967

Youngest competitors
Britain: Nick Faldo, 20 years 1 month 28 days, 1977
USA: Horton Smith, 21 years 4 days, 1929

Form of the match
1927–59: Two days, 36-hole matches, four foursomes, eight singles
1961: Two days, first day, two series 18-hole foursomes. Second day, two series 18-hole singles
1963–71: Three days, one day each of two series of 18-hole foursomes, fourballs and singles

1973–75: Three days, first two days, 18-hole foursomes and fourballs. Third day two series of singles
1977: Three days, first day, 18-hole foursomes; second day, 18-hole fourballs; third day 18-hole singles
1979–81: Three days, first two days, four foursomes and four fourballs, third day twelve singles

Teams winning all the foursomes or fourballs
1947: the United States won the foursomes 4–0
1963: the United States won the second series of foursomes 4–0

1975: the United States won the first series of foursomes 4–0
1967: the United States won the first series of fourballs 4–0
1971: the United States won the first series of fourballs 4–0

Teams winning all the singles
None, but in 1963 the United States won 7½ out of 8 in the second series of singles

The United States have won 20 matches, Great Britain and Ireland 3 and 1 halved

---

OUTSTANDING INDIVIDUAL RECORDS
UNITED STATES

(Number of individual matches shown in brackets)

Name	%
Larry Nelson (9)	100
Jimmy Demaret (6)	100
Billy Maxwell (4)	100
Ben Hogan (3)	100
Johnny Golden (3)	100
Billy Burke (3)	100
Wilfrid Cox (2)	100
Ralph Guldahl (2)	100
Chick Harbert (2)	100
Lew Worsham (2)	100
Bob Rosburg (2)	100
Jim Turnesa (1)	100
Gardner Dickinson (10)	90
Lanny Wadkins (8)	88.88
Jack Burke (8)	87.5
Clayton Heafner (4)	87.5
Horton Smith (4)	87.5
Mike Souchak (6)	83.3
Walter Hagen (9)	83.3
Tony Lema (11)	81.81
Tom Kite (8)	81.25
Tom Weiskopf (10)	75
Lloyd Mangrum (8)	75

Tommy Bolt (4)	75
Ted Kroll (4)	75
Tommy Jacobs (4)	75
Henry Picard (4)	75
Ed Dudley (4)	75
Byron Nelson (4)	75
Hubert Green (3)	75

Other players of interest

Hale Irwin (16)	71.87
Tom Watson (7)	71.42
Gene Sarazen (12)	70.83
Arnold Palmer (32)	68.75
Julius Boros (16)	68.75
Lee Trevino (29)	67.24
Gene Littler (27)	66.66
Jack Nicklaus (28)	66.07
Billy Casper (37)	63.51

Billy Casper's 37 matches is a record for America.

A total of 117 players have actually *played* for the United States.

OUTSTANDING INDIVIDUAL RECORDS
GREAT BRITAIN AND IRELAND

(Number of individual matches shown in brackets)

Name	%
John Jacobs (2)	100
John Fallon (1)	100

Peter Mills (1)	100
Nick Faldo (10)	70.0
Abe Mitchell (6)	66.66
Sid Easterbrook (3)	66.66
Percy Alliss (6)	58.33
Charles Whitcombe (9)	55.55
Peter Oosterhuis (28)	55.35
Bernard Gallacher (29)	53.44
Ken Bousfield (10)	50
Harry Bradshaw (5)	50
Arthur Lees (8)	50
Arthur Havers (6)	50
W H Davies (4)	50
Norman Drew (1)	50
Aubrey Boomer (4)	50
Eric Brown (8) won in all 4 singles	50

Other players of interest

Tony Jacklin (36)	47.22
Brian Huggett (24)	45.83
Brian Barnes (26)	44.23
Fred Daly (8)	43.75
Peter Alliss (30)	41.66
Dai Rees (18)	41.66
Neil Coles (40)	38.75
Christy O'Connor (36)	36.11
Henry Cotton (6)	33.33

Neil Coles's 40 matches is a record for either side.

A total of 87 players have actually *played* for Great Britain and Ireland or Europe.

RYDER AND WALKER CUP MATCHES

Golfers who have played in both
British: Norman Drew, Peter Townsend, Peter Oosterhuis, Howard Clark, Mark James, Clive Clark, Sandy Lyle and Michael King.
American: Fred Haas, Gene Littler, Ken Venturi, Jack Nicklaus, Tommy Aaron, Mason Rudolph, Lanny Wadkins, Bob Murphy, Tom Kite, Jerry Pate and Bill Rogers.
Tommy Armour played for Britain against America in the forerunner to the Walker Cup in 1921 and for America against Britain as a professional in 1926.
Mark James and Sandy Lyle are the only players to have made the change from Walker to Ryder Cup in two years. James played in the Walker Cup of 1975 and the Ryder Cup of 1977, Lyle in the Walker Cup of 1977 and the Ryder Cup of 1979.

Neil Coles (Dunlop Sports)

RYDER CUP

Year	Venue	Winners	USA Total	Great Britain and Ireland Total	Captains USA	Britain
1927	Worcester, Massachusetts	USA	9½	2½	Walter Hagen	Ted Ray
1929	Moortown, Leeds	Britain	5	7	Walter Hagen	George Duncan
1931	Scioto, Ohio	USA	9	3	Walter Hagen	Charles A Whit-combe
1933	Southport and Ainsdale, Lancashire	Britain	5½	6½	Walter Hagen	*J H Taylor
1935	Ridgewood, New Jersey	USA	9	3	Walter Hagen	Charles A Whit-combe
1937	Southport and Ainsdale, Lancashire	USA	8	4	*Walter Hagen	Charles A Whit-combe
1947	Portland, Oregon	USA	11	1	Ben Hogan	Henry Cotton
1949	Ganton, Scarborough, Yorkshire	USA	7	5	*Ben Hogan	*Charles A Whit-combe
1951	Pinehurst, North Carolina	USA	9½	2½	Sam Snead	*Arthur Lacey
1953	Wentworth, Surrey	USA	6½	5½	Lloyd Mangrum	*Henry Cotton
1955	Palm Springs, California	USA	8	4	Chick Harbert	Dai Rees
1957	Lindrick, Sheffield	Britain	4½	7½	Jack Burke	Dai Rees
1959	Palm Desert, California	USA	8½	3½	Sam Snead	Dai Rees
1961	Royal Lytham and St Annes, Lancashire	USA	14½	9½	Jerry Barber	Dai Rees
1963	Atlanta, Georgia	USA	23	9	Arnold Palmer	*Johnny Fallon
1965	Royal Birkdale, Lancashire	USA	19½	12½	*Byron Nelson	*Harry Weetman
1967	Houston, Texas	USA	23½	8½	*Ben Hogan	*Dai Rees
1969	Royal Birkdale, Lancashire	(tie)	16	16	*Sam Snead	*Eric C Brown
1971	St Louis, Missouri	USA	18½	13½	*Jay Hebert	*Eric C Brown
1973	Muirfield, East Lothian	USA	19	13	*Jack Burke	*Bernard J Hunt
1975	Laurel Valley, Pennsylvania	USA	21	11	*Arnold Palmer	*Bernard J Hunt
1977	Royal Lytham and St Annes, Lancashire	USA	12½	7½	*Dow Finsterwald	*Brian G C Huggett
1979	Greenbrier, White Sulphur Springs	USA	17	11	*Billy Casper	*John Jacobs
1981	Walton Heath, Surrey	USA	18½	9½	*Dave Marr	John Jacobs

*Non-playing captains

Mixed emotions. Part of the European team at the Hennessy Cup at Sunningdale, 1980 (Phil Sheldon)

World Cup
(formerly Canada Cup)

Unlike soccer, the World Cup at golf is not regarded as the most important international tournament. It was founded in 1953 as the Canada Cup by John Jay Hopkins, an American industrialist for 'the furtherance of good fellowship and better understanding among the nations of the world through the medium of international golf competition'.

It consists of two-man teams representing their countries, the competition taking the form of 72 holes of strokeplay, the combined score of both players producing a team total. For the first two years, it was a 36-hole event and in two other years it was decided over 63 and 54 holes. In 1963, fog in Paris meant curtailment by 9 holes and in 1972 at Royal Melbourne, heavy rain washed out a day's play.

One of the problems of organisation is in finding dates suitable to everyone in view of such expansion in the golfing fixtures over the last 25 years. Nowadays, the International Golf Association settle for the end of the year but, despite a succession of worries, the competition has managed to survive although there was no competition in 1981.

Sam Snead and Peter Thomson who met in the final of Palm Beach Invitation Tournament in 1955

United States (Ben Hogan and Sam Snead) winners of the World Cup 1956 (D R Stuart)

It has been held in several countries where golf is not widely played and has traded on goodwill, modest prize-money and long hours of play. With such a variety of standard, rounds can take five or six hours.

The individual award is secondary but gives players who may have weak partners some extra interest.

DETAILED RECORDS

Most victories
15, United States
3, Australia
2, South Africa, Spain and Canada

Member of the most winning teams
6, Arnold Palmer and Jack Nicklaus (both United States)

Lowest winning team aggregate
544, Australia (Bruce Devlin and David Graham) at Jockey Club, Buenos Aires, 1970
(In 1963 and 1972, the competition was reduced to three rounds owing to the weather.)

Highest winning team aggregate
591, Spain (Severiano Ballesteros and Antonio Garrido) Manila, Philippines, 1977

Lowest individual score
269, Roberto de Vicenzo (Argentina), Jockey Club, Buenos Aires, 1970

Most consecutive victories
5, United States, 1960–64

Most individual lowest scores
3, Jack Nicklaus (USA)

Most times runner-up (team)
4, United States, Argentina and South Africa

Lowest 9-hole record—individual (29)
Juan Sereda, Uruguay (Buenos Aires, 1962)

Lowest 18-hole record—individual (63)
Jack Nicklaus, USA (Palm Beach, 1971)

Holes in one
Ake Bergkvist, Sweden, 12th hole, Portmarnock, 1960
Juan Sereda, Uruguay, 16th hole, Royal Kaanapali, Hawaii, 6 December 1964
Cees Cramer, Holland, 11th hole, Club de Campo, Madrid, 2 October 1965
Jean-Charles Rey, Monaco, 7th hole, Circolo Golf Olgiata, Rome, 15 November 1968
Dave Thomas, Wales, 12th hole, Bukit Course, Singapore Island Country Club, 3 October 1969
Henrik Lund, Denmark, 12th hole, Jockey Club, Buenos Aires, 12 November 1970
José Maria Canizares, Spain, 2nd hole, Lagunita Country Club, Caracas, 24 November 1974
Antonio Evangelista, Brazil, 13th hole, Navatanee Golf Course, Bangkok, 6 December 1975

Youngest competitor:
Marko Vovk, 15 years, Yugoslavia, 1979 (Athens)
Ossie Gartenmaier, 17 years, Austria, 1965 (Madrid)

Oldest competitor:
Flory van Donck, 67 years, Belgium, 1979 (Athens)
Juan Dapiaggi, 66 years, Uruguay, 1973 (Marbella)

Most number of appearances
Jean Garaialde (France) 23 in 1979
Mohamed Moussa (Egypt) 21 in 1979
Roberto de Vicenzo (Argentina) 19 in 1974
Gary Player (South Africa) 17 in 1977
Flory van Donck (Belgium) 19 in 1979

RESULTS

Year	Total
1953 Beaconsfield GC, Montreal, Canada, 2–3 June	
Argentina: Roberto de Vicenzo 147, Tony Cerda 140	287
Canada: Stan Leonard 144, Bill Kerr 153	297
Individual: Tony Cerda 70, 70	140
1954 Laval Sur Le Lac GC, Montreal, Canada, 19–22 August	
Australia: Peter Thomson 277, Kel Nagle 279	556
Argentina: Roberto de Vicenzo 283, Tony Cerda 277	560
Individual: Stan Leonard (Canada) 66, 68, 71, 70	275
1955 Columbia CC, Washington DC, USA, 9–12 June	
United States: Chick Harbert 281, Ed Furgol 279	560
Australia: Peter Thomson 279, Kel Nagle 290	569
Individual: Ed Furgol 73, 70, 69, 67	279
1956 Wentworth GC, Surrey, England, 24–26 June	
United States: Ben Hogan 277, Sam Snead 290	567
South Africa: Bobby Locke 285, Gary Player 296	581
Individual: Ben Hogan 68, 69, 72, 68	277
1957 Kasumigaseki GC, Tokyo, Japan, 24–27 October	
Japan: Torakichi Nakamura 274, Koichi Ono 283	557
United States: Sam Snead 281, Jimmy Demaret 285	566
Individual: Torakichi Nakamura 68, 68, 67, 71	274
1958 Club de Golf Mexico, Mexico City, 20–23 November	
Ireland: Harry Bradshaw 286, Christy O'Connor 293	579
Spain: Angel Miguel 286, Sebastian Miguel 296	582
Individual: Angel Miguel 72, 73, 71, 70	286
1959 Royal Melbourne GC, Australia, 18–21 November	
Australia: Peter Thomson 275, Kel Nagle 288	563
United States: Sam Snead 281, Cary Middlecoff 292	573
Individual: Stan Leonard (Canada) 70, 66, 69, 70	275
1960 Portmarnock GC, Dublin, Eire, 23–26 June	
United States: Arnold Palmer 284, Sam Snead 281	565
England: Bernard Hunt 289, Harry Weetman 284	573
Individual: Flory van Donck (Belgium) 68, 71, 70, 70	279
1961 Dorado Beach GC, Puerto Rico, 1–4 June	
United States: Sam Snead 272, Jimmy Demaret 288	560
Australia: Peter Thomson 280, Kel Nagle 292	572
Individual: Sam Snead 67, 67, 70, 68	272
1962 Jockey Club, Buenos Aires, Argentina, 8–11 November	
United States: Arnold Palmer 278, Sam Snead 279	557
Argentina: Roberto de Vicenzo 276, Fidel de Luca 283	559

Individual: Roberto de Vicenzo 71, 68, 69, 68   276

1963 St Nom La Breteche, Paris, France, 24–27 October
United States: Jack Nicklaus 237, Arnold Palmer 245   482
Spain: Sebastian Miguel 242, Ramon Sota 243   485
Individual: Jack Nicklaus 67, 72, 66, 32 (63 holes only)   237

1964 Royal Kaanapali GC, Maui, Hawaii, 3–6 December
United States: Arnold Palmer 278, Jack Nicklaus 276   554
Argentina: Roberto de Vicenzo 281, Leopoldo Ruiz 284   565
Individual: Jack Nicklaus 72, 69, 65, 70   276

1965 Club de Campo, Madrid, Spain, 30 September–3 October
South Africa: Gary Player 281, Harold Henning 290   571
Spain: Ramon Sota 285, Angel Miguel 294   579
Individual: Gary Player 70, 69, 68, 74   281

1966 Yomiuri GC, Tokyo, Japan, 10–13 November
United States: Jack Nicklaus 273, Arnold Palmer 275   548
South Africa: Harold Henning 276, Gary Player 277   553
Individual: George Knudson (Canada) 64, 68, 66, 74   272

1967 Club de Golf, Mexico, Mexico City, 9–12 November
United States: Arnold Palmer 276, Jack Nicklaus 281   557
New Zealand: Bob Charles 281, Walter Godfrey 289   570
Individual: Arnold Palmer 68, 70, 71, 67   276

1968 Olgiata GC, Rome, Italy, 14–17 November
Canada: Al Balding 274, George Knudson 295   569
United States: Lee Trevino 283, Julius Boros 288   571
Individual: Al Balding 68, 72, 67, 67   274

1969 Singapore Island CC, Singapore, 2–5 October
United States: Lee Trevino 275, Orville Moody 277   552
Japan: Takaaki Kono 279, Haruo Yasuda 281   560
Individual: Lee Trevino 71, 70, 69, 65   275

1970 Jockey Club, Buenos Aires, Argentina, 12–15 November
Australia: David Graham 270, Bruce Devlin 274   544
Argentina: Roberto de Vicenzo 269, Vicente Fernandez 285   554
Individual: Roberto de Vicenzo 64, 67, 68, 70   269

1971 PGA National GC, Palm Beach, USA, 11–14 November
United States: Jack Nicklaus 271, Lee Trevino 284   555
South Africa: Gary Player 278, Harold Henning 289   567
Individual: Jack Nicklaus 68, 69, 63, 71   271

1972 Royal Melbourne, Australia, 9–12 November
Taiwan: Hsieh Min Nam 217, Lu Liang Huan 221   438
Japan: Takaaki Kono 219, Takashi Murakami 221   440
Individual: Hsieh Min Nam 70, 69, 78 (54 holes only)   217

1973 Golf Nueva Andalucia, Marbella, Spain, 22–25 November
United States: Johnny Miller 277, Jack Nicklaus 281   558
South Africa: Gary Player 280, Hugh Baiocchi 284   564
Individual: Johnny Miller 73, 65, 72, 67   277

1974 Lagunita CC, Venezuela, 21–24 November
South Africa: Bobby Cole 271, Dale Hayes 283   554
Japan: Isao Aoki 283, Masashi Ozaki 276   559
Individual: Bobby Cole 66, 70, 67, 68   271

1975 Navatanee, Bangkok, Thailand, 4–7 December
United States: Lou Graham 279, Johnny Miller 275   554
Taiwan: Hsieh Min Nam 277, Hsiung Kuo Chi 287   564
Individual: Johnny Miller 66, 71, 70, 68   275

1976 Mission Hills CC, Palm Springs, California, 9–12 December
Spain: Manuel Pinero 285, Severiano Ballesteros 289   574
United States: Jerry Pate 285, Dave Stockton 291   576
Individual: Ernesto Perez Acosta (Mexico) 69, 74, 69, 70   282

1977 Wack Wack CC, Manila, Philippines, 8–11 December
Spain: Severiano Ballesteros 295, Antonio Garrido 296   591
Philippines: Rudy Lavares 292, Ben Arda 302   594
Individual: Gary Player (South Africa) 72, 68, 73, 76   289

1978 Princeville Maka GC, Hanalei, Hawaii, 30 November–3 December
United States: John Mahaffey 281, Andy North 283   564
Australia: Greg Norman 286, Wayne Grady 288   574
Individual: John Mahaffey 68, 72, 69, 71   281

1979 Glyfada GC, Athens, Greece, 8–11 November
United States: John Mahaffey 290, Hale Irwin 285   575
Scotland: Ken Brown 293, Sandy Lyle 287   580
Individual: Hale Irwin 74, 70, 72, 69   285

1980 El Rignon, Bogota, Columbia, 11–14 December
Canada: Dan Halldorson 285, Jim Nelford 287   572
Scotland: Sandy Lyle 282, Steve Martin 293   575
Individual: Sandy Lyle 69, 69, 74, 70   282

1981 No competition

The foundation of what is today known as the Asia Golf Circuit was laid in 1959 when the late Eric Cremin, a former Australian Open champion, and the late Kim Hall, a Welsh international then serving in the Royal Air Force, had the idea of running a small tournament for eight Australian professionals who would be playing in the Philippines Open. In those days, the Philippines Open was the only truly 'Open' professional event played in Southeast Asia.

As things turned out, Cremin and Hall managed to produce 24 professionals including Kel Nagle, Bob Charles and Mr Lu, as he later became known. With these names and an offer of £1000 in prize-money, Hall approached the Royal Hong Kong GC who accepted a proposal to run the first Hong Kong Open.

Together with the Philippines Open, the Far East Circuit was started and in 1961 Peter Thomson convinced the Singapore golfers to join in with the Singapore Open. The following year, the Malaysian Open followed suit while the Yomiuri Country Club in Tokyo staged the first Japan Invitational tournament.

India, Taiwan and Thailand followed in quick succession and, with the inclusion of Korea in 1970 and Indonesia in 1974, the family circle was complete. The circuit became firmly established with ten tournaments.

In 1961, Hall retired from the Royal Air Force and returned to Hong Kong to become co-ordinator of the circuit. He continued until 1968 when he handed over to Leonardo 'Skip' Guinto, then President of the Philippines Golf Association.

Sukree Onsham, Thailand (Phil Sheldon)

Guinto did much to build up the prize-money and in 1977 the first $100 000 tournament was reached. This was the Tokyo event whose sponsorship had been taken over by the Sobhu Company. This is the only tournament on the circuit which is not a national title.

In the early 1970s the minimum prize-money for inclusion in the circuit, renamed the Asia Golf Circuit in 1970, was $15 000. This increased to $25 000 and in 1977 to $30 000.

However, in 1978 the various bodies got together and agreed to make a grand circuit prize of $100 000 to encourage more leading overseas competitors.

Unfortunately, this had only limited success, but by 1979 the Philippines, Hong Kong and Japan had all raised their prize-money to $100 000 and in the same year, there was a record total prize-money of $700 000.

Also in 1979, 'Skip' Guinto retired; Kim Hall returned as Circuit Director and it is thought that in the near future prize-money for the circuit will reach $1 million.

Entries normally cover 16 different countries, with support from young Americans who cannot gain entry to their own tour and from the increasing number of Japanese professionals.

In 1979, there were 1300 professionals in Japan and it became necessary to restrict entries to 30 professionals from any one country with pre-qualifying, known in Asia as the 'Monday tournament', becoming an essential part of the circuit.

More countries such as Papua, New Guinea and Okinawa made requests to join the circuit, but with ten tournaments fitted in between the end of the Australian circuit and the beginning of those in Japan and Europe, there was no room to accept any more prize-money.

In 1979, Lu Hsi Chuen won $43 670, four Taiwanese players finishing in the first five in the order of merit and seven in the first eleven.

THAILAND OPEN

Year	Winner	Country	Venue	Score
1965	Hsieh Yung Yo	Taiwan	Royal Thai Air Force	283
1966	Tadashi Kitta	Japan	Royal Thai Air Force	283
1967	Tomoo Ishii	Japan	Royal Thai Air Force	283
1968	Randall Vines	Australia	Royal Thai Air Force	285
1969	Hsieh Yung Yo	Taiwan	Royal Thai Air Force	277
1970	David Graham	Australia	Bangphra GC	286
1971	Lu Liang Huan	Taiwan	Royal Thai Air Force	278
1972	Hsieh Min Nam	Taiwan	Royal Thai Air Force	278
1973	Graham Marsh	Australia	Siam CC	286
1974	Toshihiro Hitomi	Japan	Bangphra GC	291
1975	Howard Twitty	United States	Bangphra GC	285
1976	Ben Arda	Philippines	Navatanee GC	270
1977	Yurio Akitomi	Japan	Siam CC	284
1978	Hsu Sheng San	Taiwan	Siam CC	280
1979	Mike Krantz	United States	Royal Thai Air Force	282
1980	Lu Hsi Chuen	Taiwan	Royal Thai Air Force	274
1981	Tom Sieckmann	United States	Bangkok	281
1982	Hsu Sheng-San	Taiwan	Bangkok	281

SINGAPORE OPEN

Year	Winner	Runner-up	Venue	By
1957	H Knaggs	G Balleine	Royal Island	3 and 2
1958	D W McMullen	R Craik		

Year	Winner	Club/Country	Venue	Score
1959	R C W Stokes		Royal Island	—
1961	F Phillips	Australia	Island Course	275
1962	Brian Wilkes	South Africa	Bukit Course	283
1963	A Brookes	South Africa	Island Course	276
1964	T Ball	Australia	Bukit Course	291
1965	F Phillips	Australia	Bukit Course	279
1966	R Newdick	New Zealand	Bukit Course	284
1967	B Arda (after a tie)	Philippines	Bukit Course	282
1968	Hsieh Yung Yo	Taiwan	Bukit Course	275
1969	T Kamata	Japan	Bukit Course	278
1970	Hsieh Yung Yo	Taiwan	Bukit Course	276
1971	H Yasuda	Japan	Bukit Course	277
1972	T Kono	Japan	Bukit Course	279
1973	B Arda	Philippines	Bukit Course	284
1974	E Nival	Philippines	Bukit Course	275
1975	Y Suzuki	Japan	Singapore Island	284
1976	K Uchida	Japan	Bukit Course	273
1977	Chi-San Hsu	Taiwan	Bukit Course	277
1978	T Gale	Australia	Bukit Course	278
1979	Lu Hsi Chuen	Taiwan	Bukit Course	280
1980	Kurt Cox	United States	Bukit Course	276
1981	Mya Aye	Burma	Bukit Course	273
1982	Hsu Sheng-San	Taiwan	Bukit Course	274

INDIA OPEN

Year	Winner	Country	Venue	Score
1963	P W Thomson	Australia	New Delhi	292
1965	P G Sethi (Am.)	India	Calcutta	282
1966	P W Thomson	Australia	Delhi	284
1968	K Hosoishi	Japan	New Delhi	285
1969	B Arda	Philippines	Royal Calcutta	291
1970	C Chung Chen	Taiwan	Royal Calcutta	279
1971	G Marsh	Australia	New Delhi	275
1972	B Jones	Australia	Royal Calcutta	282
1973	G Marsh	Australia	New Delhi	280
1974	Chie-Hsiung Kuo	Taiwan	Royal Calcutta	287
1975	T Ball	Australia	New Delhi	282
1976	P W Thomson	Australia	New Royal Calcutta	288
1977	B Jones	Australia	New Delhi	284
1978	B Brask	United States	Royal Calcutta	284
1979	G Burrows	United States	New Delhi	284
1980	Kurt Cox	United States	Tollygunge	286
1981	Payne Stewart	United States	New Delhi	284
1982	Hsu Sheng-San	Taiwan		277

MALAYSIAN OPEN

Year	Winner	Country	Venue	Score
1963	Billy Dunk	Australia	Kuala Lumpur	276
1964	T Ishii	Japan	Kuala Lumpur	282
1965	T Ishii	Japan	Kuala Lumpur	282
1966	H R Henning	South Africa	Kuala Lumpur	278
1967	I Legaspi	Philippines	Kuala Lumpur	286
1968	K Hosoishi	Japan	Kuala Lumpur	271
1969	T Kono	Japan	Kuala Lumpur	280
1970	B Arda	Philippines	Kuala Lumpur	273
1971	T Kono	Japan	Kuala Lumpur	269
1972	T Murakami	Japan	Kuala Lumpur	276
1973	Hideyo Sugimoto	Japan	Kuala Lumpur	277
1974	G Marsh	Australia	Ipoh	278
1975	G Marsh	Australia	Kuala Lumpur	276
1976	Hsu Sheng-San	Taiwan	Kuala Lumpur	279
1977	S Ginn	Australia	Kuala Lumpur	276
1978	B Jones	Australia	Kuala Lumpur	276
1979	Lu Hsi Chuen	Taiwan	Kuala Lumpur	277
1980	M McNulty	South Africa	Kuala Lumpur	270
1981	Lu Hsi-Chuen	Taiwan	Kuala Lumpur	276
1982	Denny Hepler	United States	Kuala Lumpur	208

PHILIPPINES OPEN

Year	Winner	Country	Venue	Score
1962	C Tugot	Philippines	Manila	284
1963	B Arda	Philippines	Manila	289
1964	P W Thomson	Australia	Manila	285
1965	Lu Liang-Huan	Formosa	Manila	288
1966	L Silverio (Am.)	Manila	Manila	287

1967	Hsu Sheng San	Formosa	Manila	283
1968	Hsu Chi San	Formosa	San Pedro	278
1969	Haruo Yasuda	Japan	Manila	279
1970	Hsieh Yung-Yo	Taiwan	Manila	282
1971	C Chien Chung	Taiwan	Manila	282
1972	H Sugimoto	Japan	Manila	286
1973	King Seung Hack	South Korea	Manila	289
1974	Lu Liang Huan	Taiwan	Manila	281
1975	Kuo Chie Hsiong	Taiwan	Manila	276
1976	Q Mancao	Philippines	Manila	281
1977	Hsieh Yung Yo	Taiwan	Manila	281
1978	Lu Liang Huan	Taiwan	Manila	278
1979	B Arda	Philippines	Manila	286
1980	Lu Hsi Chuen	Taiwan	Manila	287
1981	Tom Sieckmann	United States	Manila	287
1982	Hsieh Min-Nan	Taiwan	Manila	292

REPUBLIC OF CHINA OPEN

Year	Winner	Country	Score
1965	Hsu Chi San		290
1966	Lu Liang Huan		281
1967	Hsieh Yung Yo		277
1968	Hsieh Yung Yo		282
1969	Hideyo Sugimoto	Japan	284
1970	Chang Chung-Fa		215
1971	Chang Chung-Fa		286
1972	A Yasuda	Japan	284
1973	E Nival	Philippines	283
1974	Kuo Chi Hsiung		282
1975	Kuo Chi Hsiung		277
1976	Hsu Chi San		288
1977	Hsieh Min Nam		276
1978	Hsieh Yung Yo		283
1979	Lu Liang Huan		287
1980	Kuo Chi Hsiung		277
1981	Ho Ming-Chung		276
1982	Chen Tze-Ming		289

KOREA OPEN

Year	Winner					Score
1970	Hahn Chang Sang	71	72	76	70	289
1971	Hahn Chang Sang	68	71	71	71	281
1972	Hahn Chang Sang	74	65	70	67	276
1973	Kim Seung Hak	71	68	72	71	282
1974	Cho Tae Woon	70	75	72	69	286
1975	Kuo Chie Hsiung	74	70	69	71	284
1976	Kazunari Takahashi	71	73	70		214
1977	Ho Ming Chong	73	70	70	72	285
1978	Kim Seung Hak	70	69	67	71	277
1979	Shen Chung Shyan	70	72	71	76	289
1980	Chen Tze-Ming	68	72	74		214
1981	Chen Tze-Ming	72	67	70	76	285
1982	Kim Joo-Heun	74	69	72	70	285

INDONESIA OPEN

Year	Winner	Country	Score
1974	Ben Arda	Philippines	
1975	Hsu Sheng San	Taiwan	
1976	Mya Aye	Burma	
1977	Gaylord Burrows	United States	
1978	Kuo Chi Hsiung	Taiwan	275
1979	Lu Hsi Chuen	Taiwan	272
1980	Lu Hsi Chuen	Taiwan	265
1981	Payne Stewart	United States	283
1982	Eleuterio Nival	Philippines	281

HONG KONG OPEN

Year	Winner	Venue	Score
1959	Lu Liang Huan	Fanling	281
1960	Peter Thomson	Fanling	272
1961	Kel Nagle	Fanling	261
1962	Len Woodward	Fanling	271
1963	Hsieh Yung Yo	Fanling	272
1964	Hsieh Yung Yo	Fanling	269
1965	P W Thomson	Fanling	278
1966	F Phillips	Fanling	275
1967	P W Thomson	Fanling	273
1968	R Vines	Fanling	271
1969	T Sugihara	Fanling	274
1970	I Katsumata	Fanling	274
1971	O Moody	Fanling	266
1972	W Godfrey	Fanling	272
1973	F Phillips	Fanling	278
1974	Lu Liang Huan	Fanling	280
1975	Hsieh Yung Yo	Fanling	288
1976	Ming-Chung Ho	Fanling	279
1977	Hsieh Min Nam	Fanling	280
1978	Hsieh Yung Yo	Fanling	275
1979	G Norman	Fanling	273
1980	Kuo Chi-Hsiung	Fanling	274
1981	Chen Tze-Ming	Fanling	279
1982	Kurt Cox	Fanling	276

The Amateurs

British Amateur Championship

MILESTONES

1885 First played 20 April to 23 April. Not recognised as the official start of the championship until much later. It was started by the Royal Liverpool Club as a 'tournament open to all amateur golfers' and the first champion at Hoylake was Allan F MacFie, a Scottish member of the home club.

However, it was unusual in that the tournament rules decreed that halved matches were not to be decided on an extra hole basis, but were simply replayed. Byes were not eliminated in the first round and, as there were 48 entries, three players reached the semi-final.

MacFie was the man in receipt of a bye into the final where he beat Horace Hutchinson by 7 and 6. If that part was fortunate, he also halved two matches in the fourth round with Walter M de Zoete (Blackheath) and was only successful in the third meeting.

He won on the last green, but was helped by a hole in one at the 13th, the first recorded in the event.

In the third round, John Ball beat his father by 4 and 2.

1886 After the highly successful start, the championship was officially instituted at St Andrews and won by Horace Hutchinson, runner-up at Hoylake. Straight matchplay. 44 entries but two disqualified as having at one time 'carried clubs' and therefore ranked as professional.

1887 Hutchinson won a second victory back at Hoylake against John Ball, the local player who was to become so famous. There were only 33 entries.

1887 to 1895 A period dominated by John Ball and Johnny Laidlay. They won the title alternately. Ball in 1888–90–92–94, and Laidlay in 1889–91. In addition, Laidlay was runner-up to Ball in 1888–90 and to Peter Anderson in 1893. Ball was runner-up in 1895. Ball won the Open in 1890 and shares the distinction with Bobby Jones of winning both the Open and Amateur titles in the same year.

In 1895, the winner was Leslie Balfour (afterwards Leslie Balfour-Melville) who won his last three matches at the 19th hole. His opponents were William Grey, Laurie Auchterlonie and John Ball who all hit their second shots into the Swilcan Burn at St Andrews. It was the last time the final was played over 18 holes except for 1966—due to adverse weather conditions.

1896 Freddie Tait beat Harold Hilton at Sandwich in the first 36-hole final. It was Hilton's third defeat in the final. Tait was something of a bogyman to Hilton and had earlier beaten Charles Hutchings, Johnny Laidlay, John Ball and Horace Hutchinson in succession.

1897 Something of a surprise win for Jack Allan, a medical student at Edinburgh University who never touched a club until 1891. At the time, he was the youngest winner and seemed destined for a fine career, but he died of lung disease the following year after taking up a medical appointment at Lasswade, near Edinburgh.

1898 A second victory for Freddie Tait who two years later was killed in the South African War. Reports of his victory at Hoylake say he was sadly out of form in the early rounds, saving himself with remarkable recovery play, but he was at his best in the final against S Mure-Fergusson.

1899 Entry of over 100 for the first time. John Ball scored his fifth win, this time against the defending champion, Freddie Tait, at Prestwick. He won at the 37th in Tait's last championship.

1900 Victory for Harold Hilton after three previous defeats in the final.

1901 Hilton conducted a successful defence of his title, the first to do so since 1887 and the last until Lawson Little in 1935.

1902 Both Charles Hutchings and Sidney Fry, the two finalists, used the new Haskell ball at Hoylake. Hutchings, the winner, was 53. The Hon Michael Scott, the oldest winner ever, was 54.

1903 First of two victories for Robert Maxwell. He won both at Muirfield where he was a member.

1904 Title taken overseas for the first time by Walter J Travis, an Australian-born resident of America, famous for his black cigars and centreshafted Schenectady putter. He beat James Robb, Harold Hilton, Horace Hutchinson and, in the final at Sandwich, Edward Blackwell.

1905 In a final remembered for consistent heavy rain A Gordon Barry defeated the Hon Osmund Scott by 3 and 2. It was felt that in these conditions Scott was at a considerable disadvantage with rubber grips. Two weeks later he had had them changed. Barry, 19, was a student at St Andrews University.

1906 James Robb, runner-up in 1897 and 1900, became champion at last.

1907 A record entry of 200 for the sixth victory of John Ball, apparently more interested in his garden and motor cycle since his last win.

1908 A Yorkshireman, E A Lassen caused a surprise by winning at Sandwich, but he proved his worth and reached the final again in 1911. An earlier round produced the longest match in the championship's history; C A Palmer beat Lionel Munn at the 28th.

1907, 1910 and 1912 The final chapters in the remarkable record of John Ball. At Westward Ho! in 1912, he completed his eighth victory, a record that will surely stand for ever. Michael Bonallack has come nearest to it with five successes. In 1912, Ball defeated Abe Mitchell, later a celebrated professional, in the final. The final lasted 38 holes, the second longest in the championship's history. They met in the 1910 semi-final when Ball also won. In 1912 Ball was 5 down and 7 to play in the fifth round.

In 1910 Ball scored the first double-figure victory in the final against C Aylmer.

1909 Of Robert Maxwell's second victory at Muirfield against Cecil Hutchison, the golf-course architect, Bernard Darwin wrote: 'They produced a never to be forgotten match by those who saw it. The golf was so faultless, the speed at which it was played so great, that they seemed to be playing not a championship final but one of the friendly, almost casual games which they had often played together on the links of the Lothians.'

1911 and 1913 Confirmation of Harold Hilton's skill in something of a revival. When he won at Prestwick in 1911, 20 years had passed since his first appearance in the final and ten since his previous victory. Hilton was also American champion in 1911.

1914 The champion, J L C Jenkins, was the player of the year who would no doubt have done greater things but for an injury in the war.

1920 In the first championship final for six years Cyril Tolley defeated Bob Gardner, twice American champion and the second American to reach the final of the British. At Muirfield, Tolley was 3 up and 4 to play in the final, but Gardner, at one time world record holder for the pole vault and US rackets doubles champion, won the 33rd, 34th and 36th. However, Tolley won the 37th with a superb 2, the old 1st hole at Muirfield being a short one.

1921 Willie Hunter, the son of the professional at Deal, won his championship over a burned-up course at Hoylake. He was a player of no great length but putted finely on very fast greens and handed a double-figure defeat in the final to Allan Graham. Earlier Graham beat Bobby Jones 6 and 5 with a queer brass putter. In the afternoon, he was still in such a

A F MacFie, the first Amateur champion in 1885, in later life

daze, he had towards the end to ask his caddie to score. Later that year, Hunter beat Jones in the US Amateur. He then turned pro. Graham's father died the day before the final.

1922 At this time the amateur triumvirate of Tolley, Roger Wethered and Ernest Holderness were dominant. In 1922, Holderness, the epitome of steadiness, won his first title at Prestwick.

1923 Sandwiched between Holderness's two victories was one for Roger Wethered at Deal, two years after losing a play-off for the Open championship at St Andrews. Wethered

Two of the early giants, John Ball (in white boots) and Johnny Laidlay prepare for battle at Hoylake in the final of the championship in 1890

A respected figure on both sides of the Atlantic, William Campbell, now President of the United States Golf Association (Action Photos)

1968 Bruce Fleisher became the fourth youngest winner in his first championship. He scored 284 at Scioto and edged out Vinny Giles who had a final round of 65.
The entry was 2057—a record at the time.
1969 In a championship at Oakmont in which there were only four rounds under par and only six which equalled it, Steve Melnyk won by 5 strokes with a total of 286. This was convincing enough, but it was hard on Vinny Giles who finished runner-up for the third year in succession.
The entry increased to 2142.
1970 In a close finish, Lanny Wadkins just got the better of Tom Kite. His total of 279 was the lowest for the eight years during which the championship was decided by strokeplay.
1971 Canadian Gary Cowan won his second title with a dramatic finish at the Wilmington Country Club. One shot ahead of Eddie Pearce playing the 72nd hole, he drove into deep rough and was in some danger of dropping a stroke, but his 9 iron recovery finished in the hole for an eagle 2. This made his winning margin a rather more comfortable 3 strokes. Entry 2327.
1972 Deserved triumph for Vinny Giles at the Charlotte CC, North Carolina, when he beat Mark Hayes and Ben

Crenshaw by 3 strokes. It was the last championship to be decided by strokeplay; in the eight years of this form, the only champions to remain as amateurs were Giles and Gary Cowan who did not defend his title.
1973 With matchplay restored, Craig Stadler defeated David Strawn at Inverness. Vinny Giles, having played in the Walker Cup, reached the semi-final in defence of his title where he lost to Stadler. In the other semi-final, Strawn beat William C Campbell, playing in his 30th championship at the age of 50.
1974 Jerry Pate won the championship at Ridgewood, New Jersey, two years before he added the US Open at Atlanta Athletic Club. He beat John Grace 2 and 1 in the final after being 3 down after 20 holes. It was the first time that Pate qualified for the championship.
Entry 2420.
1975 Fred Ridley defeated Keith Fergus in the final but Ridley's best performances were in beating Curtis Strange and Andy Bean on the way.
1976 In the final at Bel-Air CC, Bill Sander beat C Parker Moore by 8 and 6, the biggest victory margin since 1961. Entry 2681.
1977 John Fought defeated Doug Fischesser by 9 and 8 in the final at Aronimink, the largest margin of victory since 1955. He won the last 4 holes of the morning round and the 1st hole after lunch to go 7 up.
In his 34th championship, Bill Campbell won his 52nd match over all.
1978 John Cook won the championship at Plainfield CC, New Jersey, with consistently good play. He beat Scott Hoch by 5 and 4 in the final but, for the first time, both semi-finals went to extra holes. Cook beat Michael Peck and Hoch beat Bob Clampett, both at the 20th.
1979 Cook was deposed as champion by Mark O'Meara, 22, the California State champion. O'Meara was persuaded to play by Cook and stayed during the championship at the Cook's condominium at the course. No champion has won back to back since Harvie Ward in 1956, but Cook started favourite in the final. He survived a long day on Friday, defeating Lennie Clements at the 8th extra hole and then accounting for Gary Hallberg. In the final, O'Meara lunched 4 up with a round of 70 and was 8 up after 26 holes.
1980 Hal Sutton completed a memorable week at the Country Club of North Carolina by beating Bob Lewis, a former professional, by 9 and 8 in the 36-hole final. Sutton was 4 under par for the match, making an overall total of 12 under par for 145 holes, strokeplay and matchplay. Using the format introduced in 1979, 282 players took part after sectional qualifying, 36 holes of strokeplay determining the leading 64 for matchplay. Pinehurst No 2 was the other course used for the strokeplay.
William C Campbell made his 36th appearance, a record only surpassed by Chick Evans. The USGA accepted a record 4008 entries, overtaking the previous best of 3916 the year before.
1981 One of the great sentimental victories, Nathaniel Crosby, son of Bing, winning at the Olympic Club, San Francisco, only a few miles from the Crosby home at Hillsborough. He had a few close calls in the matchplay section but showed a remarkable flair for producing the right shot or holing the crucial putt when needed. He beat Brian Lindley at the 37th, the first final to go to extra holes since 1950. Crosby had been 3 down and 7 to play.

DETAILED RECORDS

Most victories
5, Bobby Jones, 1924–25–27–28–30
4, Jerome D Travers, 1907–08–12–13
3, Walter J Travis, 1900–01–03

Most times runner-up or joint runner-up
3, Chick Evans, 1912–22–27; Ray Billows, 1937–39–48; Marvin Giles II, 1967–68–69

Oldest winner
Jack Westland, 47 years 8 months 9 days, 1952

Youngest winner
Robert A Gardner, 19 years 5 months, 1909
Jack Nicklaus, 19 years 8 months 29 days, 1959
Nathaniel Crosby, 19 years 10 months 8 days, 1981

Consecutive winners
2, Walter Travis, 1900–01; H Chandler Egan, 1904–05; Jerome D Travers, 1907–08, and 1912–13; Bobby Jones, 1924–25, and 1927–28; W Lawson Little, 1934–35; E Harvie Ward, 1955–56

Biggest span between first and last victories
17 years, Francis Ouimet, 1914–31

Biggest span between finals
21 years, Jack Westland, 1931–52

Overseas winners
Harold Hilton (England), 1911; C Ross Somerville (Canada), 1932; Gary Cowan (Canada), 1966 and 1971

Longest final
39 holes: Sam Urzetta beat Frank Stranahan, Minneapolis GC, 1950

Longest match (18 holes)
28 holes; Maurice McCarthy beat George von Elm, Merion, 1930

Most finals
7, Bobby Jones
5, Jerome D Travers and Chick Evans

Identical finals
None

Most appearances
50, Chick Evans, Jr
37, William C Campbell

Most golf in one day
63 holes, Maurice McCarthy, Jr, Merion, 1930. In the second qualifying round, he came to the 17th needing two birdies or an eagle to tie for the last qualifying place. He made a hole in one at the 17th to get the tie. Next morning, he won the play-off match lasting 16 holes, followed by a 19-hole match with Watts Gunn and in the afternoon beat George von Elm at the 28th, the longest 18-hole match ever played in the championship

First player to win the US Amateur and US Open
Francis Ouimet, Open 1913; Amateur, 1914

First player to win US Amateur and US Open the same year
Chick Evans, Jr, 1916, followed by Bobby Jones, 1930

Other amateur winners of both events
Jerome D Travers and John Goodman

Record entry
4008, Country Club of North Carolina, 1980

Youngest qualifier
Bobby Jones, 14 years 5½ months, 1916

Strokeplay—biggest margin of victory
5 strokes, Steve Melnyk, Oakmont, 1969

Lowest aggregate
279 (67, 73, 69, 70), Lanny Wadkins, Waverley CC, Oregon, 1970

Lowest individual round
65, Marvin Giles III, Scioto CC, 1968; Kurt Cos, Waverley CC, Oregon, 1970

Courses most often used
The Country Club, Brookline, 5
Merion, Oakmont, Chicago GC, 4

Champion twice on same course
Bobby Jones, Merion, 1924 and 1930; Jerome Travers, Garden City, 1908 and 1913

RESULTS

1895 Newport, Rhode Island
C B Macdonald, Chicago
Semi-finals: Macdonald beat C Claxton 8 and 7; C E Sands beat F I Amory 3 and 2
Final: Macdonald beat Sands 12 and 11

1896 Shinnecock Hills, New York
H J Whigham, Onwentsia
Semi-finals: Whigham beat A M Coats 8 and 6; J G Thorp beat H P Toler 4 and 3
Final: Whigham beat Thorp 8 and 7

1897 Chicago, Illinois
H J Whigham, Onwentsia
Semi-finals: Whigham beat F S Douglas 6 and 5; W R Betts beat C B Macdonald 1 up
Final: Whigham beat Betts 8 and 6

1898 Morris County, New Jersey
F S Douglas, Fairfield
Semi-finals: Douglas beat W J Travis 8 and 6; W B Smith beat C B Macdonald 2 and 1
Final: Douglas beat Smith 5 and 3

1899 Onwentsia, Illinois
H M Harriman, Meadow Brook
Semi-finals: F S Douglas beat W J Travis 2 and 1; Harriman beat C B Macdonald 6 and 5
Final: Harriman beat Douglas 3 and 2

1900 Garden City, New York
W J Travis, Garden City
Semi-finals: Travis beat A G Lockwood

4 and 3. It was felt that an annual match was too much and thereafter the sides agreed to meet in alternate years.

1926 Another narrow victory for the Americans at Muirfield, the highlight being the 12 and 11 victory of Bobby Jones over Cyril Tolley. Jess Sweetser began the long sequence of victories in the Amateur championship in Walker Cup years in Britain.

1928 A heavy defeat (11–1) for Britain and the beginning of a lean period. Bobby Jones beat Phil Perkins at the Chicago Golf Club by 13 and 12, the biggest margin in the history of the Walker Cup. Tony Torrance won Britain's lone point, a 1-hole victory over Chick Evans.

1930 At Royal St George's, Sandwich, the United States won 10–2. In his Grand Slam year, Bobby Jones beat Roger Wethered 9 and 8 and preserved his 100 per cent record in his fifth and last single, but the most notable victory was that of Donald K Moe. He was 7 down with 13 to play but won with a birdie on the last hole. He was round in 67.

1932 Francis Ouimet took over the captaincy from Bobby Jones, appropriately enough on his own course, the Country Club, Brookline where he had won the US Open in 1913. He was Captain until 1949 although in a non-playing role after 1934.

The British had the brothers, Rex and Lister Hartley playing together in the first foursome, but they won only one match, that in which Leonard Crawley defeated George Voigt. Crawley also dented the Walker Cup with an overstrong second at the 18th in the morning, the Cup being on display.

1934 The Americans won their eighth successive victory at St Andrews. Michael Scott became the oldest participant at 56, but the British won only one foursome and one single. The singles winner was Tony Torrance who won three and halved one of his last four singles.

1936 The first and only time that Britain failed to win a match. It meant that they had only won two foursomes and four singles in the five matches from 1928. At Pine Valley, a complete whitewash was avoided by 2 half points in the foursomes. In the fourth foursome, Alec Hill and Cecil Ewing

were 7 down to George Voigt and Harry Givan with 11 holes to play. They squared on the 35th and the Americans had to hole an awkward putt on the 36th to gain a half.

1938 In two years, Britain went from their worst result to their best. Prior to the Walker Cup, Charlie Yates had won the Amateur championship at Troon but at St Andrews, amid scenes of wild delight, Britain won the foursomes 2½–1½ and the singles 5–3. It was only the second time that Britain had won a series of singles and they were not to do so again until 1963.

1947 Because of post-war conditions, a two-year gap resulted and the Americans agreed to come to Britain although it was Britain's turn to go to America. St Andrews was once again the venue but this time there was a comfortable American victory. Bud Ward was the only survivor of 1938 in the American team; Leonard Crawley, Alec Kyle and Cecil Ewing for Britain and Ireland. The match, however, saw the introduction of several outstanding players: Joe Carr, Ronnie White, Frank Stranahan and Dick Chapman.

1949 A one-sided contest at Winged Foot, but encouragement for Britain in the golf of Ronnie White who won both his foursome (with Joe Carr) and single.

1951 Britain led in three foursomes and were square in the fourth after 18 holes on the first day, but they failed to win any of them. The best they could manage was two halves.

This was one of many disappointments over the years but in the singles, Ronnie White, playing on his home course, Royal Birkdale, beat Charlie Coe, Joe Carr beat Frank Stranahan and Alec Kyle beat Willie Turnesa.

1953 Notable for the incident on the first morning when James Jackson, paired with Gene Littler, discovered that he was carrying 16 clubs. In those days, the penalty was disqualification, but the British, captained by Tony Duncan, refused to accept victory in that way. The penalty was therefore modified to the loss of 2 holes. As the incident occurred on the 2nd hole, America, having lost the 1st at Kittansett, they were 3 down on the fourth tee where the match resumed. Jackson and Littler were still 3 down at the turn, but they lunched 2 up and went on to win 3 and 2.

The outstanding single was that in which Ronnie White, 3 down after 30 holes, beat Dick Chapman by 1 hole. He had 3 birdies in the last 6 holes and so won his fourth successive single—a British record. John Morgan won both his matches for Britain.

1955 Back at St Andrews, America won all four foursomes and six of the eight singles; even Ronnie White suffered his first defeat for Britain in the singles. The American Captain, Bill Campbell, did not play himself although he was one of their best players and had reached the final of the British Amateur at Muirfield the previous summer.

1957 One of the best British sides and one of the best matches at Minikhada, but still a victory (8½–3½) for America. However, Charlie Coe, the American Captain, commented at the presentation that he thought during the afternoon the Walker Cup was half-way back across the Atlantic!

He referred to the moment when three crucial singles were all square with 6, 5, and 2 holes to play, but America won them all. The best recovery was that of Billy Joe Patton, 5 down at lunch, who was round in 68 in the afternoon to beat Reid Jack, British champion, on the last green.

1959 Another big disappointment for the British side at Muirfield. They lost all four foursomes, but the Americans, who included the young Jack Nicklaus, fielded what many regard

Francis Ouimet, the American captain, lends his opposite number, John Beck, a helping hand; St Andrews 1947

as their best team ever.

1961 The matches were held for the first time on the west coast, at Seattle where the Americans equalled their record victory margin (11–1) in 1928. Martin Christmas, the youngest member of the British side, was their only winner.

1963 A change in the form of the match took place at Turnberry, 18-hole matches being introduced for the first time. Foursomes and singles were played each day and at the end of the first day, Britain led 7½–4½. They lost the foursomes and then won only their second series of singles since the matches began.

However, despite promising to win at least two of the second series of foursomes, they lost them all—the 16th hole proving enormously costly. Suitably reprieved, America then won five singles in the afternoon.

1965 The only halved match in the history of the series, America making a dramatic recovery on the last afternoon and then Clive Clark having to hole from 30 ft (9 m) to prevent a British defeat. Britain had a lead of five matches going into the last afternoon at Five Farms, Baltimore, but America made an historic rally.

1967 Not even the cold May weather at Royal St George's, Sandwich, could deter the Americans. They had the match well won on the first day and though Britain won three foursomes on the second morning, there were no dramatic recoveries, as there had been in Baltimore. Bill Campbell won four matches for America. Last match for Joe Carr who was picked for a record ten teams.

1969 A fine, close match at Milwaukee Country Club, Britain staging an effective rally after America had won the first day 8–4. On the second day, America won only three matches, but they held on to win 10–8 with six halved.

1971 A second victory for Great Britain and Ireland at St Andrews, the scene of their first in 1938. It was the 50th anniversary of the first informal match in 1921 and was made possible by their winning six of the final afternoon's singles. They lost the second series of foursomes 2½–1½ to go 2 points behind, but they got the better of six close singles, two on the 17th green and four on the last green. The deciding point was supplied by David Marsh who hit a 3 iron to the famous 17th to go dormie 1 on Bill Hyndman.

The British and Irish side included Roddy Carr, son of Joe. It is the only instance of a father and son winning Walker Cup honours.

1973 A good defence of the Cup by Britain at the Country Club, Brookline. Having managed only a half on the first morning, they won five singles, but again on Saturday the foursomes were their undoing. They went down 14–10 without winning one foursomes match. It was the last appearance of Michael Bonallack whose 25 individual matches is a record.

1975 Steady control for the Americans at St Andrews, the eighth time the match has been played over the Old course. They were four points clear on the first day, shared the second series of foursomes and won the final singles 5½–2½.

1977 Great Britain and Ireland travelled to Shinnecock Hills with obvious hopes of victory, but they were destroyed on the first day by a new, young American side who led 9–3 at the end of it. Only Dick Siderowf had played in a previous match. Britain did better on the second day, but it was too late.

1979 Another young American side went to Muirfield although it was not at full strength owing to a clash with the

National Collegiate championship which deprived them of Bob Clampett, Gary Hallberg and John Cook. It was a close match, America gaining a 1 point lead on the first day and preserving it on the second morning.

Britain made the better start in the last series of singles and, at one stage, were down in only one. However, in the end, they won only one.

America won by the margin of 15½–8½.

1981 A Californian venue for the first time, Cypress Point, provided a fine match in which the Americans won 15–9. However, there were several notable performances by the British and Irish who won the second series of foursomes 3–1. This gave interest to the last afternoon but America produced unbeatable golf.

Ronan Rafferty and Philip Walton won both their foursomes, the first all Irish pair to win a point in the history of the Walker Cup. On the first morning, they finished their match by holing two chip shots. Roger Chapman won three matches out of four including both singles.

DETAILED RECORDS

Most appearances
10, Joe Carr (for Great Britain and Ireland). In addition he was Captain in 1965 but did not play.

Most consecutive appearances
9, Joe Carr, 1947–63
8, Francis Ouimet 1922–34. In addition, he was Captain in 1934–36–38–47–49. Michael Bonallack, 1959–73. He was a member of the 1957 side, but did not play.

Biggest margin of victory in individual matches
Over 36 holes (1922–61)
Foursomes: **9 and 8**, E Harvie Ward and Jack Westland, 1953; Billy Joe Patton and Charles Coe, 1959, both for the United States
Singles: **13 and 12**, Bobby Jones, 1928
Over 18 holes
Foursomes: **7 and 5**, Marvin Giles and G Koch (United States) 1973
Singles: **9 and 7**, Scott Hoch 1979; **8 and 7**, Douglas Clarke 1979; **7 and 6**, Scott Simpson 1977 (all United States)

Largest winning margin by team
11–1, United States, 1928 and 1961

Outstanding individual records
William C Campbell won seven singles, halved one and never lost. He also won six foursomes, lost three and halved one. Bobby Jones won all his five singles matches and four of his five foursomes.

Best team recovery
The United States trailed by 3–1 after the foursomes in 1923, but won 6–5. In 1963 they trailed 6–3 after the first day and won 12–8. In 1965 they were 8–3 down on the first day and 10–5 down at lunch on the second day; and earned a halved match.

Brothers
In 1932, Rex and Lister Hartley played in the British side and were paired together in the foursomes.

Most consecutive team victories
9, United States 1922–36, 1947–63

Courses most often used
Britain: St Andrews, 8
America: The Country Club, Brookline, 2

Oldest competitor
Hon Michael Scott (Great Britain and Ireland) 56 years, 1934

Youngest competitor
Ronan Rafferty (Great Britain and Ireland) 17 years 8 months 15 days, 1981
James Bruen (Great Britain and Ireland) 18 years 25 days, 1938
John Langley (Great Britain and Ireland) 18 years 4 months 7 days, 1936
Peter Oosterhuis (Great Britain and Ireland) 19 years 2 weeks, 1967

Team winning all the foursomes
United States: 1928–32–55–59–61. They also won the second series of foursomes in 1963.
Great Britain and Ireland won 4–0 in the first series of foursomes in 1971.

Team winning all the singles
None, but the United States won 7½ out of 8 in 1936 at Pine Valley.

Form of the match
Foursomes and singles. From 1922 until 1961, there were four foursomes matches and eight singles—all played over 36 holes.
From 1963, one series of foursomes and one series of singles have taken place each day, all the matches being over 18 holes.
In all cases, halved matches count; the exception was in 1922 when Hooman and Sweetser played 37 holes before anyone could rectify the mistake. The result, victory for Hooman, was allowed to stand.

Unusual facts
In 1930, Jack Stout of Britain was 7 up with 13 holes to play on Donald Moe. However, when Moe had completed the second 18 in 67 at Sandwich, he had recovered to win on the last green.
In 1936, George Voigt and Harry Givan were 7 up with 11 holes to play in their foursomes match at Pine Valley. However, the British pair Alec Hill and Cecil Ewing squared on the 35th and halved the match—the Americans holing an awkward putt on the last green.
In 1971, Cecil Ewing and Frank Pennink, both members of Britain's first winning side in 1938, were selectors on the occasion of Britain and Ireland's second victory.
Up to and including 1979, the United States have won 25 matches, Great Britain and Ireland two, with one halved.

OUTSTANDING INDIVIDUAL RECORDS
UNITED STATES

(Number of individual matches played shown in brackets)
Over 30 players have a 100% record. They include:

Name	%
E Harvie Ward (6)	100
Don Cherry (5)	100
Jack Nicklaus (4)	100
G T Moreland (4)	100
Skee Riegel (4)	100
O F Willing (4)	100
Watts Gunn (4)	100
Sam Urzetta (4)	100
Danny Edwards (4)	100
John Fought (4)	100
L Miller (4)	100
Scott Hoch (4)	100
Jay Haas (3)	100
Dr Frank Taylor (3)	100
Joe Rassett (3)	100
Jodie Mudd (3)	100
Gene Littler (2)	100
Ken Venturi (2)	100

Other players of interest

Bobby Jones (10)	90
Charlie Yates (4)	87.50
Johnny Fischer (4)	87.50
Curtis Strange (4)	87.50
James B McHale (3)	83.3
H R Johnston (6)	83.3
Ed Tutwiler (6)	83.3
Corey Pavin (3)	83.3
Douglas Clarke (3)	83.3
Roland R Mackenzie (5)	80.0
Jack Westland (5)	80
Billy Joe Patton (14)	78.57
Bill Hyndman (9)	77.77
Jay Sigel (11)	77.27
R A Gardner (8)	75
George von Elm (6)	75
Deane Beman (11)	72.72
Vinny Giles (15)	70
William C Campbell (18)	66.66
Jess Sweetser (12)	62.50
Francis Ouimet (16)	62.5
Dick Chapman (5)	60
Charlie Coe (13)	57.69

Bill Campbell whose total of 18 matches is a record, won seven and halved one of his eight singles. Bobby Jones won all five of his singles matches.
A total of 146 competitors have played for the United States.

OUTSTANDING INDIVIDUAL RECORDS
GREAT BRITAIN AND IRELAND
(Number of individual matches played shown in brackets)

Name	%
John Wilson (2)	100
Robert Scott, Jr (1)	100
Roddy Carr (4)	87.5
Roger Chapman (4)	75
Mark James (4)	75
Peter Townsend (4)	75
Clive Clark (4)	75
Gordon Cosh (4)	75
Allan Brodie (8)	68.75
Gordon Peters (4)	62.50

One of only two Great Britain and Ireland teams in the position of defending the Walker Cup. At the trial at St Andrews 1947. Back row (left to right) Ronnie White, Hamilton McInally. Centre: Joe Carr, Sam McCready, Cecil Ewing, Charlie Stowe, Laddie Lucas. Front: Leonard Crawley, Gerald Micklem, John Beck (captain), Alec Kyle, Jimmy Wilson (Central Press)

American Walker Cup team 1947. From the left: Bud Ward, Willie Turnesa, Fred Kammer, Frank Stranahan, Stanley Bishop, Smiley Quick, Skee Riegel, George Hamer and Francis Ouimet, non-playing captain (Associated Press)

Quite a landing party. Possibly the best Walker Cup team of all. The Americans landing at Prestwick, 1959. From the top: Ward Wettlaufer, Tommy Aaron, Jack Nicklaus, Harvie Ward, Billy Joe Patton, Dr Frank Taylor, Deane Beman, Billy Hyndman and Charlie Coe (captain) (Action Photos)

continued

Roger Wethered (9)	61.11
Ronnie White (10)	60
Leonard Crawley (6)	50
Bernard Darwin (2)	50
Hon Michael Scott (4)	50
Hector Thomson (4)	50
C C Aylmer (2)	50
Laddie Lucas (2)	50
Charlie Stowe (4)	50
Frank Pennink (2)	50
Ronnie Shade (14)	50
Ronan Rafferty (4)	50
Philip Walton (4)	50
Paul Way (4)	50
David Sheahan (4)	50
B Marchbank (4)	50
A E Shepperson (3)	50
Alan Bussell (2)	50

Other players of interest

Sandy Saddler (10)	40
Tony Torrance (9)	38.88
Michael Bonallack (25)	38
Cyril Tolley (12)	33.33
Joe Carr (20)	25

Michael Bonallack's 25 matches are a record. Ronnie White won four of his five singles matches. His opponents were A Frederick Kammer, Willie Turnesa, Charles Coe and Dick Chapman.

A total of 135 competitors have played for Great Britain and Ireland.

Below: Charlie Green holing a putt on the last green at St Andrews to win his Walker Cup foursomes match with Roddy Carr. Vinny Giles approaches to shake hands (Action Photos)

WALKER CUP

Year	Venue	Winners	US Total	Great Britain and Ireland Total	Captains USA	Britain
1922	National Links, Long Island, New York	USA	8	4	William C Fownes, Jr	Robert Harris
1923	St Andrews, Scotland	USA	6½	5½	Robert A Gardner	Robert Harris
1924	Garden City, New York	USA	9	3	Robert A Gardner	Cyril J H Tolley
1926	St Andrews, Scotland	USA	6½	5½	Robert A Gardner	Robert Harris
1928	Chicago GC, Wheaton, Illinois	USA	11	1	Robert T Jones, Jr	Dr William Tweddell
1930	Royal St George's, Sandwich	USA	10	2	Robert T Jones, Jr	Roger H Wethered
1932	Brookline, Massachusetts	USA	9½	2½	Francis D Ouimet	Tony A Torrance
1934	St Andrews, Scotland	USA	9½	2½	Francis D Ouimet	Hon Michael Scott
1936	Pine Valley, New Jersey	USA	10½	1½	*Francis D Ouimet	Dr William Tweddell
1938	St Andrews, Scotland	GB & I	4½	7½	*Francis D Ouimet	John B Beck
1947	St Andrews, Scotland	USA	8	4	*Francis D Ouimet	John B Beck
1949	Winged Foot, New York	USA	10	2	*Francis D Ouimet	Percy B 'Laddie' Lucas
1951	Royal Birkdale, Lancashire	USA	7½	4½	*William P Turnesa	Raymond Oppenheimer
1953	Kittansett Club, Massachusetts	USA	9	3	*Charles R Yates	Lt-Col Tony Duncan
1955	St Andrews, Scotland	USA	10	2	*William C Campbell	*G Alec Hill
1957	Minikhada Club, Minnesota	USA	8½	3½	*Charles R Coe	*Gerald H Micklem
1959	Muirfield, Scotland	USA	9	3	Charles R Coe	*Gerald H Micklem
1961	Seattle, Washington	USA	11	1	*Jack Westland	*Charles D Lawrie
1963	Ailsa Course, Turnberry, Scotland	USA	14	10	*Richard S Tufts	*Charles D Lawrie
1965	Baltimore, Maryland	(tie)	12	12	*John W Fischer	*Joe B Carr
1967	Royal St George's, Sandwich	USA	15	9	*Jess W Sweetser	Joe B Carr
1969	Milwaukee, Wisconsin	USA	13	11	*Billy Joe Patton	Michael Bonallack
1971	St Andrews, Scotland	GB & I	11	13	*John M Winters, Jr	Michael Bonallack
1973	Brookline, Massachusetts	USA	14	10	*Jess W Sweetser	Dr David Marsh
1975	St Andrews, Scotland	USA	15½	8½	*Dr Ed R Updegraff	*Dr David Marsh
1977	Shinnecock Hills, New York	USA	16	8	*Lou W Oehmig	*Sandy C Saddler
1979	Muirfield, Scotland	USA	15½	8½	*Richard Siderowf	*Rodney Foster
1981	Cypress Point, California	USA	15	9	*Jim Gabrielsen	*Rodney Foster

*Non-playing captains.

World Amateur Team Championship

EISENHOWER TROPHY

The idea for this championship was put by the United States Golf Association to the Royal and Ancient Golf Club in March 1958. It was agreed that the two governing bodies should join forces in running the event which was first played in October 1958 and has since been held every other year. A handsome trophy was presented bearing the name of President Eisenhower and the inscription, 'To foster friendship and sportsmanship among the Peoples of the World'.

The form of the tournament is strokeplay for teams of four, the best three scores to count for the four rounds played. The lowest aggregate of the four daily totals constitutes the winner.

1958 Played appropriately at St Andrews, the first championship was one of the best and certainly the closest. It produced a tie (the only tie so far) between Australia and the United States with Great Britain and Ireland 1 stroke behind in third place. It is the only time that 1 stroke has divided three teams. Australia set the target of 918 thanks largely to Bruce Devlin, later such a well-known professional. In the first round, all four Australians took over 80 and they finished 17 strokes behind Britain.

On the last day, the United States, captained by Bobby Jones, looked out of it but Bill Hyndman had a 72, the lowest of all the fourth-round scores. He even had a 3 at the 17th to force the tie.

In the play-off, the Australians, with Devlin again leading the way, won by 2 strokes with a total of 222.

1960 The championship in which the Americans set all sorts of records at Merion which may never be broken. Led by Jack Nicklaus whose four rounds of 66, 67, 68, 68 for an 11 under par 269 is easily a record, they won by 42 strokes—another record.

Yet a further record was their team total of 834. No other championship has ever been so completely dominated by one team.

Thirty-two teams took part, three more than in 1958.

Left: Gladys Ravenscroft and Cecil Leitch meeting in the 1911 Ladies' British Open Amateur championship at Royal Portrush 1911 (BBC Hulton Pic. Lib.) *Above:* One of golf's historic matches. Glenna Collett against Joyce Wethered, Troon 1925 (BBC Hulton Pic. Lib.) *Opposite right:* Semi-finalists in the Ladies' championship at St Andrews 1929. (Standing) Miss Doris Park, Mrs H Guedella. (Seated) Miss Glenna Collett and Miss Joyce Wethered (BBC Hulton Pic. Lib.)

Any port in a storm. Makeshift starter's hut at a ladies championship at Prince's (BBC Hulton Pic. Lib.)

Right: Miss A Macbeth driving off, Stoke Poges 1921 (BBC Hulton Pic. Lib.)

GLENNA COLLETT VARE

In an age when successful women golfers are lured by the professional circuit, Glenna Collett's six victories in the US Women's Amateur championship are no more likely to be matched than Bobby Jones's Grand Slam.

Throughout the 1920s and early 30s, she was the outstanding player in America although Virginia van Wie won three times in succession and Glenna was twice runner-up, once to van Wie. However, Glenna Vare, as she had then become, won again in 1935, beating Patty Berg in the final.

As well as capturing the imagination of galleries by her skill, she was popular away from the course but her attempts to win the British were twice thwarted by Joyce Wethered, once in an epic final, and then by Diana Fishwick in the final of 1930.

JOANNE GUNDERSON CARNER

An amateur who stood comparison with Glenna Collett Vare and Babe Zaharias, JoAnne Carner then embarked upon a wonderfully successful professional career which shows no sign of waning.

She turned professional in 1970 after winning the US

LADIES' BRITISH OPEN AMATEUR CHAMPIONSHIP

Year	Winner	Runner-up	Venue	By
1893	Lady Margaret Scott	Isette Pearson	St Annes	7 and 5
1894	Lady Margaret Scott	Isette Pearson	Littlestone	3 and 2
1895	Lady Margaret Scott	Miss E Lythgoe	Portrush	3 and 2
1896	Amy Pascoe	Miss L Thomson	Hoylake	3 and 2
1897	Edith C Orr	Miss Orr	Gullane	4 and 2
1898	Miss L Thomson	Miss E C Neville	Yarmouth	7 and 5
1899	May Hezlet	Miss Magill	Newcastle, Co Down	2 and 1
1900	Rhona Adair	Miss E C Neville	Westward Ho!	6 and 5
1901	Miss Graham	Rhona Adair	Aberdovey	3 and 1
1902	May Hezlet	Miss E C Neville	Deal	19th hole
1903	Rhona Adair	Miss F Walker-Leigh	Portrush	4 and 3
1904	Lottie Dod	May Hezlet	Troon	1 hole
1905	Miss B Thompson	Miss M E Stuart	Cromer	3 and 2
1906	Mrs Kennion	Miss B Thompson	Burnham	4 and 3
1907	May Hezlet	Florence Hezlet	Newcastle, Co Down	2 and 1
1908	Miss M Titterton	Dorothy Campbell	St Andrews	19th hole
1909	Dorothy Campbell	Florence Hezlet	Birkdale	4 and 3
1910	Miss Grant Suttie	Miss L Moore	Westward Ho!	6 and 4
1911	Dorothy Campbell	Violet Hezlet	Portrush	3 and 2
1912	Gladys Ravenscroft	Miss S Temple	Turnberry	3 and 2
1913	Muriel Dodd	Miss Chubb	St Annes	8 and 6
1914	Cecil Leitch	Gladys Ravenscroft	Hunstanton	2 and 1
1915–18	No Championship owing to World War I.			
1919	Should have been played at Burnham in October, but abandoned owing to Railway Strike.			
1920	Cecil Leitch	Molly Griffiths	Newcastle, Co Down	7 and 6
1921	Cecil Leitch	Joyce Wethered	Turnberry	4 and 3
1922	Joyce Wethered	Cecil Leitch	Prince's, Sandwich	9 and 7
1923	Doris Chambers	Miss A Macbeth	Burnham, Somerset	2 holes
1924	Joyce Wethered	Mrs Cautley	Portrush	7 and 6
1925	Joyce Wethered	Cecil Leitch	Troon	37th hole
1926	Cecil Leitch	Mrs Garon	Harlech	8 and 7
1927	Miss Thion de la Chaume (France)	Miss Pearson	Newcastle, Co Down	5 and 4
1928	Nanette Le Blan (France)	Miss S Marshall	Hunstanton	3 and 2
1929	Joyce Wethered	Glenna Collett (USA)	St Andrews	3 and 1
1930	Diana Fishwick	Glenna Collett (USA)	Formby	4 and 3
1931	Enid Wilson	Wanda Morgan	Portmarnock	7 and 6
1932	Enid Wilson	Miss C P R Montgomery	Saunton	7 and 6
1933	Enid Wilson	Miss D Plumpton	Gleneagles	5 and 4
1934	Helen Holm	Pam Barton	Royal Porthcawl	6 and 5
1935	Wanda Morgan	Pam Barton	Newcastle, Co Down	3 and 2

From 1893 to 1912, the final was played over 18 holes. From 1913 to 1964, the final was played over 36 holes. In 1965, the final should have been played over 36 holes but bad weather earlier in the week caused it to be 18 holes and in 1966 it reverted to 18 holes on a permanent basis.

Women's Amateur five times and, within a year, had added the US Women's Open. She won again in 1976 but her best year was 1974 and though her game is based on an obvious inclination to attack, she has retained a remarkable consistency.

JOYCE WETHERED (**Lady Heathcoat-Amory**)

Thought by Bobby Jones to be the best golfer, man or woman, he had seen—a view nobody could possibly contradict. Certainly, she and Jones were the best players of their generation—perhaps of all time.

They had other things in common, too. They

combined style, ease and elegance in their play and managed, while concentrating fiercely, to act as the most gracious and courteous opponents. However, it was their achievements which stood them apart.

Joyce Wethered won the Ladies' British Open Amateur championship four times and was runner-up on another occasion; she dominated the English championship, winning it five times in a row, and won the Worplesdon mixed foursomes which, in those days, attracted the best amateurs, eight times with seven different partners.

Yet, having achieved supremacy, she withdrew from

Year	Winner	Runner-up	Venue	By
1936	Pam Barton	Miss B Newell	Southport and Ainsdale	5 and 3
1937	Jessie Anderson	Doris Park	Turnberry	6 and 4
1938	Helen Holm	Elsie Corlett	Burnham	4 and 3
1939	Pam Barton	Mrs T Marks	Portrush	2 and 1
1940–45	No Championship owing to World War II.			
1946	Jean Hetherington	Philomena Garvey	Hunstanton	1 hole
1947	Babe Zaharias (USA)	Jacqueline Gordon	Gullane	5 and 4
1948	Louise Suggs (USA)	Jean Donald	Royal Lytham	1 hole
1949	Frances Stephens	Val Reddan	Harlech	5 and 4
1950	Vicomtesse de Saint Sauveur (France)	Jessie Valentine	Newcastle, Co Down	3 and 2
1951	Mrs P G MacCann	Frances Stephens	Broadstone	4 and 3
1952	Moira Paterson	Frances Stephens	Troon	39th hole
1953	Marlene Stewart	Philomena Garvey	Porthcawl	7 and 6
1954	Frances Stephens	Elizabeth Price	Ganton	4 and 3
1955	Jessie Valentine	Barbara Romack (USA)	Portrush	7 and 6
1956	Margaret Smith	Mary P Janssen	Sunningdale	8 and 7
1957	Philomena Garvey	Jessie Valentine	Gleneagles	4 and 3
1958	Jessie Valentine	Elizabeth Price	Hunstanton	1 hole
1959	Elizabeth Price	Belle McCorkindale	Ascot	37th hole
1960	Barbara McIntire (USA)	Philomena Garvey	Harlech	4 and 2
1961	Marley Spearman	Diane Robb	Carnoustie	7 and 6
1962	Marley Spearman	Angela Bonallack	Royal Birkdale	1 hole
1963	Brigitte Varangot (France)	Philomena Garvey	Newcastle, Co Down	3 and 1
1964	Carol Sorenson (USA)	Bridget Jackson	Prince's, Sandwich	37th hole
1965	Brigitte Varangot (France)	Belle Robertson	St Andrews	4 and 3
1966	Elizabeth Chadwick	Vivien Saunders	Ganton	3 and 2
1967	Elizabeth Chadwick	Mary Everard	Harlech	1 hole
1968	Brigitte Varangot (France)	Claudine Rubin (France)	Walton Heath	20th hole
1969	Catherine Lacoste (France)	Ann Irvin	Portrush	1 hole
1970	Dinah Oxley	Belle Robertson	Gullane	1 hole
1971	Michelle Walker	Beverley Huke	Alwoodley	3 and 1
1972	Michelle Walker	Claudine Rubin (France)	Hunstanton	2 holes
1973	Ann Irvin	Michelle Walker	Carnoustie	3 and 2
1974	Carol Semple (USA)	Angela Bonallack	Royal Porthcawl	2 and 1
1975	Nancy Syms (USA)	Suzanne Cadden	St Andrews	3 and 2
1976	Cathy Panton	Alison Sheard (S Africa)	Silloth	1 hole
1977	Angela Uzielli	Vanessa Marvin	Hillside	6 and 5
1978	Edwina Kennedy (Australia)	Julia Greenhalgh	Notts	1 hole
1979	Maureen Madill	Jane Lock (Australia)	Nairn	2 and 1
1980	Anne Sander (USA)	Liv Wollin (Sweden)	Woodhall Spa	3 and 1
1981	Belle Robertson	Wilma Aitken	Caernarvonshire	20th hole
1982	Kitrina Douglas	Gillian Stewart	Walton Heath	4 and 2

the competitive scene for three years but returned to win the 1929 British final against Glenna Collett who had been 5 up after 11 holes.

Glenna Collett was the leading American woman golfer of that era and the match was inevitably seen as a comparison of strength but the other quality Joyce Wethered had in common with Jones was an innate modesty and, as a result, an unawareness of just how good she was.

Though most pictures show her on her toes at impact, she had perfect balance and once told Leonard Crawley: 'On the rare occasions that I am playing my best, I feel nobody could push me off my right heel at the top of the swing and, at the other end, I feel nobody could push me off my left foot.' You cannot define balance better than that.

LADY MARGARET SCOTT

The first lady champion and an outstanding one in her own right. She won the first three British championships (1893–95) and only once, the semi-final of 1895, was she ever in danger of defeat. She came from a great golfing family, her three brothers, Michael, Osmund and Denys, were all fine players but she gave up the game after her third win. She became Lady Margaret Hamilton-Russell on her marriage.

CECILIA LEITCH

Cecil Leitch, one of five daughters of a Cumberland doctor, was a multiple champion of Britain, England, France and Canada but it was her rivalry with Joyce Wethered, ten years her junior, which made women's golf front page news for the first time.

Altogether, she won four British and two English titles. In the four finals she played against Joyce Wethered, Cecil Leitch won only one, the British of 1921, but their match at Troon in 1925 was one of the best and most famous in women's history which lasted 37 holes.

ENID WILSON

Apart from Joyce Wethered, Enid Wilson was regarded as the best British player to grow up between the two wars. She won three successive victories in the British championship (1931–33) and two, by commanding margins, in the English.

She played in the first Curtis Cup match in 1932 but, after an early retirement, became well known as a writer and respected authority on the game.

PAM BARTON

Pam Barton's career, tragically ended by her death in a plane crash in 1943, was short but highly distinguished. At the age of 19, she won the British and American championships within the space of a few weeks in the summer of 1936, the first player to do so since Dorothy Campbell in 1909. She won the British again in 1939 and seemed destined for many more successes.

MAY HEZLET

May Hezlet, the youngest winner of both Irish and British women's championships, belonged to a remarkable golfing family. May, Florence and Violet played in the first three of the singles order for Ireland and their brother, Charles, played in three Walker Cup matches. However, May was the outstanding champion although in four finals, three Irish and one British, May was opposed by Florence. Her first victory in the Irish came a few days before her 17th birthday and her first in the British a few days after.

JESSIE VALENTINE

The last three-time winner of the Ladies' British Open championship, Jessie Valentine won her first title in 1937, the year after she had holed a fine putt on the last green to win her Curtis Cup single and halve the entire contest.

In a notable post-war era which included Frances Smith, Jean Donald, Elizabeth Price, Jeanne Bisgood and Philomena Garvey, Jessie Valentine confirmed her competitive qualities by winning the British twice more and the Scottish championship a total of six times. Noted for control rather than power, she became the first woman to be recognised for her services to the game, receiving the MBE in 1959.

CATHERINE LACOSTE

Catherine Lacoste, the finest woman golfer from the continent of Europe, holds a special place in the history of the game. She is the only amateur to have won the US Women's Open and belongs to the distinguished handful of players who have won the British and American Amateur championships.

She inherited her sporting talents from her parents. Few women have matched her power, particularly with a 1 iron, and there is no doubt that she could have made a highly successful professional. Her victory in the US Women's Open was an acute embarrassment to the American professionals but it was an achievement matched by her winning the Amateur titles of Britain and America in the same summer of 1969; she is the last player to have done this.

ANNE QUAST
(later Decker, later Welts, later Sander)

One of the American amateurs who resisted the temptation to turn professional, Anne Sander was an outstanding champion whose reign was spread over four decades. She won the first of three American titles in 1958 and surprised and delighted everyone by winning the British in 1980 when she had virtually given up hope of so doing.

She reached the quarter-finals of the American in 1955 as a girl of 17 but her greatest performance was winning the national title in 1961. She was 9 under par for the week at Tacoma, lost only 6 holes and set a record winning margin in the final by defeating Phyllis Preuss by 14 and 13.

US Women's Amateur Championship

DETAILED RECORDS

Most victories
6, Glenna Collett Vare, 1922–25–28–29–30–35
5, JoAnne Gunderson Carner, 1957–60–62–66–68
3, Beatrix Hoyt; Margaret Curtis; Dorothy Campbell Hurd; Alexa Stirling; Virginia van Wie; Anne Quast (later Decker, later Welts, later Sander)

Oldest winner
Dorothy Campbell Hurd, 41 years 4 months, 1924

Youngest winner
Laura Baugh, 16 years 2 months 21 days, 1971;
Beatrix Hoyt, 16 years 3 months 4 days, 1896
Peggy Conley reached the 1963 final at 16 years 2 months 2 weeks, and Roberta Albers reached the semi-final in 1961 aged 14 years 8 months.

Biggest margin of victory in final
14 and 13, Anne Quast beat Phyllis Preuss at Tacoma in 1961. Anne Quast was 12 up at lunch—also a record.

Longest final
41 holes, JoAnne Gunderson Carner beat Marlene Stewart Streit in 1966 at Sewickley Heights, Pennsylvania. This was the longest final in any USGA competition.
In 1954, the second 18 holes of the final was halted by storms and played on Sunday. It thus took 29 hours 15 minutes to complete.

Most times in the final
8, Glenna Collett Vare

Most times runner-up
3, Mrs William A Gavin, 1915–19–22; Anne Quast, 1965–68–73

Longest 18-hole match
27 holes, Mae Murray beat Fay Crocker in the fourth round at East Lake, Atlanta in 1950.
27 holes Denise Hermida (USA) beat Carole Caldwell (GB) in the first round at Plymouth Meeting, Pennsylvania in 1978.

Consecutive winners
3, Beatrix Hoyt, 1896–97–98; Alexa Stirling, 1916–19–20. No championship in 1917–18; Glenna Collett Vare, 1928–29–30; Virginia van Wie, 1932–33–34
2, Genevieve Hecker, 1901–02; Dorothy Campbell, 1909–10; Margaret Curtis, 1911–12; Betty Jameson, 1939–40; Juli Inkster 1980–81

Family records
In 1907, the final was contested by the sisters Margaret Curtis and Harriot Curtis. Margaret won 7 and 6, succeeding Harriot as champion. In 1962, Jean Trainor defeated her daughter Anne Trainor by 4 and 3 in the fourth round.

First to win American and British championships
Dorothy Campbell (later Dorothy Hurd), 1909

First American to win American and British championships
Mildred 'Babe' Didrikson Zaharias, 1946 and 1947

Overseas winners
Dorothy Campbell; Gladys Ravenscroft; Pam Barton; Marlene Stewart; Catherine Lacoste

Winner of British and American championships the same year
Catherine Lacoste, 1969; Pam Barton, 1936; Dorothy Campbell, 1909

Longest span between victories
15 years, Dorothy Campbell, 1909–24

Club hosting most championships
4 times, Merion, Pennsylvania

Winners of British and American championships
'Babe' Zaharias; Gladys Ravenscroft; Pam Barton; Louise Suggs; Dorothy Campbell; Barbara McIntire; Marlene Stewart; Catherine Lacoste; Carol Semple; Anne Sander

Winners of British, American and Canadian championships
Marlene Stewart and Dorothy Campbell Hurd

Repeat finals
1928 and 1930, Glenna Collett Vare beat Virginia van Wie

US WOMEN'S AMATEUR CHAMPIONSHIP

Year	Winner	Runner-up	Venue	Score
1895	Mrs C S Brown	Miss N C Sargeant	Meadow Brook	132
Matchplay				By
1896	Beatrix Hoyt	Mrs Arthur Turnure	Morris County	2 and 1
1897	Beatrix Hoyt	Miss N C Sargeant	Essex CC	5 and 4
1898	Beatrix Hoyt	Maude Wetmore	Ardsley Club	5 and 3
1899	Ruth Underhill	Mrs Caleb Fox	Philadelphia CC	2 and 1
1900	Frances Griscom	Margaret Curtis	Shinnecock Hills	6 and 5

Flying the flag. Ball spotters in the Curtis Cup match of 1936 (BBC Hulton Pic. Lib.)

promising start by sharing the foursomes. The foursomes were played in a severe rainstorm, but the weather improved the next day when America won five of the six singles. Mrs J B Walker was the lone British winner. Mrs L D Cheney beat Pam Barton who, two years later, won the British and American Women's championship the same summer.

1936 The year of the first tie. At Gleneagles, the foursomes were again shared, but the real excitement came in the singles. Two last-green victories by Charlotte Glutting and Maureen Orcutt for America were countered by Helen Holm and Marjorie Ross Garon for Britain. Glenna Collett Vare had won the top match for America and so all depended on Mrs L D Cheney and Jessie Anderson (later Jessie Valentine), a 21-year-old who was born just down the road in Perth. In the first of a record seven appearances in the Curtis Cup, she became the British heroine, holing a putt of 20 ft (6 m) on the last green to win her match and tie the whole contest.

1938 At the Essex Country Club, Massachusetts, a very British-sounding name, the British had high hopes of their first victory after winning the foursomes 2½–½, but they won only one single. The deciding match was between Nan Baird and Charlotte Glutting who won the last 3 holes for a 1-hole victory.

1948 After a gap of ten years because of World War II, the Americans resumed with a victory at Royal Birkdale. A newcomer, Jean Donald, won both her matches for Britain, but after her singles win and a half at the top from Philomena Garvey against Louise Suggs, who won the last 2 holes, America won the remaining four matches.

1950 Britain's defeat by 7½–1½ at the Country Club of Buffalo was the largest margin to date. There was never any doubt about the result, but there was encouragement for the British in the first appearance of Frances Stephens. She won her foursome with Elizabeth Price and halved the leading single with Dorothy Germain Porter.

1952 An historic first victory for Britain at the Honourable Company of Edinburgh Golfers, Muirfield, a club with no lady members and no provision for them. In cold blustery conditions, Britain won the foursomes by the odd match but they suffered a shock before winning three of the singles through Frances Stephens, Jeanne Bisgood and Elizabeth Price. Jean Donald, 5 up and 11 to play, lost on the 18th to Dorothy Kirby but, by then, Elizabeth Price had control of the bottom match with Grace DeMoss.

1954 Britain lost the Cup at Merion by losing all three foursomes by wide margins. However, they showed their strength by sharing the singles. In the top match, Frances Stephens beat Mary Lena Faulk by 1 hole. Mary Lena Faulk squared with a 2 at the 35th but Frances Stephens holed from 6 yd (5.4 m) on the 36th for victory.

1956 Great Britain confirmed their strength throughout the fifties by winning again, this time at Prince's, Sandwich, scene of Gene Sarazen's Open championship victory. They lost the foursomes 2–1, but they had three commanding victories in the singles; Mrs George Valentine beat Patricia Lesser 6 and 4, Angela Ward (later Mrs Michael Bonallack) won her first Curtis Cup on a course where she was a member by 4 and 3 against Mary Ann Downey; and Elizabeth Price beat Jane Nelson 7 and 6.

This left Frances Stephens Smith and Polly Riley in the deciding match, both players being undefeated in singles matches. Polly Riley squared on the 32nd and again on the 34th but, after a half at the 35th, Mrs Smith won the 36th.

1958 The second halved match of the series occurred at Brae Burn Country Club, Massachusetts. It was the first time that any British team in Walker, Ryder or Curtis Cup had avoided defeat in America, a feat which only the 1965 Walker Cup equalled subsequently.

As holders, the British side retained the Cup. They won the foursomes 2–1, but America had a slight edge in the singles. In the end, the whole match depended, as in 1956, on the match between Frances Smith and Polly Riley, this time playing in the last match. Mrs Smith, 1 up playing the 18th, won the hole to win by 2 holes.

1960 At Lindrick, Yorkshire, scene of Britain's Ryder Cup victory in 1957, America won the Curtis Cup for the first time since 1954. Since then, they have won all the matches. The Americans won the foursomes 2–1 and there was none of the excitement of the previous three matches. The Americans won 4½ singles.

Mrs Frances Stephens Smith's remarkable Curtis Cup career ended after the foursomes. She did not play in the singles in which she was unbeaten in five matches.

1962 A British team, with five new names in its midst, suffered their worst defeat, 8–1 at Broadmoor Golf Club, Colorado Springs. They lost all three foursomes and only Mrs Alistair Frearson won her single. She beat Judy Bell 8 and 7.

1964 A change to 18-hole matches produced a fine contest at Royal Porthcawl. Peggy Conley, 17, was the youngest competitor in the Curtis Cup at the time and she played a decisive part at the end of a close match.

After the first three singles on the last afternoon, the teams were level but Peggy Conley, Barbara Fay White and Carol Sorenson, who went on to win the British Women's championship, beat Bridget Jackson, Angela Bonallack and Ruth Porter to settle things for America. Mrs Marley Spearman halved both singles and won both foursomes with Angela Bonallack for the British side.

1966 A big victory by 13–5 for the Americans at Virginia Hot Springs. All the Americans had previous Curtis Cup experience compared to three of the British. On the second day, the British won only two matches.

1968 As in 1964, the result hung in the balance for a long time on the second day of the match held at Royal County Down, Newcastle, Northern Ireland. It was the first time that the Curtis, Walker or Ryder Cup had been held on the other side of the Irish Sea; it was a huge success in two days of glorious weather.

Ann Irvin was the outstanding British player, but once again the last three American victories in the singles made the difference between the teams.

1970 Back at Brae Burn, Massachusetts, the Americans won 11½–6½, but the British began by winning the first foursomes series. However, they got only two points from the next nine matches which made all the difference.

1972 A match at Western Gailes, Ayrshire, notable for the play of the two young champions, Michelle Walker and Laura Baugh. The single between the two was halved; Walker won the foursome in which they were both involved, but they won their other matches, Walker dropping only that one half point in two days.

Over all, it was a match which swung in the Americans' favour on the first afternoon. They had lost the foursomes in the morning, but won the singles 4½–1½. The second day's play was halved.

1974 For the first time, the match was held on America's west coast at the San Francisco Golf Club. After the first morning's play was halved, the Americans gained and maintained a steady advantage. They won 13–5 with Mrs Anne Sander who played her first Curtis Cup match in 1958, winning all her three matches.

1976 An 11½–6½ victory for the United States was never seriously in doubt after they led 6½–2½ on the first day at Royal Lytham St Annes. The American side included Nancy Lopez who, though winning her matches, played only twice.

1978 Britain made an encouraging start on the first morning at Apawamis, New York. They won the foursomes 2½–½, but thereafter were disappointing. They finished the first day behind at 5–4 and then lost all the second day's foursomes.

1980 A one-sided match at St Pierre, Chepstow, after the first morning. The Americans ran away on Friday afternoon and Saturday morning to win 13–5. The new British Professional tour had its effect upon the strength of the British. Jane Connachan was the youngest to take part in any Curtis Cup.

DETAILED RECORDS 1932–1980

Most appearances
7, Mrs George Valentine (Great Britain and Ireland)
6, Philomena Garvey (Great Britain and Ireland); Elizabeth Price (Great Britain and Ireland); Frances Smith (Great Britain and Ireland); Angela Bonallack (Great Britain and Ireland); Polly Riley (United States); Barbara McIntire (United States); Anne Quast Sander (United States); Mary McKenna (Great Britain and Ireland)

Most consecutive appearances
6, Elizabeth Price; Frances Smith; Angela Bonallack; Polly Riley

Biggest margin of victory
Over 36 holes (1932–62)
Foursomes: **8 and 7,** Jean Ashley and Lee Johnstone (United States) beat Mrs Alistair Frearson and Ruth Porter, 1962

Singles: **9 and 8,** Margaret 'Wiffi' Smith (United States) beat Philomena Garvey, 1956
Polly Riley (United States) beat Elizabeth Price, 1954

Over 18 holes (from 1964 onwards)
Foursomes: **8 and 7,** Carol Sorenson and Barbara Fay White (United States) beat Bridget Jackson and Susan Armitage, 1964
Singles: **7 and 5,** Jane Booth (United States) beat Julia Greenhalgh, 1974

Largest winning margin by team
13–5, United States over Great Britain and Ireland 1966, 1974 and 1980.
Prior to 1964, when 18 points became at stake, the largest winning score was 8–1 to the United States in 1962.

Ties
There have been two tied matches: in 1936 and 1958.

Best comebacks
In 1938, United States won 5½–3½ after trailing 2½–½ in the foursomes.
In 1956, Great Britain and Ireland won 5–4 after losing the foursomes 2–1.

Team winning all the foursomes
In 1932, 1954 and 1962 all by the United States

Team winning all the singles
None. The United States won 5½ out of 6 in 1950

Most consecutive victories
11, United States, 1960–80

Youngest competitor
Jane Connachan, 16 years 3 months, 1980

Members of the 1948 American Curtis Cup team. From the *left*: Amelia Goldthwaite, Maureen Orcutt, Patty Berg, Charlotte Glutting

**OUTSTANDING INDIVIDUAL RECORDS
UNITED STATES**
(Number of individual matches played shown in brackets)

Name	%
Debbie Massey (5)	100
Dorothy Kielty (4)	100
Claire Doran (4)	100
Clifford Ann Creed (2)	100
Beverly Hanson (2)	100
Nancy Lopez (2)	100
Barbara White Boddie (8)	93.75
Beth Daniel (8)	87.50
Virginia van Wie (4)	87.50
Mrs L D Cheney (6)	83.33
Carol Sorenson Flenniken (8)	81.25
Jane Bastenchury Booth (12)	75
Martha Wilkinson (4)	75
Charlotte Glutting (5)	70
JoAnne Gunderson Carner (10)	65
Glenna Collett Vare (7)	64.28

A total of 84 players have played for the United States in the 21 matches. The United States have won 17. Great Britain and Ireland two with two halved.

**OUTSTANDING INDIVIDUAL PERFORMANCES
GREAT BRITAIN AND IRELAND**
(Number of individual matches played shown in brackets)

Name	%
Clarrie Tiernan (2)	100
Michelle Walker (4)	87.50
Marjorie Ross Garon (2)	75
Frances Smith (11)	68.18
Muriel Thomson (3)	66.66
Ita Burke (3)	66.66
Elizabeth Price (12)	62.50
A M Holm (5)	60
Ruth Porter (7)	50
Marley Spearman (6)	50
Jean Donald Anderson (6)	50
Joyce Wethered (2)	50
Enid Wilson (2)	50
Elsie Corlett (2)	50
Jacqueline Gordon (2)	50
Julia Greenhalgh (17)	47.05
Mary Everard (15)	46.60
Angela Ward Bonallack (15)	43.33
Mary McKenna (23)	41.30
Jessie Anderson Valentine (13)	30.76

Mrs Frances Stephens Smith was unbeaten in her five singles matches. She won four and halved one.
A total of 74 players have taken part in the 21 matches.

Joyce Wethered pictured in the Worplesdon Mixed Foursomes, 1931. She won eight times, only twice with the same partner (Topical Press)

CURTIS CUP

Year	Venue	Winners	US Total	Great Britain and Ireland Total	Captains USA	Britain
1932	Wentworth GC, Surrey, England	USA	5½	3½	Marion Hollins	Joyce Wethered
1934	Chevy Chase Club, Maryland	USA	6½	2½	Glenna Collett Vare	Doris Chambers
1936	King's Course, Gleneagles, Scotland	(tie)	4½	4½	Glenna Collett Vare	Doris Chambers
1938	Essex CC, Massachusetts	USA	5½	3½	Frances Stebbins	Kathleen Wallace-Williamson
1948	Royal Birkdale, Lancashire, England	USA	6½	2½	Glenna Collett Vare	Doris Chambers
1950	Buffalo CC, New York	USA	7½	1½	Glenna Collett Vare	Diana Critchley
1952	Links of the Honourable Company of Edinburgh Golfers, Muirfield, Scotland	Britain	4	5	Aneila Goldthwaite	Lady Katherine Cairns
1954	Merion GC (East course), Pennsylvania	USA	6	3	Edith Flippin	Dorothy 'Baba' Beck
1956	Prince's GC, Sandwich, England	Britain	4	5	Edith Flippin	Zara Bolton
1958	Brae Burn GC, Massachusetts	(tie)	4½	4½	Virginia Dennehy	Daisy Ferguson
1960	Lindrick GC, Yorkshire, England	USA	6½	2½	Mildred Prunaret	Maureen Garrett
1962	Broadmoor GC, Colorado Springs	USA	8	1	Polly Riley	Frances Smith
1964	Royal Porthcawl GC, Wales	USA	10½	7½	Helen Hawes	Elsie Corlett
1966	Cascades Course, Hot Springs, Virginia	USA	13	5	Dorothy Porter	Zara Bolton
1968	Royal County Down GC, Newcastle, Northern Ireland	USA	10½	7½	Evelyn Monsted	Zara Bolton
1970	Brae Burn GC, Massachusetts	USA	11½	6½	Carol Cudone	Jeanne Bisgood
1972	Western Gailes, Scotland	USA	10	8	Jean Crawford	Frances Smith
1974	San Francisco GC, California	USA	13	5	Allison Choate	Belle Robertson
1976	Royal Lytham and St Annes, Lancashire	USA	11½	6½	Barbara McIntire	Belle Robertson
1978	Apawamis, New York	USA	12	6	Helen Sigel Wilson	Carol Comboy
1980	St Pierre, Chepstow, England	USA	13	5	Nancy Syms	Carol Comboy

Well played girls! The Americans congratulating each other after their victory in the 1980 Curtis Cup match (Phil Sheldon)

Women's World Amateur Team Championship

For the Espirito Santo Trophy

MILESTONES

The championship was instituted by the French Golf Federation on a suggestion of the United States Golf Association. The inaugural event was held at the Saint-Germain Club in Paris in October 1964. Each team consists of three players, the two best each day making up the team's score. The sum of the four daily totals decides the winner.

1964 Appropriately, the first championship was won by France, the host country who, at that time, had three of the best players in the world, Claudine Cros, Catherine Lacoste and Brigitte Varangot.

They had a close duel with the United States who led by only 1 stroke after 54 holes. Lacoste had a final round of 73 and Cros 74, but the issue was decided when the American, Barbara McIntire, played the last 2 holes in 3 over par. France won by 1 stroke with a total of 588.

1966 A comfortable victory in Mexico City for the Americans despite losing the services of Mrs JoAnne Gunderson Carner. She was replaced by 17-year-old Shelley Hamlin who, after failing to count in the first two rounds, finished with two 72s, the best last 36-hole score by any player. The Americans won by 9 strokes from Canada and 17 from France, the holders.

1968 In a championship of high scoring, the United States won for the second time at the Victoria Golf Club, near Melbourne. After three rounds, America and Australia were level on 463, 1 ahead of France, but America won by 5 strokes.

1970 America won a desperate victory over France by a single stroke at the Club de Campo in Madrid. They had trailed after three rounds by 2 strokes but, with Martha Wilkinson, the US champion, paired with Catherine Lacoste, there were fluctuations in plenty before America squeezed home. The individual title was won by the South African, Sally Little.

1972 The United States won for the fourth time in a row at the Hindu Country Club, Buenos Aires. They won by 4 strokes from France who were 18 strokes behind America at the halfway. Then Claudine Rubin and Brigitte Varangot had a 68 and a 71 to make up 14 strokes. Good finishing rounds of 72 and 73 by Laura Baugh and Jane Bastanchury Booth, whose 68 in the first round equalled the lowest round ever in the championship, saw America home.

1974 The United States made it five victories in a row at the Campo de Golf, Cajuiles, Dominica, beating South Africa and Great Britain and Ireland into second place by a record 16 strokes. It was none the less, the highest winning total—620. America were close to disaster on the first day—or so it seemed. Deborah Massey almost withdrew after 9 holes, having been heavily medicated, but in the end her score of 84 counted, because Carol Semple committed a breach of the rules and was disqualified. Cynthia Hill had 76, the lowest first round and one of the few under 80. They were only a stroke behind Italy and never looked back.

The lowest score of the championship was a 71 by Catherine Lacoste de Prado of France in the last round. The first six teams had only 25 rounds under 80 out of a possible 72.

1976 The United States yet again at Vilamoura, Portugal. They were never headed and steadily built up the record-winning margin of 17 strokes, 1 more than the previous championship. Nancy Lopez, whose 72 in the first round was the lowest of all the four days, had the best aggregate of all—297.

France, the only other country to have won, were second for the third time.

1978 First victory for Australia and the first time that the United States have finished outside the first two. They were tied fourth.

At Pacific Harbour, Fiji, Australia won by a single stroke in a desperate finish with Canada who started the final round 6 strokes behind. France had a good last day to finish third on 602, 6 strokes behind the winners.

1980 United States claimed revenge on Australia over Pinehurst No 2 although at halfway the two countries were level. In the third round, the United States returned 74s from Carol Semple and Juli Inkster to take a 3-stroke lead and on the final day Semple and Inkster shot 71 and 73 respectively, the lowest daily total of the week. This made their winning margin 7 strokes. The third member of the American team, Patti Rizzo had the lowest individual total, 294 (73–70–75–76). There were a record 28 team entries. It was the first time the Espirito Santo Trophy had been contested in the United States.

DETAILED RECORDS

Most victories
7, United States
1, France
1, Australia

Lowest aggregate total
580, United States, 1966

Highest winning total
620, United States, 1974

Lowest individual round
68, Jane Bastanchury Booth, Marlene Stewart and Claudine Cros Rubin, all in 1972

Lowest individual aggregate
289 (74, 71, 70, 74) Marlene Stewart, Mexico City CC, 1966

Lowest individual first round
68, Marlene Stewart and Jane Bastanchury Booth, Hindu CC, Buenos Aires, 1972

Lowest individual second round
71, Catherine Lacoste, St Germain GC, Paris, 1964
71, Mrs Teddy Boddie and Marlene Stewart, Mexico City CC, 1966
71, Liv Forsell (Sweden), Hindu CC, Buenos Aires, 1972

Lowest individual third round
68, Claudine Cros Rubin, Hindu CC, Buenos Aires, 1972

Lowest individual fourth round
71, Claudine Cros Rubin and Isa Goldschmid, Hindu CC, Buenos Aires, 1972
71, Catherine Lacoste de Prado, Campo de Golf, Cajuiles, Dominican Republic, 1974
71, Carol Semple and Marie Laure de Lorenzi, Pinehurst No 2, 1980

Largest lead after 18 holes
5 strokes, United States, 1972

Largest lead after 36 holes
13 strokes, United States, 1972

Largest lead after 54 holes
10 strokes, United States, 1974

Largest margin of victory
17 strokes, United States, 1976

Smallest lead after 18 holes
1 stroke, France in 1964, United States in 1966, Italy in 1974 and Great Britain and Ireland in 1978

Smallest lead after 36 holes
United States and Australia were tied after 36 holes, 1980

Smallest lead after 54 holes
United States and Australia tied in 1968

Smallest margin of victory
1 stroke, France in 1964, the United States in 1970 and Australia in 1978

Most teams to compete
28 in 1980

Youngest competitors
Maria de la Guardia and Silvia Corrie, both of the Dominican Republic, were both only 14 years old in 1974

RESULTS

Espirito Santo Trophy
1964 Saint-Germain GC, Paris 1–4 October
France 588 (Claudine Cros, Catherine Lacoste, Brigitte Varangot)
1966 Mexico City Country Club 20–23 October
United States 580 (Marjorie Boddie, Shelley Hamlin, Anne Welts)
1968 Victoria GC, Nr Melbourne, Australia 2–5 October
United States 616 (Jane Bastanchury, Shelley Hamlin, Anne Welts)
1970 Club de Campo, Madrid 30 September–3 October
United States 598 (Jane Bastanchury, Cynthia Hill, Martha Wilkinson)
1972 Hindu CC, Buenos Aires 11–14 October
United States 583 (Laura Baugh, Jane Bastanchury Booth, Mary Anne Budke)
1974 Campo de Golf, Cajuiles, Dominica 22–25 October
United States 620 (Cynthia Hill, Deborah Massey, Carol Semple)
1976 Vilamoura GC, Algarve, Portugal 6–9 October
United States 605 (Donna Horton, Nancy Lopez, Deborah Massey)
1978 Pacific Harbour, Fiji 10–13 October
Australia 596 (Lindy Goggin, Edwina Kennedy, Jane Lock)
1980 Pinehurst No 2, North Carolina, USA 1–4 October
United States 588 (Juli Inkster, Patti Rizzo, Carol Semple)

MICKEY WRIGHT

In any argument about the greatest woman golfer of all time, the name of Mickey Wright would be on the shortest of short lists. Her scoring, unparalleled in women's golf, set new standards but it also brought her victory after victory.

Altogether she scored 82 victories on the LPGA circuit and was one of those primarily responsible for the expansion of the tour but she holds other records. In 1961, she won ten tournaments, four of them in a row, and she shares with Betsy Rawls the highest number (4) of victories in the US Women's Open.

Daughter of an attorney, she turned professional after losing the final of the US Women's Amateur to Barbara Romack in 1954 and quickly established her supremacy. In addition to her four Open wins, she won the LPGA championship four times and holds the record for the lowest 18 holes on the tour—62.

MILDRED 'BABE' ZAHARIAS

A legendary name in women's golf and in the field of athletics where she won two gold medals and one silver in the 1932 Olympic Games.

She took up golf relatively late but soon earned the reputation as the longest hitter the game had seen at that time, although she possessed all the control in the short game as well.

The war hindered her career but she won US Women's Amateur in 1946, became the first American to win the British the following year and promptly reverted to the professional status she was forced to acquire in 1935.

Her strong sense of publicity and her spectacular play were a godsend to the women's tour and she was the star of the show. She won more than 30 events including three US Opens, but her most famous victory was in 1954 less than a year after a major operation for cancer.

She won by a record 12 strokes, added a further four events as well as two more in 1955 but a year later cancer had claimed another victim and one of the great figures was lost.

PATTY BERG AND LOUISE SUGGS

With Babe Zaharias, the pioneers of the women's tour; Berg, a teenage prodigy and a great personality, was a tireless tournament player and giver of clinics. Louise Suggs, who won four tournaments in her first two years as a professional, was the first woman to be elected to the LPGA Hall of Fame, and, like Berg, won both US Amateur and Open championships.

KATHY WHITWORTH

Winner of 81 tournaments, one behind the record of Mickey Wright, Kathy Whitworth has been a model of consistency on the LPGA tour although victory in the US Open has eluded her.

She became the first woman to top the million dollar mark in prize-money, has been leading money-winner in a year a record eight times and Player-of-the-Year seven times.

US Women's Open

A championship started in 1946 and adopted by the United States Golf Association in 1953, it is the leading championship in women's golf. Unlike all the others, there is no sponsorship, but the popularity of women's golf has grown out of all recognition in recent years and in 1979, the Open was watched by crowds averaging 12 000 for the last three days.

The championship is decided by 72 holes of stroke-play and is one of the very few occasions when amateurs and professionals compete together.

MILESTONES

1946 The first Women's Open produced one of the most famous players as winner. Patty Berg headed the qualifying field with 73, 72 for 145 at Spokane, Washington. In the matchplay section, she then beat Betty Jameson 5 and 4 in the final.
1947 Adoption of 72 holes of strokeplay. Betty Jameson, the previous year's runner-up, came back to win at Starmount Forest CC, Greensboro, North Carolina. She won by 6 strokes with a total of 295. Two amateurs were second.
1948 The great Mildred Zaharias, the 'Babe', triumphed with an even-par total of 300 at Atlantic City CC, New Jersey. In bad weather, she won by 8 strokes.
1949 Under the guidance of the Ladies' Professional Golf Association, Louise Suggs beat 'Babe' Zaharias by 14 strokes to register a total of 291—a record at that time.
1950 At the Rolling Hills CC, Wichita, Kansas, Mildred Zaharias wasted no time in equalling Louise Suggs's record of 291. She won by 9 strokes from the amateur Betsy Rawls, now Tournament Director of the LPGA.
1951 Betsy Rawls, now a professional, won the title at Druid Hills GC, Atlanta. Her score was 293, five better than Louise Suggs.
1952 Louise Suggs became champion for the second time with a record-breaking aggregate of 284 (70, 69, 70, 75) at the Bala GC, Philadelphia. Marilynn Smith set a low individual round record with 67 in the second round, but Marlene Bauer and Betty Jameson were joint runners-up on 291.
1953 A total of 37 entrants of whom 17 were professionals competed for the first championship to be run, at the request of the LPGA, by the USGA. It took place at the Country Club of Rochester, New York, and was won by Betsy Rawls after a play-off with Jacqueline Pung of Honolulu. Their 72-hole score was 302, Rawls winning the 18-hole play-off with 71 to 77.

1954 In a manner akin to Ben Hogan winning the US Men's Open after his terrible car crash, 'Babe' Zaharias ran away with the Women's championship at the Tam O'Shanter CC just over a year after her serious cancer operation. She won by 12 strokes from Betty Hicks, a victory which confirmed her as the leading American woman golfer of her time. It was her last appearance in the Open.
Mickey Wright, later one of the most famous names herself, was fourth and the leading amateur.
1955 Fay Crocker of Montevideo, Uruguay, became the first foreign winner at the Wichita CC, Kansas. In high winds, she led after every round and won by 4 strokes with a total of 299. 'Babe' Zaharias was unable to defend owing to another operation just before the event.
1956 Kathy Cornelius defeated Barbara McIntire, later to become US Women's Amateur champion, after they had tied on 302 at Northland CC, Minnesota. 'Babe' Zaharias was too ill to take part and died later in the year.
1957 Betsy Rawls won her third title at Winged Foot with a total of 299 without it actually being the lowest score. That was the 298 of Jacqueline Pung. However, she signed and returned the card as kept by her marker on which the 6 she had taken at the 4th hole was shown as a 5. The total was correct, but Jacqueline Pung was disqualified since a player is solely responsible for his or her score at each hole. If the mistake had been in the addition, it would not have mattered.
It was a tragedy even worse than that befalling Roberto de Vicenzo at the 1968 Masters who was not disqualified— simply prevented by his error from taking part in a play-off. The members of Winged Foot promptly raised a collection for Jacqueline Pung which reached over $3000 and exceeded the first prize of $1800 which she lost. Total prize-money was $7200.
Competitors were asked to wear skirts not shorts in order to conform with a club rule.
1958 Start of a great burst of victories by Mickey Wright. She won three times in four years and four times in seven years. Her first success at Forest Lake CC, Michigan, was by 5 strokes after she had led throughout. A total of 290 left her 5 strokes clear of Louise Suggs. It was a new record total for championships under the USGA's direction. At 23, she was also the youngest winner to date. The leading amateur was Anne Quast, 20.
1959 Mickey Wright lowered her record total to 287 and Louise Suggs again followed her home, this time only 2 strokes behind. To maintain the uniformity, Anne Quast was again leading amateur, her 299 being the first by an amateur under 300. At Churchill Valley CC near Pittsburgh, Mickey Wright sought advice on the telephone for her putting troubles from Paul Runyan.
1960 Betsy Rawls became the first four-time winner with a score of 292 at Worcester CC, Massachusetts. This Club housed the men's Open in 1925 and became the first to complete the double. Mickey Wright led for three rounds before posting a final 82. Joyce Ziske was second, 1 stroke behind Rawls.
Judy Torluemke, 15, finished leading amateur.
1961 Mickey Wright's third victory and one of her best over the Lower course at Baltusrol. The course measured 6372 yd (5826 m) and Wright's controlled power was seen to excellent advantage. She played the final 36 holes in 141 strokes and won by 6 strokes from Betsy Rawls with a total of 293.

1962 High scores and a surprising winner at the Dunes Golf and Beach Club, Myrtle Beach, South Carolina. Murle Mac-Kenzie Lindstrom made up 5 strokes in the last round to win with 301. It was her first professional victory and she won by 2 strokes from Ruth Jessen and JoAnn Prentice. Her prize was $1800.

In contrast to the previous year, Mickey Wright scored 158 for the final 36 holes. The weather was bad throughout.

1963 Another winner, Mary Mills, scoring her first success in professional golf. Having set a record of 141 for the first two rounds, she won by 3 strokes with a total of 289 at Kenwood Country Club, Cincinnati. Mickey Wright did not play.

Prize-money totalled $9000 and the event was televised locally for the first time.

1964 Wright won her fourth title under USGA direction at her old home club, the San Diego CC, California, after a play-off with Ruth Jessen. They had tied on 290, but at the 72nd hole, Wright got down in 2 from a bunker whereas Jessen hit a wood to 3 ft (0.9 m) and made a birdie. In the play-off, Wright had 70 against 72.

1965 Carol Mann, 6 ft 3 in (1.88 m) tall, came back to win at Atlantic City CC, New Jersey, after an opening round of 78 which put her 7 strokes behind the leader, Cathy Cornelius. Cornelius had a closing round of 69 to finish on 292, 2 strokes behind Mann who had second and third rounds of 70.

Mickey Wright was unable to defend her title, but Catherine Lacoste was second amateur, 8 strokes behind Mrs Helen Sigel Wilson whose 296 set an amateur record.

The last two rounds were played over two days and the final round was televised nationally for the first time.

1966 Sandra Spuzich, 29, became yet another to celebrate her first professional victory in the national Open. At Hazeltine CC, Chaska, she defeated defending champion Carol Mann by 1 stroke with 297. The lowest round of the championship was an opening 71 by Mickey Wright.

1967 A famous victory by Catherine Lacoste of France at the Cascades course in Hot Springs, Virginia. She became the first amateur to win the title after leading at the half-way stage by 5 strokes. She preserved this lead in the third round and increased her lead to 7 at one point, but her play deteriorated and, in the end, she had only a couple of strokes to spare from Susie Maxwell and Beth Stone. At one stage, Louise Suggs, 9 behind after 54 holes, had made up 8 of them.

1968 A triumph from start to finish for Susie Maxwell Berning who married only seven weeks before the championship began at Moselem Springs, Pennsylvania. She won by 3 strokes from Mickey Wright with a total of 289, her 71 equalling the lowest last round by a champion. However, Wright's 68 was the lowest last round by any player.

There was a record entry of 104; first prize was $5000.

1969 Another first professional victory in the Open. Donna Caponi held off the challenge of Peggy Wilson by 1 stroke at the Scenic Hills CC, Pensacola, Florida.

She took the lead late on and was delayed 15 minutes by an electric storm as she waited to play the 18th. After taking shelter in the clubhouse, she then got a birdie for a round of 69, the best by a champion.

1970 Donna Caponi joined Mickey Wright as the only champion at that time to successfully defend her title. In so doing she also equalled Wright's record score of 287. At Muskogee CC, Oklahoma, she was almost caught by Sandra Haynie and Sandra Spuzich after being 4 ahead with a record 54-hole total of 210.

1971 A commanding win for JoAnne Carner at the Kahkwa Club, Pennsylvania. She led after every round and won by 7 strokes from Kathy Whitworth with a total of 288. She thus became the fourth player to have won the US Women's Amateur and Open championships; she won her last Amateur title in 1968.

Three amateurs finished in the first ten.

Prize-money totalled $34 450.

1972 Susie Berning joined a select group of six who have won the Open at least twice. At Winged Foot, New York, she won with a score of 299, 1 stroke ahead of Judy Rankin, Pam Barnett and Kathy Ahern. However, after an opening 79, she did not look the likely champion. The defending champion JoAnne Carner also began with a 79, but despite the heavy rains that made 70 the best round of the week, Susie Berning's final round of 71 saw her home. In that round, she had a 2 at the 17th to Pam Barnett's 4.

Marilynn Smith finished 72 holes in her 20th consecutive Open—a record. Nine amateurs from the entry of 176 also completed 72 holes although the USGA set a limit of 150 competitors. Prize-money exceeded $38 000 with the winner claiming $6000—both records.

1973 Susie Berning successfully defended her title and so became only the third player to win the Open three times. At Rochester, New York, she won by 5 strokes from Shelley Hamlin and Gloria Ehret with a total of 290.

Marilynn Smith played through her 21st consecutive Open and the amateur Cynthia Hill set a new record with a first round of 68.

1974 Sandra Haynie of Texas had birdies on the last 2 holes of La Grange CC, Illinois, to win by a single stroke from Carol Mann and Beth Stone. JoAnne Carner who led the field by 2 strokes with 9 holes to play, tied for 4th place on 297, 2 strokes behind Haynie.

Prize-money totalled $40 000.

1975 There were only two sub-par rounds all week in the 23rd championship at Atlantic City CC. One of these was a third round of 71 by Sandra Palmer who added a final par round of 72 to win by 4 strokes on 295. Among those who tied for 2nd place was Nancy Lopez, then still an amateur. It was the best finish by an amateur since Catherine Lacoste won in 1967.

1976 JoAnne Carner, champion in 1971, denied Sandra Palmer a successful defence of her title. After they had tied on 292, 8 over par, at Rolling Green GC, Pennsylvania, Carner won the play-off with 76 to 78, further indication of the difficulty of the course. It was the first play-off since 1964.

Miss Nancy Porter made a hole-in-one on the 16th (135 yd (123 m)) in the second round. It was only the fourth in the history of the championship, but two of the four have been by Nancy Porter.

Sectional qualifying was necessary for the first time. The entry reached 205.

1977 Hollis Stacy, 23, had a creditable victory at Hazeltine National GC, Chaska, Minnesota, scene of Tony Jacklin's US Open victory in 1970. She led after all four rounds and won by 2 strokes with a total of 292. Nancy Lopez and JoAnne Carner were 2nd and 3rd. All three were former Girls' Junior champions. It was Lopez's first tournament as a professional. Prize-money totalled a record $75 000.

1978 Hollis Stacy joined the band of those who have successfully defended their titles. She is also the youngest to win twice. It was her fifth USGA title; she won three consecutive Girls' titles.

Above: **Many times a Curtis Cup heroine. The simple grace of Frances Smith (Sport and General)**

Right: **Belle Robertson successful at last in winning the 1981 Ladies British Open Amateur championship after reaching her first final in 1959 (Phil Sheldon)**

Sally Little set a new individual round record with 65.

1979 Jerilyn Britz chose a good moment to win her first tournament as a professional. She captured the 27th Women's Open at Brooklawn CC, Connecticut, by 2 strokes from Debbie Massey and Sandra Palmer. Her total of 284 (70, 70, 75, 69) was 3 strokes lower than any returned by a winner since the USGA took over the running of the event. Louise Suggs won with 284 in 1952, but the Bala course measured only 5460 yd (4993 m) compared with 6010 yd (5496 m) at Brooklawn.

Jerilyn Britz, who did not turn professional until she was 30 in 1973, left a position as a teacher of physical education at New Mexico State University to try her hand on the golf tour. Twenty-third in the money list in 1978, she led the 1979 LPGA championship with 7 holes to play, but it was obviously good experience.

Susie Berning's second-round 66 was the second lowest in the championship's history. Sally Little set the record in 1978.

1980 A championship dominated by Amy Alcott, 24 of Santa Monica, California. In a temperature of over 100 degrees at Richland CC, Nashville, Tennessee, she broke the 72-hole aggregate by 4 strokes. She also set a record for the lowest first (208) and last (210) 54 holes and equalled the lowest last 36 holes, 140, by Mickey Wright in 1959.

She was 8 strokes ahead after three rounds and 10 ahead with 1 hole to play. She dropped a stroke at the 18th and won by 9. There were 337 entries and the prize-money was a record $140 000.

1981 In a thrilling finish, Pat Bradley beat Beth Daniel by 1 stroke at La Grange CC, Illinois, breaking Amy Alcott's 72-hole aggregate record, set the year before, by 1 stroke. Bradley achieved her first victory in the championship with third and fourth rounds of 68 and 66. This lowered by 6 strokes the record total for the final 36 holes held by Mickey Wright since 1959 and equalled in 1980 by Amy Alcott.

DETAILED RECORDS

Most victories
4, Mickey Wright, 1958–59–61–64; Betsy Rawls, 1951–53–57–60

Oldest winner
Fay Crocker, 40 years 11 months, 1955

Youngest winner
Catherine Lacoste, 22 years and 5 days, 1967

Biggest margin of victory
12 strokes, Mildred 'Babe' Didrikson Zaharias, 1954

Lowest winning aggregate (after 1953)
279, Pat Bradley, La Grange CC, 1981
280, Amy Alcott, Richland CC, 1980

Lowest aggregate by runner-up
280, Beth Daniel, La Grange CC, 1981

Most times runner–up
4, Louise Suggs, 1955–58–59–63

Lowest single round
65, Sally Little, fourth round, Indianapolis CC, 1978
66, Susie Maxwell Berning, second round, Brooklawn CC, 1979

Lowest first round
68, Cynthia Hill, Rochester CC, New York, 1973; Kathy Ahern, La Grange, Illinois, 1974; Donna Young, Indianapolis CC, 1978

Lowest second round
66, Susie Maxwell Berning, Brooklawn CC, 1979

Lowest third round
67, Judy Bell, San Diego CC, 1964

Lowest fourth round
65, Sally Little, Indianapolis CC, 1978

Lowest first 36 holes
139, Donna Caponi and Carol Mann, Muskogee CC, 1970; Kathy Whitworth and Bonnie Lauer, La Grange CC, 1981

Lowest last 36 holes
134, Pat Bradley, La Grange CC, 1981

Lowest first 54 holes
208, Amy Alcott, 1980

Lowest last 54 holes
208, Pat Bradley, 1981

Highest winning score
302, Betsy Rawls and Jacqueline Pung, Rochester CC, 195_ and Kathy Cornelius and Barbara McIntire, Northland CC, 1956

Largest span between victories
9 years, Betsy Rawls, 1951–60

Consecutive winners
27 Mickey Wright, 1958–59; Donna Caponi, 1969–70; Susie Maxwell Berning, 1972–73; Hollis Stacy, 1977–78

Amateur winner
Catherine Lacoste, 1967. Barbara McIntire lost a play-off to Kathy Cornelius in 1956

Overseas winners
Fay Crocker, 1955; Catherine Lacoste, 1967

Play-offs
6, 1947–52–53–56–64–76

Poorest start by champion
79, Susie Maxwell Berning, 1972

Poorest finish by champion
79, Kathy Cornelius 1956; Catherine Lacoste 1967

Youngest leading amateur winner
Judy Torluemke was 15 years, 1960

Best comebacks by champions
After 18 holes: Susie Maxwell Berning in 1972 and Carol Mann in 1965 were 7 strokes behind
After 36 holes: in 1953, Betsy Rawls was 9 behind
After 54 holes: in 1962, Murle Lindstrom and in 1969 Donna Caponi were 5 behind
In 1956, Barbara McIntire made up 8 strokes in the last round to tie Kathy Cornelius but lost the play-off.

Leaders' fate
Up until 1981, a player who has led after 18 holes has won 1_ of the 29 Opens. A player who has led after 36 holes has won 14 times. A player who has led after 54 holes has won 2_ times.

A star in his own right. Nathaniel Crosby, United States
Amateur champion, 1981 (Phil Sheldon)

Horticultural beauty of Augusta (Phil Sheldon)

Left: A popular character and the best of caddies, the
incomparable Mullins (Phil Sheldon)

A touch of Eastern magic. Lu Hsi-Chuen of Taiwan (Phil Sheldon)

Right: Bernhard Langer; no problem that a good explosion cannot solve, Royal St George's, 1981 (Phil Sheldon)

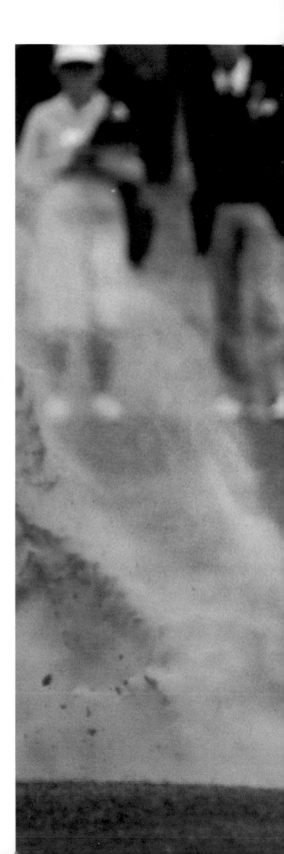

A distinguished gallery at the 1981 Ryder Cup match: (from the left) Dave Marr, Jack Nicklaus, Linda Watson, Barbara Nicklaus, Tom Watson and Dow Finsterwald. Normally the wives suffer on their own (Phil Sheldon)

Bill Rogers, runner-up in the 1981 US Open, went to capture the British and Australian Opens later in the year. The caddie holds one of Merion's unique basket 'flags' (Phil Sheldon)

Jerry Pate and Ben Crenshaw paired at the Masters (Phil Sheldon)

Far from a question of having cold feet, Severiano Ballesteros prepares for a courageous recovery (Phil Sheldon)

Greg Norman sparing nothing (Phil Sheldon)

Two quiet men of American golf, although their play speaks volumes. Larry Nelson (on left) and Tom Kite, Ryder Cup partners (Phil Sheldon)

Craig Stadler approaching his moment of triumph in the 1982 US Masters (Phil Sheldon)

Patience is a virtue. Peter Oosterhuis won his first tournament on the American circuit, the Canadian Open 1981 (Phil Sheldon)

The remote splendour of The Machrie Hotel and Golf Course, Isle of Islay, Scotland

Left: Master of his craft of clubmaking, Harry Busson (Phil Sheldon)

Tom Watson under the tutelage of Byron Nelson (Phil Sheldon)

MOST CAREER WINS

	Player	Wins	Unofficial Wins	Joined Tour
1	Mickey Wright	82		1955
2	Kathy Whitworth	81	2	1959
3	Betsy Rawls	55		1951
4	Louise Suggs	50		1949
5	Patty Berg	41		1948
6	Sandra Haynie	39		1961
7	Carol Mann	38		1961
8	Babe Zaharias	31		1948
9	JoAnne Carner	27	3	1970
10	Judy Rankin	26	2	1962

MOST VICTORIES IN A SEASON

Year	Player	Victories
1948	Patty Berg/Babe Zaharias	3
1949	Patty Berg/Louise Suggs	3
1950	Babe Zaharias	6
1951	Babe Zaharias	7
1952	Betsy Rawls/Louise Suggs	6
1953	Louise Suggs	8
1954	Louise Suggs/Babe Zaharias	5
1955	Patty Berg	6
1956	Marlene Hagge	8
1957	Patty Berg/Betsy Rawls	5
1958	Mickey Wright	5
1959	Betsy Rawls	10
1960	Mickey Wright	6
1961	Mickey Wright	10
1962	Mickey Wright	10
1963	Mickey Wright	13
1964	Mickey Wright	11
1965	Kathy Whitworth	8
1966	Kathy Whitworth	9
1967	Kathy Whitworth	8
1968	Kathy Whitworth/Carol Mann	10
1969	Carol Mann	8
1970	Shirley Englehorn	4
1971	Kathy Whitworth	5
1972	Kathy Whitworth/Jane Blalock	5
1973	Kathy Whitworth	7
1974	JoAnne Carner/Sandra Haynie	6
1975	Carol Mann/Sandra Haynie	4
1976	Judy T Rankin	6
1977	Judy T Rankin/Debbie Austin	5
1978	Nancy Lopez	9
1979	Nancy Lopez	8
1980	JoAnne Carner/Donna Caponi	5
1981	Donna Caponi	5

LEADING MONEY-WINNERS (1948–1979)

Year	Player	Amount $
1948	Babe Zaharias	3400.00*
1949	Babe Zaharias	4650.00*
1950	Babe Zaharias	14 800.00*
1951	Babe Zaharias	15 087.00*

*Approximate figure

1952	Betsy Rawls	14 505.00
1953	Louise Suggs	19 816.25
1954	Patty Berg	16 011.00
1955	Patty Berg	16 492.34
1956	Marlene Hagge	20 235.50
1957	Patty Berg	16 272.00
1958	Beverly Hanson	12 639.55
1959	Betsy Rawls	26 744.39
1960	Louise Suggs	16 892.12
1961	Mickey Wright	22 236.21
1962	Mickey Wright	21 641.99
1963	Mickey Wright	31 269.50
1964	Mickey Wright	29 800.00
1965	Kathy Whitworth	28 658.00
1966	Kathy Whitworth	33 517.50
1967	Kathy Whitworth	32 937.50
1968	Kathy Whitworth	48 379.50
1969	Carol Mann	49 152.50
1970	Kathy Whitworth	30 235.01
1971	Kathy Whitworth	41 181.75
1972	Kathy Whitworth	65 063.99
1973	Kathy Whitworth	82 864.25
1974	JoAnne Carner	87 094.04
1975	Sandra Palmer	76 374.51
1976	Judy T Rankin	150 734.28
1977	Judy T Rankin	122 890.44
1978	Nancy Lopez	189 813.83
1979	Nancy Lopez	197 488.61†
1980	Beth Daniel	231 000.42
1981	Beth Daniel	206 977.66

†Record

TOTAL PURSES (1956–1980)

Year	Amount $	Events
1956	140 447	26
1957	147 830	26
1958	158 600	25
1959	202 500	26
1960	186 700	25
1961	288 750	24
1962	338 450	32
1963	345 300	34
1964	351 000	33
1965	356 316	33
1966	509 500	37
1967	435 250	32
1968	550 185	34
1969	597 290	29
1970	435 040	21
1971	558 500	21
1972	988 400	30
1973	1 471 000	36
1974	1 752 500	35
1975	1 742 000	33
1976	2 527 000	32
1977	3 058 000	35
1978	3 925 000	37
1979	4 400 000	38
1980	5 000 000	39
1981	5 800 000	40

Great Golfing Achievements

A distinguished trio for the 1947 final of the President's Putter at Rye. Leonard Crawley (left) and Laddie Lucas flanking the President, Bernard Darwin.

Record Dimensions

Note—these records are taken from the *Guinness Book of Records*, Editor and Compiler Norris McWhirter.

CLUB *Largest*

The club with the highest membership in the British Isles is the Royal and Ancient Golf Club of St Andrews, Fife, Scotland with 1800 members. The largest in England is 1600 at the Moor Park GC, Rickmansworth, Hertfordshire, and the largest in Ireland is Royal Portrush, Co Antrim with 1215 members.

COURSE *Highest*

The highest golf course in the world is the Tuctu Golf Club in Morococha, Peru, which is 4369 m (14 335 ft) above sea-level at its lowest point. Golf has, however, been played in Tibet at an altitude of over 4875 m (16 000 ft).

The highest golf course in Great Britain is one of 9 holes at Leadhills, Strathclyde, 1500 ft (457 m) above sea-level.

COURSE *Lowest*

The lowest golf course in the world was that of the now defunct Sodom and Gomorrah Golfing Society at Kallia (Qulya) on the northern shores of the Dead Sea, 380 m (1250 ft) below sea-level. Currently the lowest is Furnace Creek, Death Valley, Calif., USA 67 m (220 ft) below sea-level.

HOLE *Longest*

The longest hole in the world is the 7th hole (par 7) of the Sano Course, Satsuki GC, Japan, which measures 831 m (909 yd). In August 1927 the 6th hole at Prescott Country Club in Arkansas, USA, measured 838 yd (766 m). The longest hole on a championship course in Great Britain is the 6th at Troon, Strathclyde, which stretches 577 yd (528 m).

GREEN *Largest*

Probably the largest green in the world is the 5th green at International GC, Bolton, Massachusetts, USA with an area greater than 28 000 ft^2 (2600 m^2).

When Gary Wright 'played' a round of golf in 28 minutes, he beat former world mile record holder Herb Elliott in the process

MOST ROUNDS
The greatest number of rounds played on foot in 24 hr is 22 rounds and five holes (401 holes) by Ian Colston, 35, at Bendigo GC, Victoria (par-73, 6061 yd (5542 m)) on 27–28 November 1971. The most holes played on foot in a week (168 hr) is 1128 by Steve Hylton at the Mason Rudolph Golf Club (6060 yd (5541 m)), Clarkesville, Tennessee, USA, from 25–31 August 1980.

MOST PERIPATETIC GOLFER
George S Salter, of Carmel, California, USA has played in 116 different 'countries' around the world from 1964 to 1977.

THROWING THE GOLF BALL
The lowest recorded score for throwing a golf ball round 18 holes (over 6000 yd or 5500 m) is 82 by Joe Flynn (USA), 21, at the 6228 yd (5694 m) Port Royal Course, Bermuda, on 27 March 1975.

LONGEST SPAN
Jacqueline Ann Mercer (née Smith) won her first South African title at Humewood GC, Port Elizabeth in 1948, and her fourth title at Port Elizabeth GC on 4 May 1979, 31 years later.

MOST CLUB CHAMPIONSHIPS
Bernard Charles Cusack has won a record total of 32 Club championships, including 31 consecutively, at the Narembeen GC, Western Australia, between 1943 and 1980. The women's record is 31 by Molly St John Pratt at the Stanthorpe GC, Queensland, Australia from 1931 to 1979. The British record for amateur club championships is 27 wins between 1925 and 1969 by Eileen Nairn (née Ashton) at the Worsley GC, Manchester. The record for consecutive wins is 22 (1959–80) by Patricia Mary Shepherd at Turriff GC, Aberdeenshire, Scotland.

RECORD TIE
The longest delayed result in any National Open Championship occurred in the 1931 US Open at Toledo, Ohio. George von Elm and Billy Burke tied at 292, then tied the first replay at 149. Burke won the second replay by a single stroke after 72 extra holes.

LARGEST TOURNAMENT
The Dunhill Trophy Open Amateur Championship in Great Britain attracted a record 124 509 competitors in 1981.

RICHEST PRIZES
The greatest first place prize-money was $½ million (total purse one million) in the Sun City tournament in Bophuthatswana, South Africa over 72 holes on 31 December 1981–3 January 1982. It was won by Johnny Miller after a sudden death play off lasting 9

Johnny Miller, a fine example of staying behind the ball (Phil Sheldon)

holes. In America the highest first place was $100 000 (total purse $500 000) in the World Open, North Carolina over 144 holes on 8–17 November 1973 won by Miller Barber. The World series of Golf also carries a first prize of $100 000. The highest British prize was £25 000 in the John Player Golf Classic at Hollinwell, Nottinghamshire, on 3–6 September 1970 won by Christy O'Connor Sr. Probably the greatest prize for one shot was the £50 000 home won by Isao Aoki (Japan) by aceing the 155 yd (142 m) 2nd hole in the World Match Play Championship at Wentworth on 12 October 1979.

HIGHEST EARNINGS *US PGA and LPGA circuits*

The all time professional money-winner is Jack Nicklaus who, up to 31 December 1980, has won $3 581 213. The record for a year is $530 808 by Tom Watson in 1980. The record for a woman is $231 000 by Beth Daniel in 1980. The record career earnings for a woman is $906 854 by Kathy Whitworth (USA) up to 31 December 1980. The most won in a year by a British golfer is £66 060 by 'Sandy' Lyle in 1980.

MOST TOURNAMENT WINS

The record for winning tournaments in a single season is 18 (plus one unofficial), including a record eleven consecutively, by John Byron Nelson from 8 March–4 August 1945. Sam Snead has won 84 official US PGA Tour events to December 1979, and has been credited with a total 134 tournament victories since 1934. Mickey Wright has won 82 professional tournaments from 1955 to December 1979, including a record 13 in 1963.

BIGGEST WINNING MARGIN

The greatest margin of victory in a major tournament is 21 strokes by Jerry Pate of America in the Colombian Open with 262 on 13 December 1981. His scores were 64, 67, 66, 65. The previous best was 17 strokes by Randall Colin Vines of Australia, in the Tasmanian Open with 274 in 1968, and by Bernhard Langer (W Germany) in the 1979 World Under-25 tournament at Nimes, France on 30 September 1979, also with 274 (73, 67, 67, 67).

Holes in one

LONGEST

The longest straight hole ever holed in one shot is the tenth (447 yd (408 m)) at Miracle Hills Golf Club, Omaha, Nebraska, USA by Robert Mitera (b 1944) on 7 October 1965. Mitera stands 5 ft 6 in (1.68 m) tall and weighs 165 lb (74.842 kg) (11 st 11 lb). He is a two handicap player who can normally drive 245 yd (224 m). A 50 mph (80 km/h) gust carried his shot over a 290 yd (265 m) drop-off. The longest 'dog-leg' hole achieved in one is the 480 yd (439 m) fifth at Hope

Country Club, Arkansas by L Bruce on 15 November 1962. The feminine record is 393 yd (359 m) by Marie Robie on the first hole of the Furnace Brook Golf Club, Wollaston, Massachusetts, USA, on 4 September 1949. The longest hole in one performed in the British Isles is the seventh (par-4, 393 yd (359 m)) at West Lancashire GC by Peter Richard Parkinson on 6 June 1972.

In 1980 *Golf Digest* magazine recorded 31 559 'aces' reported in the US, which averages over 80 per day.

MOST

The greatest number of holes-in-one in a career is 57 by Harry Lee Bonner from 1967–1982. The British record is 31 by Charles T Chevalier of Heaton Moor Golf Club, Stockport, Greater Manchester between 20 June 1918 and 1970. Douglas Porteous, 28, holed-in-one four times over 39 consecutive holes (3rd and 6th on 26 September; 5th on 28 September at Ruchill Golf Club, Glasgow; 6th at the Clydebank and District Golf Course on 30 September 1974). Robert John Taylor (Leicestershire) holed the par-3 188 yd (172 m) 16th at Hunstanton, Norfolk on three successive days—31 May, 1 and 2 June 1974—in the Eastern Inter-Counties foursomes. Joseph Felix Vituello (USA) holed the 130 yd (119 m) 16th at the Hubbard Golf Course, Ohio, in one for the tenth time on 26 June 1979.

CONSECUTIVE

There are at least 15 cases of 'aces' being achieved in two consecutive holes, of which the greatest was Norman L Manley's unique 'double albatross' on the par-4 330 yd (301 m) 7th and par-4 290 yd (265 m) 8th holes on the Del Valle Country Club Course, Saugus, California, on 2 September 1964. The only woman to record consecutive 'aces' is Sue Prell, on the 13th and 14th holes at Chatswood Golf Club, Sydney, Australia on 29 May 1977.

There is no recorded instance of a golfer performing 3 consecutive holes in one. The closest to achieving it was by the late Dr Joseph Boydstone on the 3rd, 4th and 9th at Bakersfield GC, California, USA, on 10 October 1962 (the year he recorded a record 11 aces), and by the Rev Harold Snider who aced the 8th, 13th and 14th holes of the par-3 Ironwood course, Arizona, USA on 9 June 1976.

YOUNGEST AND OLDEST

The youngest golfer recorded to have shot a hole-in-one was Coby Orr (5 years) of Littleton, Colorado on the 103 yd (94 m) fifth at the Riverside Golf Course, San Antonio, Texas in 1975. The oldest golfers to have performed the feat are (men): 93-year-olds George Henry Miller, on the 116 yd (106 m) 11th at Anaheim GC, California on 4 December 1970; Charles Youngman, at the Tam O'Shanter Club, Toronto in

1971; and William H. Diddel, on the 142 yd (130 m) 8th at the Royal Poinciana GC, Naples, Florida on 1 January 1978. The oldest woman to perform the feat is Maude Bridget Hutton, aged 86, when she holed the 102 yd (93 m) 14th at Kings Inn Golf and Country Club, Sun City Center, Florida on 7 August 1978.

SHOOTING YOUR AGE

The lowest under his age score recorded on the PGA Circuit is 66, at age 67, by Sam Snead (USA) in the Ed McMahon Quad Cities Open, Oakwood CC, Coal Valley, Illinois on 23 June 1979. In a less important tournament he had scored 64, at Onion Creek GC (6585 yd (6021 m) par 70), Austin, Texas, in April 1978 when one month short of his 66th birthday.

The oldest player to score his age is C Arthur Thompson (1869–1975) of Victoria, British Columbia, Canada, who scored 103 on the Uplands course of 6215 yd (5682 m) aged 103 in 1973. The youngest player to score his age is Robert Leroy Klingaman who shot a 58 when aged 58 on the 5654 yd (5170 m) course at the Caledonia GC, Fayetteville, Pennsylvania, USA, on 31 August 1973. Bob Hamilton shot 59, aged 59, on the 6233 yd (5699 m) blue course, Hamilton GC, Evansville, Indiana, USA, on 3 June 1975.

Facts and Feats

A record sale for a golf ball was made at Christie's, South Kensington, London in July 1981 when a feather ball by William Robertson, dating from about 1830, was sold to dealer, Richard Emery, for £950.

In the first British Boys championship at Ascot in 1921, **Henry Cotton**, then 14, was beaten in the first round.

In 1930, **Macdonald Smith** finished runner-up to Bobby Jones in both British and American Open championships.

Bernhard Langer became the first German ever to win the German Open in 1981. It was first held in 1911.

Francois Illouz became the youngest winner and the second Continental to win the scratch medal at the Royal and Ancient Golf Club's autumn meeting in September 1980. In the same year, 1981, **Philippe Ploujoux**, also a Frenchman, won the British Amateur championship at St Andrews; the Boys championship was won by a Spaniard and the Youths championship by a Swede.

On 3 January 1966, **Harold Dean**, then 55, played 18 holes of golf at Dukinfield, Manchester, swam a mile and drank three pints of beer—all within the space of two hours. He did it as part of a £20 bet which he gave to charity. He started at 10.30 am with golf, returning a net score of 70. At 11.35, he drove to Hyde indoor baths; at 11.40, he swam a mile and at 12.19 drank three pints.

In the 1981 German Open championship at Falkenstein, Hamburg, the American, **John Fought** was disqualified for failing to sign his card after a second round of 65. It was the lowest round of the day.

In the 1981 Walker Cup match at Cypress Point, California, **Ronan Rafferty** and **Philip Walton** won their first foursome together for Great Britain and Ireland, ending the match by holing two chip shots. At the 15th, Walton holed; and at the 16th, Rafferty holed. The 15th and 16th are consecutive par-3s.

After the 1981 Walker Cup match, **Ronan Rafferty** went round Pine Valley at first sight in 68.

Royal Lytham and St Annes is the only Open championship course in Britain or America which begins with a par-3.

At the 18th hole at Merion, Philadelphia, **Paul Runyan** felt the drive involved a carry he could not make during one major championship. As a result, he chipped on to the ladies' tee and then hit a 4 wood to the fairway.

In the 1981 Bing Crosby tournament, curtailed by the weather, there was a five-way tie. The play-off was won by **John Cook**.

By winning the Irish Amateur championship at Rosses Point in 1981, **Declan Branigan** (33), became the first Irishman to have won the country's three major amateur titles in the same year. He earlier won the East and West of Ireland championships.

Joel Hirsch, runner-up in the British Amateur championship in 1981, tied for first individual place with **Corey Pavin**, the Walker Cup player, in the Maccabiah Games over the Caesarea course in Israel. The United States took the team event by 35 strokes.

In 1946, playing in the Victory Cup at Rochdale, **Ian Webster,** on leave from the Royal Navy at the time, took 50 strokes to the turn. He then came home in 32 and won the competition with a net 67.

Arnold Palmer won the second US Open Senior championship at Oakland Hills in 1981, his victory coming in a play-off with **Billy Casper** and Bob Stone. The last time Palmer and Casper met in a play-off for a national title, Palmer let slip a large lead in the 1966 US Open championship at the Olympic Club, San Francisco.

Palmer, winner also of the USPGA Seniors title, was eligible to play because the USGA lowered the age limit from 55 to 50.

Apart from the Lunts and the Carrs, two other fathers and sons have represented their countries in the Home Internationals: **Teddy** and **Michael Dawson** for Scotland; **James** and **Peter Flaherty** for Ireland.

Two fathers and sons have played for their countries in the same World Amateur team championship for the Eisenhower Trophy. In 1958 and 1960, **I S Malik** and **A S Malik** played for India; and the **Visconde de Pereira Machado** and **Nuno Alberto de Brito e Cunha** for Portugal.

The most famous golfing father and son partnership in South America is **Mario** and **Jaimé Gonzales**. Mario, equal eleventh in the 1948 British Open, has been a regular winner of the Brazilian Open. His son, Jaimé, won the Brazilian Amateur championship four times before turning professional.

In 1952, the final of the Swiss Amateur championship was contested by **Antoine** and **André Barras**, father and son, the son winning.

BROTHERS

In 1963, the brothers, **Bernard** and **Geoffrey Hunt** played for Great Britain and Ireland in the Ryder Cup in Atlanta. In 1953, they contested the final of the British Assistants' championship at Hartsbourne. Bernard won 2 and 1.

Willie and **Tony Torrance** played Walker Cup golf for Great Britain. Willie in 1922 and Tony in 1924–28–30–32 and 34.

In 1932, the brothers **Rex** and **Lister Hartley** played for Great Britain in the Walker Cup match. They were paired together in the top foursome, but were beaten 7 and 6 by Jess Sweetser and George Voigt.

The brothers **Jay** and **Lionel Hebert** both played for the United States in the Ryder Cup, Lionel in 1957 and Jay in 1959 and 1961. They have also both won the USPGA championship, Lionel in 1957 and Jay in 1960.

In 1910, **Alex Smith** defeated his brother, **Macdonald**, in a play-off for the title in the US Open, which he had previously won in 1906. His victory followed that of another brother, **Willie**, in 1899. In 1906, Alex was first and Willie second.

Charles, **Ernest** and **Reg Whitcombe** all played in the Ryder Cup. In 1935, Charles and Ernest were paired together in the foursomes. Reg Whitcombe was British Open champion in 1938.

The seven **Turnesa** brothers (sons of the greenkeeper at Fairview CC) were equally famous. Six of them were professionals.

Joe Turnesa, runner-up to Walter Hagen (beaten 1 hole) in the USPGA championship of 1927, played in the Ryder Cup match of 1927 and 1929.

Jim Turnesa, the sixth son, won the USPGA championship in 1952 which earned him a place in the Ryder Cup of 1953; and **Willie**, the youngest, won the US Amateur championship in 1938 and again in 1948. He also won the British Amateur in 1947 and played in the Walker Cup, 1947–49–51.

The Spanish professionals, **Angel** and **Sebastian Miguel** were leading players in Europe for a number of years before the European circuit was established. Both won the Spanish Open championship, Angel twice and Sebastian three times, in 1961 Angel succeeding Sebastian for the title.

In the 1958 World Cup competition in Mexico City, they were runners-up together for Spain and, additionally, in partnership with Ramón Sota, they each finished second—Sebastian in 1963 and Angel in 1965.

Harry and **Arnold Bentley** both won the English Amateur championship, the only brothers to achieve the feat. Harry won in 1936, the year in which he played in the Walker Cup at Pine Valley and halved his single, the only British success in the singles. He also played in the winning British team two years later. Arnold won the English title in 1939.

Alistair and **Walter McLeod**, and **Andrew** and **Allan Brodie** are brothers who played for Scotland in the Home International series. The McLeods played in the same team, the Brodies missed by a year. **Tony** and **George Duncan** played together in the Welsh teams of 1952–59.

In 1954, **Peter Toogood** won the final of the Australian Amateur championship with his brother, **John**, runner-up. Two years later, they finished first and third in the Tasmanian Open. In second place was their father Alfred.

More recently, **Severiano** and **Manuel Ballesteros** have succeeded the Miguels as the leading Spanish golfing brothers. Severiano, the best player ever to come out of Spain, has few peers and Manuel, though naturally overshadowed, is a good player in his own right. He has featured prominently in many European events. Incidentally, they are nephews of Ramón Sota.

In America, **Lanny** and **Bobby Wadkins** are the most notable golfing brothers. Lanny, a Walker and Ryder Cup player, was USPGA champion in 1977 and third in the money list; Bobby, the younger by about 20 months, has yet to win a big tournament in the States, but won the first European Open in London in October 1978.

The **Wilkes brothers**, **Trevor** and **Brian** of South

Africa, were both successful tournament professionals in the late fifties and early sixties.

Arthur Lacey, Ryder Cup captain in 1951, was the brother of **Charles** who finished third in the 1937 British Open championship at Carnoustie behind Reg Whitcombe and Henry Cotton.

Count John de Bendern, British Amateur champion in 1932 when he was **John de Forest**, had a brother **Alexis**, who reached the semi-final of the British Amateur in 1937.

Harold, **Alan** and **Graham Henning** were all successful tournament professionals in South Africa, Harold and Alan both winning the South African Open. A fourth brother, **Brian**, was chairman of the South African PGA.

BROTHERS IN LAW

Jerry Pate and **Bruce Lietzke**, were members of the 1981 US Ryder Cup team. Lietzke is married to Pate's sister.

SIBLINGS

Undoubtedly the most famous brother and sister combination was **Roger** and **Joyce Wethered** (later Lady Heathcoat-Amory). Joyce won the British Women's championship four times (1922–24–25–29) and the English five times in a row (1920–24). Roger, British Amateur champion in 1923, tied for the British Open championship in 1921.

The Wethereds and the **Bonallacks** (**Michael** and **Sally**) were the only brothers and sisters to have played for Britain in the Walker and Curtis Cup, until the Moodys, Griff and Terri for America in 1979–80.

However, Charles Hezlet played in the Walker Cup and his sister, May, was British Women's champion on three occasions before the Curtis Cup started.

In 1906, the brothers, the **Hon Denys Scott** and the **Hon Osmund Scott** contested the final of the second Italian Open Amateur championship. Denys won 4 and 3. Their brother, the **Hon Michael Scott**, won the British Amateur of 1933, the oldest to do so, and played in the Walker Cup. Osmund was beaten in the 1905 final of the British Amateur by A G Barry.

Their sister, **Lady Margaret Scott**, won the first three British Women's championships (1893–95) and, to complete a remarkable golfing family, Osmund's son, **Kenneth Scott**, played for England in 1937 and 1938 while an undergraduate at Oxford University. Alas, he was killed in the war.

Claudine and **Patrick Cros**, brother and sister, were both champions of France in the same years, 1964 and

1965. She also won the French Women's Open on two occasions and Patrick the Men's Open, once. Claudine's older brother, **Jean Pierre Cros**, was French Close champion in 1959.

Franco Bevione and his sister, **Isa Goldschmid Bevione**, were national amateur champions of Italy; Franco 13 times (between 1946 and 1971) and Isa ten times (between 1952 and 1969). Franco was Italian Open Amateur champion three times.

Equally well known in Italy are **Baldovino Dassu** and his sister, **Federica**, lady champion of Italy in 1976. Baldovino, Professional and Amateur champion of Italy, won the Dunlop Masters in 1976.

In the United States, the best-known brother and sister in professional golf are **Raymond** and **Marlene Floyd**. Raymond, US Masters and USPGA champion, has been one of the leading players for a number of years. Marlene, though not as successful as her brother, is making her mark on the LPGA tour.

Another brother and sister combination on the PGA and LPGA tours is **Jack** and **Jane Renner**. Jack won the 1979 West Chester Classic.

Jack Graham, semi-finalist in the British Amateur championship on four occasions, was brother of **Molly Graham**, British Women's champion in 1901. Their cousin **Allan Graham** was runner-up in the British Amateur in 1921. They were all Hoylake players and Allan's son, **John**, was captain of the Royal Liverpool GC, Hoylake, in 1956.

SISTERS

In 1897, **Edith Orr** defeated her sister in the final of the British Women's championship at Gullane. A third sister reached the fourth round.

It is said that when their father discovered that there had been betting on the outcome of the final involving his two daughters, he did not allow them to compete subsequently. They lived nearby in North Berwick.

The other instance of sisters in a British final was in 1907 when **May Hezlet** defeated **Florence Hezlet**. They also contested the Irish finals of 1905, 1906 and 1908. May Hezlet won those also.

May is the youngest winner of the British championship. She was 16 when she won the Irish for the first time; the following week she won the British on the same course, County Down, and celebrated her 17th birthday during the week-end between the two events. In 1905 Florence, May and Violet Hezlet played first, second and third in the order for the Irish Ladies' team.

In the same year that the Hezlet sisters contested the

Percy Belgrave 'Laddie' Lucas, a Walker Cup player and Captain, was a distinguished fighter pilot in World War II. He later became a Member of Parliament and Chairman of the Greyhound Racing Association.

Henry Longhurst, the well-known British writer, television commentator and former German Amateur champion, served for a time as a Member of Parliament when Winston Churchill was Prime Minister.

Tom Blackwell, Captain of the Royal and Ancient Golf Club in 1963/64, was later twice Deputy Senior Steward of the Jockey Club.

Bing Crosby was a good enough golfer to have started 3, 3, in a British Amateur championship at St Andrews. He is also one of only two players to have holed in one at the famous 16th at Cypress Point, California. The shoot involves a carry of some 180 yd (165 m) across the edge of the Pacific Ocean.

He died suddenly on 14 October 1977, after playing a round of golf in Madrid. His son **Nathaniel** who won the 1981 US Amateur championship continues to run the Bing Crosby tournament held in California in January.

Robin Cater, a Walker Cup player for Britain in 1955, later became Chairman of the Distillers' Company.

Guy Wolstenholme, well-known professional and former Walker Cup golfer, is a capable pianist.

Bobby Locke, four times British Open champion, flew as a bomber pilot with the South African Airforce during World War II.

Bernard Darwin, twice a semi-finalist in the British Amateur championship and winner of his Walker Cup single, when he was called in to replace the sick British captain, was an incomparable writer on golf. Grandson of Charles Darwin, he practised law on leaving Cambridge but decided on a life writing about golf. He was described by Herbert Asquith as 'the greatest living essayist in the English language' and was said by another eminent critic to be 'one of the six best essayists since Charles Lamb'. He was also a great authority on the works of Dickens.

Arnold Palmer and **Jerilyn Britz**, the 1979 US Women's Open champion, are qualified pilots.

Peter Thomson stood as Liberal candidate for Prahran in the Victoria State government election, Australia, in 1982. He is also Chairman of the James McGrath Foundation which established Odyssey House in Melbourne which helps and cares for the problems of drug addicts.

Stop Press

US Open 1982

Tom Watson won the title he wanted most and, by so doing, moved into the category of authentically great players. In one of the most thrilling of all finishes in the US Open, he won by two strokes at Pebble Beach where he played quite a bit as a boy. By taking 5 at the 16th in the final round, Watson and Nicklaus, who had just completed his round, were level.

Watson missed the green at the long par-3, 17th on the left but, to everyone's surprise and his own delight, he holed a chip for a 2 and finished with a 4 at the famous par-5, 18th—the first US Open champion to finish with two birdies. Of the chip which he holed at the 17th, Watson said, 'It meant more to me than any other single shot in my whole life'.

It is probable that no other single stroke by an opponent stunned Nicklaus more than that one, but his second place finish in Pebble Beach's second Open (Nicklaus won its first) was a further example of his phenomenal consistency.

Tom Watson, Kansas City, Mo	72 72 68 70	**282**
Jack Nicklaus, Muirfield Village, Dublin, Ohio	74 70 71 69	**284**
Bill Rogers, Texakarna, Texas	70 73 69 74	**286**
Bobby Clampett, Carmel Valley Ranch, Calif	71 73 72 70	**286**
Dan Pohl, Canadian Lakes CC, Mecosts, MI	72 74 70 70	**286**

In the Westchester Classic at Harrison, New York in June, Bob Gilder equalled Mike Souchak's 54 hole record of 192 (64, 63, 65). A final round of 69 left him four strokes behind Souchak's 72 hole record for an event on the US tour.

British Open 1982

Tom Watson won his fourth Open title at Royal Troon and his seventh major championship, equalling the number of Sam Snead and Gene Sarazen. His four Opens have been won in the space of eight years, all in Scotland. He also became only the 5th player to win the British and American Opens in the same summer.

The pace for the first two rounds was set by the Californian, Bobby Clampett whose total of 133, the lowest since Henry Cotton in 1934, gave him a lead of 5 strokes in his first British Open over Nick Price of South Africa.

Tom Watson, seven behind at halfway, had 3rd and 4th rounds of 74 and 70 to finish on 284, the highest winning score since 1968, but after Clampett, one ahead at the end of the 3rd round, had faded, Price had the best chance. With 6 holes to play, he was 3 ahead of Watson, but he dropped four strokes on the last 6 holes.

For the second year running, Jack Nicklaus put himself out of the running with his first round (77) but he had a 69 on the final day, his 27th round under 70 in his 21st consecutive Open.

Despite a rail strike, the crowd figures were the second best ever, below the record set in 1979.

USLPGA

Kathy Whitworth equalled Mickey Wright's record of 82 LPGA victories at the CPC Women's International and then broke it a month later at the Lady Michelob Classic.

Curtis Cup

By her selection for the 1982 Curtis Cup match in America, Mary McKenna equalled the record number of appearances (7) held by Mrs Jessie Valentine.

1982 Royal Troon

Tom Watson, USA	69 71 74 70	**284**
Nick Price, South Africa	69 69 74 73	**285**
Peter Oosterhuis	74 67 74 70	**285**
Nick Faldo	73 73 71 69	**286**
Tom Purtzer, USA	76 66 75 69	**286**
Des Smyth, Ireland	70 69 74 73	**286**
Masahiro Kuramoto, Japan	71 73 71 71	**286**

Sterling — US Dollar Exchange Rates

$4·50–$5·00	Post War of Independence	1776
$12·00	All-time Peak (Civil War)	1864
$4·86 21/32	Fixed parity	1880–1914
$4·76 7/16	Pegged rate World War I	Dec. 1916
$3·40	Low point after £ floated, 19 May 1919	Feb. 1920
$4·86 21/32	Britain's return to gold standard	28 Apr. 1925
$3·14½	Low point after Britain forced off Gold Standard (20 Sept. 1931 [$3·43])	Nov. 1932
$5·20	High point during floating period	Mar. 1934
$4·03	Fixed rate World War II	4 Sept. 1939
$2·80	First post-war devaluation	18 Sept. 1949
$2·40	Second post-war devaluation	20 Nov. 1967
$2·42	Convertibility of US dollar into gold was suspended on	15 Aug. 1971
$2·58	£ Refloated	22 June 1972
$1·99	£ broke $2 barrier	5 Mar. 1976
$1·56	£ at new all-time low	28 Oct. 1976
$1·76	Bank of England buying pounds	10 Oct. 1977
$2·00	£ breaks back to $2 level (1978 av. $1·91)	15 Aug. 1978
$2·26	Dollar weakens	June 1979
$2·19	Iranian crisis unresolved	8 Dec. 1979
$1·99	£ again falls below $2 (lowest: $1·77 12 Sept 1981)	3 June 1981
$1·90	One year of 'Reaganomics'	20 Jan. 1982
$1·73	Falklands crisis	5 July 1982

Trainor, Jean (USA), 234
Travers, Jerome (USA 1887–1951), 77, 83, 87
US Amateur, 161, 162, 168
Travis, Walter J (USA 1862–1927), 151, 159, 161, 167, 168
Trevino, Lee (USA b 1–12–1939), 27, 120, 225
British Open, 56–57, 61, 62, 63, 72
prize money, 127, 128
US Open, 80, 84, 92
USPGA, 114, 117
Trinidad, 19
Troon, *102*
British Amateur, 160, 161
British Open, 55, 58, 63, 71, 72
Tumba, Sven (Swe), 238
Tunisia, *18*, 19
Tupling, Leonard Peter (GB b 6–4–1950), 215
Turnberry, *103*
British Open, 57, 62, 63, 72
Turnesa, Jim (USA 1912–1971), 112, 113, 116, 232
Turnesa, Joe (USA b 21–1–1901),
Ryder Cup, 133
USPGA, 111, 232
Turnesa, Willie (USA b 20–1–1914), 155, 160
US Amateur, 163, 169, 232
Walker Cup, 172, *175*
Tutwiler, Ed (USA b 20–7–1919), 164
Tway, Robert (USA), 179
Tweddell, Dr William (GB b 21–3–1897), *152*, 153, 154, 159
Twitty, Howard (USA b 15–1–1949), 127

U

Uganda, 19
Ulrich, Wall, 126
Underhill, Ruth, 187
United States, 19
Ryder Cup victories, 140
Women's Professional Tour, 7
World Cup, 142–43
US Amateur, 25, 161–70
Bobby Jones, 34, 35, 36, 37
Nicklaus, 32, 34
Palmer, 44
records, 167
results, 167
supreme champions, 26–28
United States Golf Association, 22, 76
US Ladies' Professional Golf Association, 210–12
US Masters, *see* Masters
US Open, 7, 25, *75*, 76–92
Bobby Jones, 34, 35, 36, 37
first, 22, 76
Hagen, 37, 38, 39
Hogan, 40, 41
Nicklaus, 31, 32, 33, 34
Palmer, 43, 44, 45
Player, 41, 42, 43
prize money, 85
records, 82–85
results (1895–1981), 85–92
Sarazen, 45, 46, 47
Snead, 47, 48, 49
supreme champions, 26–28
United States Professional Golfers' Association (USPGA), 19, 23, 111
USPGA championship, 23, 111–17
Hagen, 38, 39
Hogan, 40, 41
Nicklaus, 32, 33, 34
Palmer, 44, 45

Player, 42, 43
results (1916–1981), 115–117
Sarazen, 46, 47
Snead, 47, 48, 49
supreme champions, 26–28
USPGA tour, 125–28
leading money winners, 127
tour purses, 127
US Women's Open, 197–209
records, 200–209
results, 209
US Women's Amateur Championship, 187–89
University Match, 22
Updegraff, Ed (USA b 1–3–1922), 156
Uruguay, 19
Urzetta, Sam (USA b 1926), 164, 169
USSR, 19
Uzielli, Angela (GB b 1–2–1940), 185, 234

V

Vagliano, André (Fra b 16–5–1896), 234
Valentine (née Anderson), Jessie (GB b 18–3–1915), 191
Valentine, Jessie (GB b 18–3–1915), 185, 186, 191, *235*
Van Donck, Flory (Bel b 23–6–1912), 55, 56, 131
Vanderbeck, Mrs C H (USA), 188
Varangot, Brigitte (Fra b 1–5–1940), 185, 195, 196
Vardon, Harry (GB 1870–1937), 7, 26, 28, *29*, 30, *113*
British Open, 51, 61, 62, 66, 67, 231
US Open, 86
Vardon Trophy, 130
Vare, Glenna Collett (USA b 20–6–1903), *182*, *183*, 186,
Curtis Cup, 189, 191, 194
Ladies' British Open Amateur, 184
US Women's Amateur, 184, 188
Venezuela, 19
Venturi, Ken (USA b 15–5–1931), 80, 83, 90
Masters, 94, 106
Ryder Cup, 135
Verwey, Bobby (SA b 21–1–1941), 236
Vicenzo, Roberto de (Arg b 14–4–1923), 55, 56, 61, 63, 72
Masters, 96
World Cup, 142
Vines, Ellsworth (USA b 28–9–1911), 237
Vines, Randall Colin (Aus b 22–6–1945), 220
Vitullo, Joseph (USA), 220
Voigt, George (USA b 1894), 154
Walker Cup, 172, 174
Von Elm, George (USA 1901–1961), 218
US Amateur, 163, 168
US Open, 78

W

Wadkins, Bobby (USA b 26–7–1951), 232
Wadkins, Lanny (USA b 5–12–1949), *120*, 232
Eisenhower Trophy, 179
prize money, 127
US Amateur, 166, 170
USPGA, 114, 115, 117
Wales, 19
Walker, Cyril (USA b 1892), 77, 87
Walker, George Herbert (USA 1874–1953), 170
Walker, Mrs J B (GB b 21–6–1896), 191
Walker, Jimmy (GB b 11–2–1921), 156
Walker, Michelle (GB b 17–12–1952), 185, 191
Walker Cup, 170–77
first match, 23
records, 173, 174, 176
results, 177
Wall, Art (USA b 25–11–1923), 80

Index compiled by Patrick Walters